Compliments of

C. S. Smith

Assembly 1923.

Robt. O. Thompson
Campbell Hall
N. Y.
June 18-1923,

Robt J Thompson
Campbell Hall
N.Y.
June 18-1923.

MINUTES OF THE COURT

OF

FORT ORANGE AND BEVERWYCK

1652-1656

Translated and edited
by
A. J. F. VAN LAER
Archivist, Division of Archives and History

VOLUME I

ALBANY
THE UNIVERSITY OF THE STATE OF NEW YORK
1920

The University of the State of New York
Division of Archives and History

August 17, 1920

Dr John H. Finley
    President of the University
DEAR SIR:

I herewith transmit and recommend for publication the first volume of the *Minutes of the Court of Fort Orange and Beverwyck*, April 15, 1652–December 12, 1656, translated and edited by A. J. F. van Laer, Archivist of the Division of Archives and History.

This is the first volume of a series of translations of Dutch manuscripts which form important sources for the early history of New York State. Without these translations the student or historiographer of the early annals of our State will always be seriously handicapped.

Though our historical scholars are generally competent to use French and German in their investigations, they are rarely found able to read Dutch with facility. Even those who are equipped to use the printed page in that language are unable to read correctly manuscripts written in hands which are difficult of decipherment and which frequently require patient reconstruction by an expert in Dutch palaeography.

New York is fortunate in possessing this material but its early history from a political, religious, institutional and economic viewpoint can not be easily written until the Dutch manuscripts which exist in New York City, Albany, Kingston and other places in the Hudson valley are translated and published in English.

        Very truly yours
            JAMES SULLIVAN
                State Historian and Director

Approved for publication

*President of the University and
    Commissioner of Education*

PREFACE

The court of Fort Orange and the village of Beverwyck, whose minutes are published herewith, was erected by proclamation issued by Director General Peter Stuyvesant on April 10, 1652. By virtue of this proclamation the main settlement of the colony of Rensselaerswyck was taken out of the jurisdiction of the patroon and created into an independent village by the name of Beverwyck, which afterwards became the city of Albany. The erection of the court was the final act in the high-handed proceedings whereby Director Stuyvesant brought to a close the long standing controversy between the Dutch West India Company and the authorities of the colony of Rensselaerswyck regarding the jurisdiction of the territory around the fort.

Questions in regard to this jurisdiction had arisen as early as 1632, when the patroon of the colony claimed that all the land on the west side of the Hudson river, from Beeren island to Moenemin's Castle (on Peobles island, at the mouth of the Mohawk), even including the ground on which Fort Orange stood, had been bought for him, whereas the company maintained that the territory of the fort, which was erected in 1624, six years before the purchase of the land of the colony from the Indians, belonged to the company and consequently was not included in the purchase.

Perhaps to avoid the difficulties which were likely to arise from these conflicting claims, or for other reasons connected with the control of the fur trade, the patroon intended that the main settlement of the colony, including the church, the houses of the sheriff, the minister and the sexton, as well as the brewery and the dwellings of the tradesmen and mechanics, should be located in what was known as the Greenen Bosch, a pine grove on the east side of the river, opposite the company's fort. Definite instructions to that effect were given by him in letters to Arent van Curler and Domine Megapolensis, dated August 4, 1639, and June 3, 1642, and documents of later date seem to indicate that before 1648 a substantial settlement had sprung up on the east side of the river.

In a brief submitted by Brant van Slichtenhorst in 1656 to the district court of the Veluwe, in the Netherlands, the statement is made that on his arrival in the colony, in March 1648, there were, besides the patroon's trading house, but three houses standing near the fort; that in August of the same year eight houses had been built; and that at the end of his administration, in 1652, there was a settlement of about one hundred houses. Considering these statements in connection with various allusions to building operations which occur in the records, it seems that between 1648 and 1652, apparently at Van Slichtenhorst's initiative and probably for reasons of greater safety and convenience, the settlers on the east side of the river gradually removed to the west side, in the immediate vicinity of the fort.

The erection of these new houses soon attracted the attention of Director Stuyvesant, who objected to their location on the ground that they endangered the security of the fort. Claiming that the jurisdiction of the fort included all territory within range of cannon shot, reckoned at 600 geometrical paces of 5 feet to the pace, he ordered the destruction of all buildings within a radius corresponding to this range, a distance which was afterwards estimated at 150 rods. The order called forth a vigorous protest from Van Slichtenhorst, who regarded it as an invasion of the patroon's rights and who proceeded with the erection of the buildings. A bitter controversy ensued, in the course of which various charges were brought against Van Slichtenhorst, who was summoned to appear at the Manhatans and was there thrown into prison and detained for four months. At length, in the spring of 1652, being determined to settle his dispute with Van Slichtenhorst, Director Stuyvesant repaired to Fort Orange and there issued his proclamation erecting a court for Fort Orange and the village of Beverwyck, apart from and independent of that of the colony of Rensselaerswyck.

The newly created court, which was termed a *Kleine Banck van Justitie*, an inferior bench of judicature, was a court for the trial of civil and minor criminal causes, from which an appeal lay to the Director General and Council of New Netherland. The court was composed of the *commies*, or commissary of the fort, afterwards bearing the title of vice director, and a variable number of *commissarissen*, or local magistrates, often designated in English documents of the period as " commissaries." Of these the commies, who acted as prosecuting officer and who represented the company, was appointed for an indefinite term of years directly by the Director General and Council of New Netherland, while the magistrates, at least in theory, represented the people and were appointed annually from a double number chosen by the inhabitants. When sitting as a criminal court, the officer presided and demanded justice of the magistrates, who not only found whether the accused was guilty, but also determined the penalty that should be imposed him.

The jurisdiction of the court comprised Fort Orange, the village of Beverwyck, Schenectady, Kinderhook, Claverack, Coxsackie, Catskill and, until May 16, 1661, when a court was established at the Esopus, also the region around Kingston. Excluded from the jurisdiction was the colony of Rensselaerswyck, which maintained its own court, side by side with that of Fort Orange and the village of Beverwyck until 1665, when by order of Governor Richard Nicolls the two courts were consolidated. A record of the court of Rensselaerswyck for the period 1648-52, when it was presided over by Van Slichtenhorst, has been preserved, but no record exists of judicial proceedings after the last mentioned date. Considering that the majority of the tenants of the patroon had become burghers of Beverwyck and had their cases tried before the local court, it is fair to assume that the court of the colony of Rensselaerswyck was rarely, if ever, called upon to exercise its judicial functions after 1652, and that therefore no record was kept.

As an illustration of the primitive conditions under which the court of Fort Orange and Beverwyck conducted its sessions, it is interesting to read the description of the first two buildings that were occupied by the court. This description has been preserved in a memorandum which was presented by Vice Director La Montagne to the Director General and Council of New Netherland on September 4, 1660, in justification of the expenditures incurred by him in building the second court house in 1657-58. The description of the original building is as follows:

The old house was 26 feet and 9 inches Rhineland measure in length and two stories high, built all around of one inch boards and having a pavilion shaped roof, covered with old shingles, as said before. Underneath was a cellar, 19 feet wide and as long as the width of the house. The first story had eight beams, resting on corbels, and was divided in two by a pine partition; at the north end was a room, 16 or 17 feet in width, and at the south end a vestibule, 10 feet wide. The second story consisted of a single room used by the court, without ceiling or chimney, and to reach this room one had to climb a straight flight of stairs through a trap door.

The old building, which stood close to the fort, on the present steamboat square, had by 1657 sagged at the north end in such a way as to crush almost completely the house of Lambert van Valckenburgh and its general condition was so dilapidated that repairs seemed useless. It was therefore torn down to make room for a larger brick building, which in the above-mentioned memorandum is described as follows:

A brick building was built, with two cellars, each 21 feet square, separated by a two-brick wall. The foundation of the said cellar is 3 or 4 feet in thickness, built of substantial stone (hauled a distance of 16 miles), 6 feet high, to the level of the ground, and on top of this is a brick wall, two feet high and three bricks thick, upon which rest the cellar beams. The first story is divided into three parts: at the north end is a room 21 feet square, inside measure, with a brick chimney; at the south end a kitchen 16 feet in width and 21 feet in length, also with a chimney and provided with a bedstead and cupboard of wainscot; and in the middle a hallway 5 feet wide, separated from the large room by a one-brick wall. The upper story is divided by a half-brick wall into two equal parts, each 21 feet square. At the north end is a room intended for the court; at the other end an office, in which are a wainscoted bedstead and a chimney. Access to this floor is by a winding stairway and a separate landing. On this landing there are three doors, one to the left, which gives access to the court room; another toward the front, which gives access to the office and which is faced by an oval window in the west wall; and a third door to the right, which gives access to the attic by means of a winding staircase. This attic extends over the whole house and above it there is a loft, suitable for the storage of powder and other ammunition. In short, it is a strong and substantial house, the walls below and above (upon which the beams rest without corbels) being one and a half bricks thick, provided at each gable end with a double chimney, braced by 42 anchors and built of choice clinker brick. The house is covered with well burned tiles and in every one's opinion makes a strong, commodious and handsome structure.

The records of the court, which under different names continued to exist until the erection of the mayor's court of the city of Albany in 1686, have for the greater part been carefully preserved. They consist of eight books of minutes, all written in the Dutch language, of which six, containing the minutes for 1652–56, 1658–59, 1668–73, 1675–84, 1676–80, and 1680–85, are kept in the Albany county clerk's office, and the remaining two volumes, containing the minutes for 1657 and 1660, form part of volume 16 of the *New York Colonial Manuscripts* in the New York State Library.

A complete calendar of the minutes, with the exception of those for 1657 and 1660, which are listed in the *Calendar of Historical Manuscripts*, edited by E. B. O'Callaghan, was prepared by Berthold Fernow, in 1894–95, under the direction of Wheeler B. Melius, in connection with the publication of the printed Index to the Albany county records, of which Mr Melius was the superintendent. A copy of this calendar, with editorial and genealogical notes by C. A. Hollenbeck, who used the pseudonym of " Jed," appeared under the heading " Historical Fragments " in the Sunday issues of the Albany Argus for October 18, 1903–April 23, 1905.

Translations of the minutes for 1658–59, which are entered in a record entitled *Mortgage[s] No. 1, 1652–1660*, were included among the manuscripts of the late Professor Jonathan

Pearson, which were recently placed at the disposal of the New York State Library by the author's sons and which, with the exception of these minutes, were published under the title of *Early Records of the City and County of Albany and Colony of Rensselaerswyck*, but, as far as known, no full translation of the entire series of minutes has ever been made.

That the oldest judicial and administrative records of the city and county of Albany should thus, for a period of more than two hundred years, have remained virtually a sealed book, is much to be regretted. It is surprising in view of the fact that as early as December 31, 1768, an act was passed providing for the translation of the Dutch records in the custody of the clerk of the city and county of Albany. The bill, which was introduced in the General Assembly by Col. Philip Schuyler, referred to a committee and favorably reported by Abraham Ten Broeck, makes no mention of any court records and was apparently primarily intended to provide for the preservation and translation of deeds and other writings which as the act says " greatly concern the Estates and property of the Freeholders and other Inhabitants of the said County, and in their present Condition are in danger of being lost." As another section of the act, however, refers to the turning over to the translator by the clerk of " all the Dutch Records and Writings remaining in his custody," it may be assumed that the court records were meant to be included. Whatever may have been the intention of the introducer of the bill, there is no evidence to show that any such translations as were contemplated by the act were ever made.

The first book of minutes, of which a translation appears in the present volume, is a folio volume of 321 pages, which contain the proceedings of the court from April 15, 1652, to December 12, 1656. The handwriting in the book varies, the first part being apparently that of Joannes Dyckman, who was commissary of Fort Orange from 1651 until June 1655, when he was incapacitated by insanity. During the administration of

Joannes Dyckman, Pieter Ryverdingh was court messenger and for some time also clerk, and it is possible that some of the entries are in his handwriting.

Johan de Deckere, who succeeded Dyckman, was appointed presiding commissary at Fort Orange on June 21, 1655, and the minutes from July 13th of that year until July 17, 1656, were kept by him. Johannes de La Montagne, who offered to go to Fort Orange on August 22, 1656, was appointed the same day and received his commission as vice director on September 22d of that year. The first entry signed by him occurs under date of October 13, 1656, and appears to be in the handwriting of Johannes Provoost, who during the administration of La Montagne was the clerk of the court. The court messenger at that time was Ludovicus Cobes, who received his appointment on August 7, 1656. For the period from October 4 to December 12, 1656, an engrossed copy of the minutes is found in part 2 of volume 16 of the *New York Colonial Manuscripts*, in the New York State Library, of which use has been made to supply the signatures to the entry of October 4, 1656, which are cut out of the original record, presumably for the sake of securing the autograph of Peter Stuyvesant, who on that date presided over the court.

In making the translations, the effort has been to combine close adherence to the original text with a fairly fluent English rendering, a task which in view of the technical character and often defective form of expression of the original minutes has proved most difficult.

Albany, N. Y., July 20, 1920

A. J. F. VAN LAER

COURT MINUTES

1652–1656

[1][1] In the name of the Lord, Amen

Proceedings of the Inferior Court of Justice erected and established in Fort Orange by order of the Hon. Petrus Stuyvesant and the Hon. Council of New Netherland, pursuant to the instructions and the oath taken on the 10th of April 1652, and the request of the burghers of the aforesaid fort and Beverwyck, situated within the established limits.

Monday, April 15, 1652

Present:

Joannes Dyckman   Abraham Staets   Volckert Jansz
Cornelis Theunisz van Westbroeck

Abraham Pietersz Vosburgh, appearing before the court, requests that he may proceed with the erection of his house, as the prohibition and nonallowance thereof involve his, Vosburgh's, total ruin.

Whereupon, it being taken into consideration that the house which he is erecting stands behind the dwelling of Commandant Brant Arisz van Slichtenhorst[2] and therefore does not greatly crowd or obstruct the fort, and seeing also the great expense already incurred by him, his request is granted.

---

[1] Figures within brackets indicate pages of the manuscript. Elsewhere brackets show material supplied by the editor.

[2] April 23, 1652, a patent was granted to Abraham Pietersz Vosburgh for "a parcel of land, ten rods square, adjoining on the south a lot and garden of van Slechtenhorst, on the north a vacant lot, extending from the side of the wagon road to the stockade in the rear." The original of this patent is in the possession of the Albany Institute and Art and Historical Society.

Whereas several persons have applied for permission to build on some lots between the two kills, it is after deliberation approved, wherefore Dirrick Jansz and Abraham Pietersz Vosburgh are chosen and appointed surveyors to make a proper survey.

[2] Upon the petition of Rut Arentsz to have a lot near his house, it is resolved to refer the same to a committee to be appointed for that purpose.

Upon the petition of Hermen Bastiaensz, carpenter, for permission to erect a house commenced by him, as the petitioner incurred great expense even before the date of the prohibition by the Director General and Council and his house is not especially crowding the fort, being situated near the mouth of the first kill, consent is hereby given him to proceed with the building.

Commissary Joannes Dyckman, Volckert Jansz and Cornelis Theunisz van Westbroeck are appointed a committee to look after the surveying of lots and gardens, but the Hon. Abram Staets is unanimously requested, in case his honor can be present, to assist the aforesaid committee.

In accordance with the instructions, it is resolved that the regular sessions of the court shall be held on Tuesday of each week, at ten o'clock in the forenoon.

Extraordinary Session, April 17, 1652. Post Meridiem

Present:

Jo: Dyckman   Ab: Staets   Vol: Jansz
Cor: Theu: v: Westbroeck

Jan Machielsz and Jacob Luyersz, plaintiffs, about charges of theft

Sander Leendertsz, defendant

The defendant states under oath that he brought no complaint against the plaintiffs, but that his negress circulated the story. Resolved, to examine the negress for further information.

[3] The instructions drawn up for the surveyors, Dirrick Jansz and Abraham Pietersz Vosburgh, having been examined, are adopted, whereupon, being summoned to come into the room, they have taken the usual oath before this court.

Jan Verbeeck, an inhabitant of Beverwyck, having appeared before the court, has taken the usual burgher oath.

Jan Thomasz and Marten Hendrixsz, inhabitants of Beverwyck, confirmed by oath before the court a certain affidavit for the behoof of Pieter Hertgers and Jan Verbeeck, concerning the discharge of the said persons from their duties as magistrates of the colony of Rensselaerswyck.

The court messenger, Pieter Ryverdingh, has been allowed the following fees, to wit:

For each citation, 6 stivers
For each attachment, 12 stivers
For each presentation of a petition, 4 stivers

Tuesday, April 23, 1652

Present:

J: Dyckman   V: Jansz   C: T: Westbroeck
J: Labatie   A: Herpertsz

Thomas Chambre, plaintiff, against Isaack de Forrest, defendant.

Plaintiff in default.

Volckgen Juriaens, plaintiff, about a blow with the fist and abusive words, according to deposition, against Geertruyt [Jeronimus],[3] defendant.

The defendant is for her abusive language and assault and threats made here against the court condemned to pay a fine of six guilders, with order to leave the plaintiff henceforth in peace.

[4] Jan van Hoesem, plaintiff, against Willem Juriaensz, defendant.

---

[3] She was the wife of Jochem Becker, the baker.

The dispute between the parties about the lot having been heard, it is resolved to adjourn the case until further advice from the Hon. General, who will be written to about it.

Pieter Bronck, appearing in court, requests that he may take possession of the lot as staked out. The court, having heard Cornelis Theunisz van Westbroeck and listened to verbal arguments on both sides, refers the matter to magistrates Jan Labite, Volckert Jansz and Andries Herpertsz, to examine the same and dispose thereof.

Jacob, the brewer, having requested permission to build an addition to his house, standing near the first kill, [the court,] taking into consideration that he has everything ready thereto and that the work can not be left undone without considerable loss to him, grants his request for very urgent reasons.

JOANNES DYCKMAN
JAN LABATIE
VOLCKART JANSZ
ANDRIES HERBERTS
CORNELUS TONISEN

Ordinary Session, April 30, 1652

Jan van Hoesem, plaintiff, for slander
Jochem Becker, baker, defendant

Jochem, the baker, is ordered to bring proof of his accusations at the next session of the court.

Caspar Jacopsz appearing before the court and requesting that he may have the lot granted him by this court, between Jacob Adriaensz, wheelwright, and Tunis Jacopsz, consent thereto is given for certain reasons.

[5] The court having considered the request of Jan van Hoesem to have the use of the lot on which he dwells and his garden, according to the resolution of the court of the colony, dated the 18th of January last, it is upon examination of the said

resolution decided by this court that the lot and garden shall from now on be assigned to Jan van Hoesem, upon condition that Willem Juriaensz shall have the right to occupy the house in which he now dwells as long as he lives, it being recommended that he furnish proper accommodation for Jan van Hoesem.

Commissary Dyckman, plaintiff, against Jochem Becker, defendant.

Defendant is ordered this day week to bring proper proof of the slanderous charges against the aforesaid commissary and president.

JOANNES DYCKMAN
JAN LABATIE
VOLCKART JANSZ
ANDRIES HERBERTS
CORNELUS TONISEN

Ordinary Session, May 7, 1652

Present:

Jo: Dyckman   J: Labatie   Andries Herpertsz
Rut Jacobsz   V: Jansz
Cornelis Theunisz van Westbroeck

Volckgen Juriaens, the wife of Jan van Hoesem, plaintiff, on account of slander

Geertruyt, the wife of Jochem, the baker, defendant

Styntge Symants declares that she knows nothing of the plaintiff but what is honorable and virtuous.

Defendant is ordered, on pain of severe punishment, to bring the proofs of which she has boasted into court on the next court day, when a decision will be rendered by this court.

[6] Reyer Elbertsz, residing outside the limits of this fort, has been granted the use of some low land near the third kill, allotted to him to be fenced in and cleared of trees, and to have the use thereof until further order.

Upon the request of Wouter Aertsz van Putten to have a piece of land for a house lot and a vegetable garden situated near the cripple bush, behind Marten, the brewer's, it is decided to let him have the same as soon as he shall have taken the oath of allegiance to the company, Rut Jacobsz and Jan Labatie being appointed a committee to lay out the aforesaid land for him. This day the aforesaid Wouter Aertsen has taken the oath of allegiance.

This day Juriaen Theunisz has denied under oath in court the charges brought a week ago in the matter of Commissary Dyckman and Jochem, the baker.

Commissary Dyckman entering a complaint about insults offered to him by the person of Jacob Jansz Schermerhooren, it is ordered that the court messenger shall summon him to appear on the next court day.

The ordinance prohibiting the tapping of wine and beer on Sunday during divine service is taken up again and adopted and published this day.

JOANNES DYCKMAN
RUTGER JACOBSEN
VOLCKART JANSZ
ANDRIES HERBERTS
CORNELUS TONISEN

Ordinary Session, May 14, 1652

Present:

J: Dyckman   J: Labatie   A: Herbertsz
A: Staets   V: Jansz   C: T: v: Westbroeck

Jan Machielsz, plaintiff, against Cathalina Sandertsz, defendant.
The defendant's first default.

[7] Joost, the baker, plaintiff, against Pieter Bronck, defendant.
Defendant's first default.

Hendrick van Driest, being summoned to appear, is asked why he enlarged his garden on his own account by moving his clapboard fence? The accused admits his guilt, whereupon Mr

Abraham Staets and Jan Labatie are appointed to make an inspection and to take such measures as they shall see fit.

Commissary Dyckman, plaintiff, against Jacob Clomp, defendant.

Defendant acknowledges that he drew his knife twice, but says that he was provoked thereto first. Case adjourned until the next court day.

The request of Dirrick Bensingh, corporal, to have provisionally a garden next to Ariaen van Alckmaer and to fence the same with palisades, is granted on condition that in case hereafter other arrangements are made, he shall have to give up the same, and the bounds thereof shall be shown him by Mr Abraham Staets and Jan Labatie, appointed for that purpose.

Volckgen Juriaens, wife of Jan van Hoesem, plaintiff against Geertruyt, the wife of Jochem Becker, the baker.

Defendant being for the third time in default, it is decided to summon her for the last time to appear on the next court day, when final judgment will be given. Meanwhile she shall be notified that if she has any proofs to submit, she must do so before the aforesaid time, on pain of arbitrary punishment.

JOANNES DYCKMAN
ABRAM STAETS
RUTGER JACOBSZ
JAN LABATIE
VOLCKART JANSZ
CORNELUS TONISEN

[8] Extraordinary Session, May 29, 1652

Present:

J: Dyckman   V: Jansz   C: T: Westbroeck
J: Labatie   A: Herpertsz

After examination of the letter and the points of the request concerning the amplification of the instructions for this court of justice, it is resolved to send the same to the deputies, Mr Abraham Staets and Rutger Jacopsz, who are at the Manhatans.

A complaint having been made to this court by Volckgen Jans, that Jochem Becker, the baker, has put up a pigsty opposite the door of Jan van Hoesem, it is decided that whereas the said Becker has done this directly against the order of this court and also created an obstruction and nuisance to the house of the aforesaid Jan van Hoesem, it is ordered that he, Becker, must within the time of three days tear down the said pigsty and remove it to a more convenient place, on pain of forfeiting twelve guilders to the sheriff.

Upon examination of the marginal annotation on the petition presented by Willem Juriaensz to the Director General and Council of New Netherland, it is resolved to abide by the resolution passed on the 30th of the preceding month.

On the complaint of Jan Verbeeck about the running away of his boy to Margriet Willems, in view of the fact that according to the authentic copy of the contract he was bound for another year, the aforesaid boy is ordered by this court immediately to reenter his master's service, on pain of punishment to be determined for that purpose and Margriet Willems is ordered not to detain the aforesaid boy on pain of arbitrary punishment.

Upon the request of Volckgen Jans, wife of Jan van Hoesem, for permission to erect a small bark house on her lot, the Hon. Volckert Jansz and Cornelis Theunisz van Westbroeck are appointed to point out to her a suitable place therefor.

         JOANNES DYCKMAN
         JAN LABATIE
         VOLCKART JANSZ
         ANDRIES HERBERTS
         CORNELUS TONISEN

[9] Extraordinary Session, ultimo May 1652

Present:
J: Dyckman   V: Jansz   C: T: v: Westbroeck
J: Labatie   A: Herpertsz

Adriaen Jansz from Leyden, aged 25 years, and Maeriecke Ryverdinxs from Dansick, aged 24 years, having requested to enter the married state, permission is granted to have the first proclamation of the banns take place on Sunday next.

Volckert Jansz, magistrate, plaintiff, about abusive language and assault, against Jochem Becker, the baker, defendant.

The court having examined the documents in the case, it is resolved to send them to the deputies of this court at the Manhatans, to be communicated to the supreme authorities there, whose order thereon they are to write and forward to us.

JOANNES DYCKMAN
JAN LABATIE
ANDRIES HERBERTS
CORNELUS TONISEN

Post Meridiem

Whereas Jochem Becker declared this morning that some members of this court immediately reported at the house of Jan van Hoesem what had taken place here in court, this is entered here with a view of questioning and examining the aforesaid Becker further about this matter and in case of lack of proof to punish him therefor by arbitrary sentence, as this tends greatly to the disparagement of this court.

JOANNES DYCKMAN
JAN LABATIE
VOLCKART JANSZ
ANDRIES HERBERTS
CORNELUS TONISEN

[10] Ordinary Session, June 3, 1652

Present:

    J: Dyckman   V: Jansz   C: T: Westbroeck
    J: Labatie   A: Herpertsz

Volckert Jansz, in the name of Joost, the baker, plaintiff, against Pieter Bronck, defendant.

Defendant is ordered to present to the court proper proof that the point of the plowshare is broken off and that he sent back a gun undamaged. When proper proof hereof is furnished, the court shall pronounce judgment regarding the claim of 50 guilders [for damages].

Jan Machielsz, plaintiff, against Cathalina Sanderts, defendant.

The case is adjourned until the next court day.

It is resolved to have the palisades of the garden of the old Captain[4] pulled up, if he refuses to do it himself, and to give Jan van Hoesem permission to put new palisades around it and from now on to take actual and personal possession of the garden.

                          JOANNES DYCKMAN
                          JAN LABATIE
                          VOLCKART JANSZ
                          ANDRIES HERBERTS
                          CORNELUS TONISEN

Ordinary Session, Tuesday, June 11, 1652

Present:

    J: Dyckman   J: Labatie   A: Herpertsz
    A: Staets   V: Jansz   C: Theunisz van Westbroeck
    R: Jacobsz

Jacob Luyersen and Jan Machielsen, plaintiffs, against Cathalina Sanders, defendant.

The negress is ordered to depart within the space of four days, on account of the false accusations brought against the fair name of the plaintiffs, either to the island of Cornelis Segertsz, or elsewhere, provided that she shall present the bill

---

[4] Willem Juriaensz, baker. See *Van Rensselaer Bowier Mss*, p. 820.

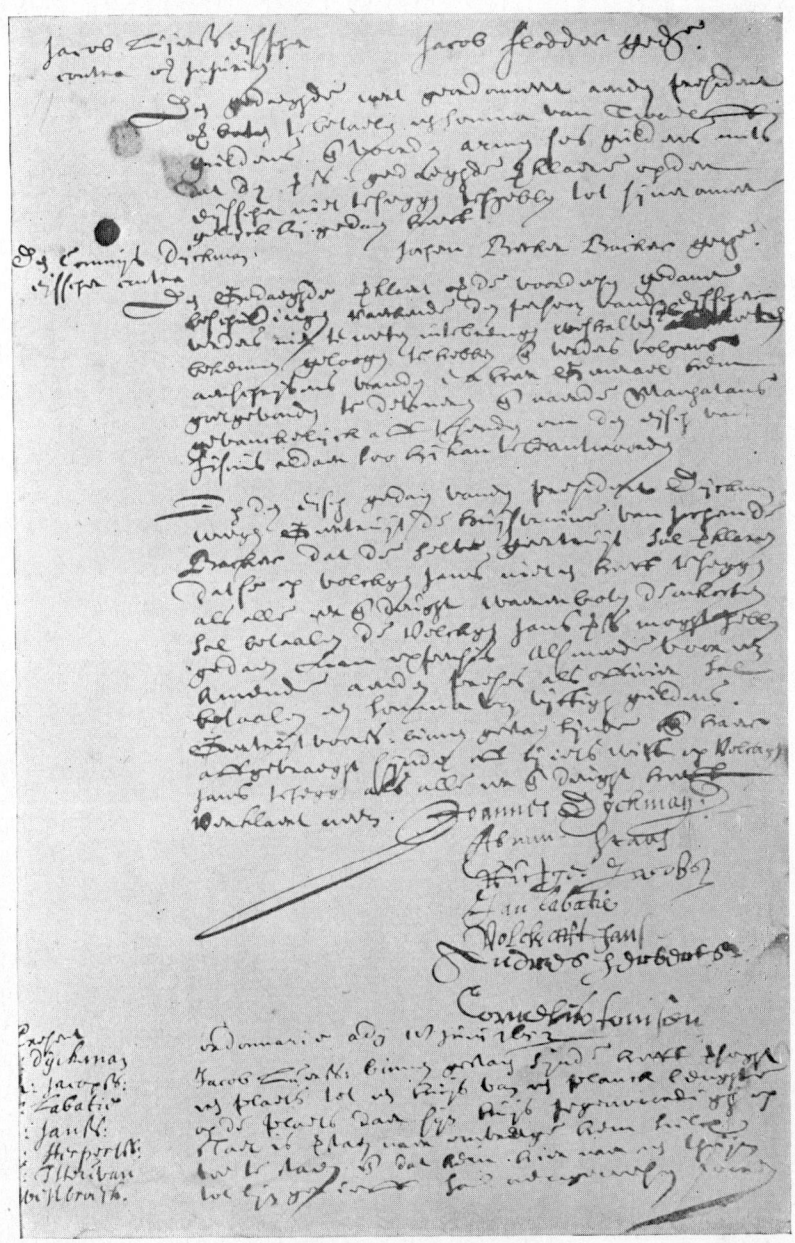

Minutes of June 11, 1652, in the handwriting of Joannes Dyckman

for the costs of the suit to the persons with whom the negress shall come to live and cause the same to be paid to the plaintiffs, but the aforesaid plaintiffs are ordered promptly to pay the court messenger what is due him.

[11] Jacob Luyersz, plaintiff, against Jacob Flodder, defendant, for slander.

The defendant is ordered to pay to the presiding officer a sum of twelve guilders by way of fine and for the poor six guilders, since the aforesaid defendant declared that he had nothing to say to the dishonor of the plaintiff, as he did.

Commissary Dyckman, plaintiff, against Jochem Becker, the baker, defendant.

The defendant declares that he has nothing further to say in regard to the charges heretofore brought against the person of the plaintiff; consequently, that he is forced to admit that he lied. Furthermore, pursuant to the directions of the Hon. General, it is resolved to detain him and to send him a prisoner to the Manhatans, to answer, if he can the complaint of the fiscal there.

On the demand made by President Dyckman, that Geertruyt, the wife of Jochem, the baker, shall declare that she has nothing to say against Volckgen Jans but what is honorable and virtuous and in addition pay the expenses which the said Volckgen Jans may have incurred, with the costs, and that furthermore the said Geertruyt shall pay to the president, in his capacity of sheriff, a fine of fifty guilders, the aforesaid Geertruyt, having appeared before the court and being asked whether she had anything to say against Volckgen Jans but what was honorable and virtuous, has declared No.

JOANNES DYCKMAN
ABRAM STAAS
RUTGER JACOBSZ
JAN LABATIE
VOLCKART JANSZ
ANDRIES HERBERTS
CORNELUS TONISEN

Ordinary Session, June 18, 1652

Present:

J: Dyckman J: Labatie A: Herpertsz
R: Jacopsz V: Jansz C: Theu van Westbroeck

Jacob Luyersz, appearing before the court, requests a place for a house, one board in length, on the spot where his present house stands. After deliberation it is resolved to grant his request and that later a garden will be assigned to him for his convenience.

[12] Geertruyt, the wife of Jochem, the baker, is ordered to deliver to the court this day week the fines which she has been condemned to pay.

This day Adriaen Jansz from Leyden and Maria Reverdinghs from Danswyck were united in marriage before the court here.

JOANNES DYCKMAN
RUTGER JACOBSZ
JAN LABATIE
VOLCKART JANSZ
ANDRIES HERBERTS
CORNELUS TONISEN

Ordinary Session, June 25, 1652

Present:

J: Dyckman J: Labatie C: T: Westbroeck
R: Jacopsz V: Jansz

After examination in court upon interrogatories of Geertruyt Jeronimus, wife of Jochem Becker, the baker, and Femmetgen Alberts, wife of Hendrick Jansz Westerkamp, regarding the abusive words spoken by Jacob Jansz Stol, commonly called Hap, against the respective magistrates, they have answered as may be seen in the said interrogatories, as was done likewise by the offender himself.

Ordinary Session, July 2, 1652

Present:

J: Dyckman   J: Labatie   C: T: v: Westbroeck
A: Staets

President Dyckman, plaintiff, against Jacob Jansz Hap, defendant.

It is resolved this first time to excuse the abusive words spoken by the defendant, but to enjoin and warn him to refrain from doing so in the future, on pain of being punished accordingly.

Willem Bout, plaintiff, against Rut Arentsz, defendant. Defendant's first default.

                J. DYCKMAN
                ABRAHAM STAAS
                JAN LABATIE
                CORNELUS TONISEN

[13] Ordinary Session, July 16, 1652

Present:

J: Dyckman   J: Labatie   A: Herpertsz
R: Jacobsz   V: Jansz   C: Theunisz van Westbroeck

Herman Bastiaensz, plaintiff against Thomas Sandertsen, defendant.

The matter in dispute is put in the hands of Rem Jansz, smith, Jan Verbeeck, Abraham Pietersz Vosburgh and Pieter Hertgers to conciliate the parties if possible and otherwise to report to the court.

Upon the complaint of Jan Machielsz and Jacob Luyersz that the negress of Sander Leendertsen continues to reside here notwithstanding the sentence of the court, it is ordered that Officer Dyckman shall conduct the negress outside the limits [of the village] and whoever harbors her again inside shall forfeit the first time six guilders and the second time twelve guilders and the third time shall receive arbitrary correction.

President Dyckman and Jan Verbeeck are appointed a committee to procure a list of burghers who are willing to subscribe for the support of the church and the minister and to make a report of their findings.

JOANNES DYCKMAN
RUT JACOBSZ
JAN LABATIE
VOLCKART JANSZ
ANDRIES HERBERTS
CORNELUS TONISEN

Tuesday, July 30, 1652

Present:

J: Dyckman   V: Jansz
J: Labatie   C: Theunisz van Westbroeck

Jan van Aecken, plaintiff, against Jan Daret, defendant. Defendant's first default.

JOANNES DYCKMAN
JAN LABATIE
VOLCKART JANSZ
CORNELUS TONISEN

[14] Tuesday, August 6, 1652

Present:

J: Dyckman   J: Labatie   V: Jansz

Joost, the baker, plaintiff, against Pieter Bronck, defendant.

The defendant having submitted for his defense that Jan van Breemen is indebted to him in the sum of fifty guilders and that last year he assigned his claim against Jan van Breemen to the plaintiff, and seeing that payment has not yet taken place and is acknowledged to have been refused, the case is adjourned until the arrival here of Jan van Bremen.

Pieter Bronck, plaintiff, against Jan Machielsz, defendant.

Defendant is condemned to pay the plaintiff the sum of one hundred and thirty-seven guilders and three stivers within the space of three months, according to his own confession, on pain of execution.

Jacob Clomp, plaintiff, against Dirrick Jansz Croon, defendant, in regard to a dispute about ax handle planks. The parties are referred to Rem Jansz, smith, and Philip Pietersz Schuler, as referees, to reconcile parties if possible.

Jan van Aecken, plaintiff, against Jan Daret, defendant.

Defendant's second default.

Geertruyt Jeronimus, plaintiff, against Styntgen Laurens, defendant.

Defendant's first default.

Dirrick van Nes, plaintiff, against Jan Verbeeck, defendant. Both parties' first default.

The petition being read of Adriaen van Ilpendam, whereby he requests that he may be promoted to the post of secretary and that to this end a letter of recommendation from this court may be sent to the Hon. Director General and the Hon. Council, his request is granted.

JOANNES DYCKMAN
JAN LABATIE
VOLCKART JANSZ

[15] Extraordinary Session, Wednesday, August 7, 1652

Present:

J: Dyckman   J: Labatie   A: Herpertsz
R: Jacobsz   V: Jansz   C: Theu: v: Westb:

Jan Labatie, plaintiff, against Jan Clomp, defendant, for 84 guilders due to Thomas Higge according to power of attorney from Jan van Bremen and attached in the hands of the Hon. Rut Jacobsz.

The court sets aside the attachment by Jacob Clomp of the aforesaid sum of 84 guilders in the hands of the Hon. Rut Jacopsz and orders him to pay the balance of the money to the plaintiff upon security, provided that the defendant may bring in his alleged claim against Thomas Higge on account of the sale of grain, which shall be his security for the recovery of the amount. Meanwhile, the defendant is ordered to pay immediately the costs of convening this court, on condition that if it is found later that his claims on account of the sale are justified, the court will order Thomas Higge promptly to reimburse the defendant for this present outlay.

Dirrick Nes, plaintiff, against Jan Verbeeck, defendant, about a debt of sixty guilders for blue linen and children's stockings.

The defendant declares that there is an overcharge of 6 guilders and in addition that he has something to claim on account of the stockings. As the parties base their claims on the writing of Dirrick Claesz Boot, at present at the Manhatans, they are ordered to write to him, Boot, about it to advise them of the truth, with offer to confirm by oath what he has to say, upon the receipt of which the court will render judgment. Meanwhile Dirck Nes is ordered promptly to pay the costs of convening this court, upon condition that they will be refunded if it is hereafter found that his claims were well founded.

The court messenger, Pieter Ryverdingh, is allowed fifteen stivers from each party for this extraordinary session.

JOANNES DYCKMAN
RUTGER JACOBSZ
JAN LABATIE
VOLCKART JANSZ
ANDRIES HERBERTS
CORNELUS TONISEN

Extraordinary Session, August 8, 1652

Present:

J: Dyckman   J: Labatie   A: Herpertsz
R: Jacopsz   V: Jansz   C: Theu: v: Westbroeck

Dirrick Jansz Kroon, plaintiff, against Herman Bastiaensz, defendant.

The plaintiff requests a receipt for some beavers taken with him to Holland for joint account, for which the defendant acknowledges that he has been paid. The defendant promises to grant the plaintiff a receipt and is hereby ordered to do so by this court in the amount of fl. 1277:15. Furthermore, the defendant is ordered to present and deliver to the court on Tuesday next the debit and credit account of the house, loss and profit, earnings and other matters outstanding between them both, when the plaintiff shall make payment and the defendant give a receipt.

Jan Jansz, plaintiff, against Willem Albertsz, defendant, for beavers in the hands of Jan Machielsz, tailor, which are attached by the defendant. The court sets aside the attachment issued against the said beavers and condemns the defendant to pay the costs of convening the court.

JOANNES DYCKMAN
RUT JACOBSZ
JAN LABATIE
VOLCKART JANSZ
ANDRIES HERBERTS
CORNELUS TONISEN

[17] Extraordinary Session, August 20, 1652

Present:

J: Dyckman   J: Labatie   A: Herpertsz
A: Staests   V: Jansz   C: Theu: v: Westb:
R: Jacopsz

Jan Labatie, plaintiff, against Hendrick Jansz Westerkamp, defendant, on account of eight beavers which the defendant owes to Philip Gerary,[5] acording to a note of the 16th of August of last year.

The court orders the defendant to pay the aforesaid eight beavers in specie to the plaintiff, by virtue of his power of attorney, within the space of ten days, on pain of execution.

Evert Tesselaer, plaintiff, against Marten, the mason, defendant, on account of some merchandise bought by the defendant from the plaintiff, amounting to the sum of fl. 141:10, which was to be paid cash.

The court orders the defendant to pay the aforesaid sum of fl. 141:10 to the plaintiff within the space of two days, or to return the plaintiff's goods, on pain of execution.

Dirrick Nes, plaintiff, against Willem Albertsz, defendant.

Defendant's first default.

Cornelis Jacopsz, plaintiff, against Jochem, the baker, for [payment of] fl. 136 in beavers for wages earned.

The court orders the defendant to pay the aforesaid sum of fl. 136 to the plaintiff in beavers within the space of ten days, on pain of execution.

Geertruyt Jeronimus, plaintiff, against Styntgen Laurens and Volckgen Jans, defendants.

The court orders each of the defendants to pay the sum of twelve guilders to the president for fighting and as they charge the plaintiff with having called them names, which [18] they have not been able to prove, the parties on both sides are fur-

---

[5] Philip Geraerdy, a tavernkeeper at New Amsterdam.

thermore ordered to hold their tongues and to leave each other in peace, as otherwise the court will take such measures as shall be found necessary.

Dirrick Bensinck, corporal here in Fort Orange in the service of the West India Company, having last year resided at the Manhatans in New Amsterdam and at that time sold to the Reverend Domine Joannes Magapolensis a certain house and garden situated there, has appeared before this court and acknowledged that he has been satisfied and paid therefor in full, the first penny with the last. In order that they may be mutually at ease and to prevent all further demands, he requests that this may be entered in the court record and that an extract therefrom be given him, the more so as he, Bensingh, can neither read nor write; which request is hereby granted him.

Philip Pietersz Scheuler is granted the lot heretofore given to Claes Croon, on the east side of Annetgen Bogardus, as it is assumed that he, Kroon, will not build upon it.

Jan van Aecken, plaintiff, against Jan Daret, defendant, for the recovery of fl. 150, loaned to him last year.

The defendant's third default. He is therefore ordered to pay the plaintiff the aforesaid fl. 150 within the space of four days and to appear and present himself here before the court a week from today to purge himself of the escape from arrest and in case of refusal he shall immediately betake himself outside of this jurisdiction and remain there, on pain of apprehension.

JOANNES DYCKMAN
ABRAHAM STAES
RUT JACOBSZ
JAN LABATIE
VOLCKART JANSZ
ANDRIES HERBERTS
CORNELUS TONISEN

[19] Ordinary Session, August 26, 1652

Present:

>J: Dyckman A: Herpertsz C: Theunisz
>R: Jacopsz J: Labatie A: Staats
>V: Jansz

Adriaen Jansz from Leyden, plaintiff, against Hendrick Jansz Westerkamp, defendant, for the sum of fl. 166, to be paid in beavers.

The defendant is ordered to pay the aforesaid sum of fl. 166 in merchantable beavers to the plaintiff on the first of June 1653 next, on pain of peremptory execution.

Adriaen Jansz from Leyden, plaintiff, against Jan Daret, defendant.

Defendant's first default.

Adriaen Jansz from Leyden, plaintiff, against Pieter Bronck, defendant, for the sum of fl. 64, to be paid in beavers.

The court orders the defendant to pay the aforesaid sum of fl. 64 in beavers to the plaintiff within the space of 24 hours, but to deduct certain fl. 33:7, which the plaintiff owes the defendant.

Adriaen Jansz from Leyden, plaintiff, against Lambert van Valckenburgh, defendant, for the sum of fl. 535 in beavers.

The court orders the defendant to pay to the plaintiff according to his promise made here, the half of the aforesaid sum of fl. 535 provisionally at the Manhatans in New Amsterdam before the departure of the ships lying ready to sail for *patria* and the balance by the middle of June of next year and in case of nonpayment execution in full is ordered.

>JOANNES DYCKMAN
>ABRAM STAES
>RUT JACOBSZ
>JAN LABATIE
>VOLCKART JANSZ
>ANDRIES HERBERTS

[20] Ordinary Session, September 3, 1652

Present:

J: Dyckman   V: Jansz   C: T: van Westbroeck
R: Jacopsz   A: Herpertsz

Cornelis Jacopsz, plaintiff, against Pieter Bronck, defendant, in regard to some claims.

The case is adjourned until the next session.

Arent Cornelisz Vogel being summoned and having appeared before the court is ordered and directed to present this day week his papers and the proofs which he may have or can secure, when judgment will be rendered.

JOANNES DYCKMAN
RUTGER JACOBSZ
VOLCKART JANSZ
ANDRIES HERBERTS
CORNELUS TONISEN

Extraordinary Session, September 4, 1652

Present:

J: Dyckman   V: Jansz   A: Herpertsz
R: Jacobsz

Willem Albertsz from Monickendam, plaintiff, against Jacob Clomp, defendant, about 100 boards of the Hon. Rut Jacopsz taken from plaintiff and put on board.

The court orders the defendant to return the one hundred boards loaded into his yacht *'t Seepaert* and to deliver them undamaged and free of charge on land, as he put them on board contrary to orders, and therefore to pay and turn over to Willem Albertsz the costs of the court. Furthermore, parties are at the first opportunity to settle with each other in regard to the accounts which they may heretofore have had together.

This day, Willem Albertsz has sworn before the court that he had given no orders to Jacob Clomp to put the aforesaid boards on board. The resolution being taken up again, it is provisionally decided to let the above written judgment take effect.

[21] There was read a certain writing and petition sent to this court by Mr de Hooges, secretary and commissioner of the colony of Rensselaerswyck, whereby he requests [relief] from annoyance caused him by the person of Willem Albertsz in demanding payment for an Edam cheese and six cans of wine, the first of which was retained as compensation for writing and the second were paid for by Joost, the baker.

After deliberation, it is resolved and decided to order Willem Albertsz to leave the aforesaid Mr de Hooges hereafter in peace and unmolested, on pain of punishment to be determined later. Meanwhile, he is to pay at once six guilders to the poor on account of the offensive conduct in the matter toward the person of the aforesaid Mr de Hooges.

As regards the fine of Willem Albertsz for fighting, the president is requested to submit his complaint and conclusion in writing on the next court day.

JOANNES DYCKMAN
RUT JACOBSZ
VOLCKART JANSZ
ANDRIES HERBERTS

Extraordinary Session, September 6, 1652

Present:

J: Dyckman   V: Jansz
R: Jacopsz   A: Herpertsz

Jan Machielsz, tailor, plaintiff, against Willem Albertsz, defendant, charging that the defendant accused the plaintiff of having stolen a cheese.

The court having examined the witnesses called and the parties and found that the plaintiff's charges are not true, they first condemn the plaintiff to pay the costs of the suit and furthermore order the parties on both sides to keep still and to behave themselves on pain of arbitrary correction.

The court having further examined the declarations made the day before yesterday by Geertruyt Jeronimus and Marritgen Jans regarding the drawing of the knife by Willem Albertsz from Monickendam, [22] sentence is passed in accordance with the complaint and conclusion, as may be seen from the documents.

JOANNES DYCKMAN
RUTGER JACOBSZ
VOLCKART JANSZ
ANDRIES HERBERTS

Present:

J: Dyckman   V: Jansz   C: Theuniszz v: Westbroeck
R: Jacopsz   A: Herpertsz

Interrogatories conducted by this court concerning the crime committed by Frans Gabrielsz from Delft against the daughter of Goosen Gerretsz, as may be seen from the contents thereof.

Upon consideration of the notice concerning the taking away of the canoes from the shore, it is resolved to post the same as drafted.

JOANNES DYCKMAN
RUT JACOBSZ
VOLCKART JANSZ
ANDRIES HERBERTS

Extraordinary Session, September 20, 1652

Present:

J: Dyckman   V: Jansz   C: Theunisz v: Westbroeck
R: Jacopsz   A: Herpertsz

In the matter of Frans Gabrielsz from Delft, at present a prisoner pursuant to the interrogatories conducted last Tuesday in regard to the crime committed by him, has accordingly confessed as shown in the margin [of said interrogatories], whereupon it is resolved to send the same to the Hon. General in order to learn his honor's very wise opinion and order thereon.

                JOANNES DYCKMAN
                RUTGER JACOBSZ
                VOLCKART JANSZ
                ANDRIES HERBERTS
                CORNELUS TONISEN

[23] Ordinary Session, October 8, 1652

Present:

J: Dyckman   A: Herpertsz   V: Jansz
R: Jacobsz   C: Theunisz v: Westbroeck

Merten, the mason, an inhabitant of Beverwyck, appears and acknowledges that he is indebted to Jan Jansz from Gottenburgh in the sum of fifty-eight beavers, which [he promises] to pay to [him] or his attorney next year before the departure of the ships, for which he hereby binds his house and goods according to the preference [of the payee].

Brecht Jacop's daughter, plaintiff, against Abram Pietersz Vosburgh, defendant, for 4½ beavers for goods supplied for his maintenance.

The defendant is ordered to pay the plaintiff within eight days three beavers in specie and twelve guilders in good, strung seawant.

                JOANNES DYCKMAN
                RUTGER JACOBSZ
                VOLCKART JANSZ
                ANDRIES HERBERTS
                CORNELUS TONISEN

Extraordinary Session, October 13, 1652

Present:

J: Dyckman   A: Herpertsz   C: T: v: Westbroeck
R: Jacopsz

The court having read and examined a certain authorization granted by the Hon. Director General and Council of New Netherland on the 28th of September last, concerning the person of Frans Gabrielsz from Delft, at present a prisoner here on account of a crime committed by him, and also the letter sent to the presiding officer and the advice contained therein, it is unanimously resolved to have the delinquent appear before this court and once more to [24] read to him his confession made heretofore upon interrogatories. Having come down and appeared before us, he has confessed as before and made the same statement that upon his confession was entered in the margin, with some additions. Whereupon, after deliberation, the president is requested to have the whipping post and its appurtenances made ready for tomorrow to punish the delinquent as an example to others.

On motion of the president made ex officio about the crime committed by Arent Cornelisz Vogel, who was imprisoned but released on bail, to have him provisionally also further examined tomorrow, his request is granted.

                               JOANNES DYCKMAN
                               RUTGER JACOBSZ
                               VOLCKART JANSZ
                               CORNELUS TONISEN
                               ANDRIES HERBERTS

Extraordinary Session, October 14, 1652

Present:

J: Dyckman   V: Jansz   C: Theunisz v: Westbroeck
R: Jacobsz   A: Herpertsz

Having seen the written bill of complaint and demand presented by the president against the delinquent, Frans Gabrielsz from Delft and duly weighed everything, we have concluded to condemn him, as we do hereby, as set forth at large in the record of the sentence, the execution of which is ordered to follow.

[The court] having examined and carefully considered the written complaint and demand presented by the president in his official capacity against the delinquent, Arent [25] Cornelisz Vogel, at present held in custody on account of the crimes committed by him, and also read the evidence against him, it was resolved to summon the witnesses to confirm their testimony by oath. Which being done, it was in accordance with legal procedure decided to have him brought to the place of justice, to be exposed to public [scorn].

However, before the sentence was read to him, the delinquent was informed that he was free to appeal, on condition of giving bail for the carrying out of the sentence. Whereupon, at the delinquent's request, two bailsmen appeared, to wit, Willem Fredrixsz and Marten Hendrixsz, who after recital of the crimes committed by the delinquent and the sentence that had been imposed upon him, begged to be excused from becoming bail. As the delinquent was unable to get any other persons to go bail for him, the sentence was left to take its course in accordance with its terms and as is to be seen more fully from the text, which to that end will be recorded in the Sentence Book.

                         JOANNES DYCKMAN
                         RUTGER JACOBSZ
                         VOLCKART JANSZ
                         CORNELUS TONISEN
                         ANDRIES HERBERTS

Ordinary Session, October 22, 1652

Present:

  J: Dyckman   V: Jansz   C: T: v: Westbroeck
  R: Jacopsz

  Volckert Jansz, plaintiff, against Pieter Bronck, defendant, for fifty guilders due by the defendant according to a note assigned in favor of Joost Theunisz, baker, at the Manhatans.

  The court orders the defendant [26] to pay the plaintiff the aforesaid sum of fifty guilders, the defendant to look to Jan van Bremen for the recovery of the sum and to make payment within the space of four weeks.

  A petition was read of Jan Thomasz and Laurens Jansz, burghers of Beverswyck, setting forth that shots are frequently fired at night by the Christians themselves, notwithstanding the ordinances against it, and requesting for the sake of preventing many accidents in the future that a warning may be issued by this court.

  Whereupon, after deliberation, it is resolved to note that proper provision in the matter will be made by the court for the future, and to request the president to make inquiries as to the persons who are guilty.

  Machiel, the *lademaker*,[6] appearing in court, requests to have a lot next to the lot[s] of Gerret, the cooper, and Annetgen Bogardus, which request is granted, notwithstanding said lot has heretofore been granted to Klaes Kroon, at the Manhatans, the president undertaking to defend the title against the claims of the said Croon.

  The president having announced that he understood and was informed that those of the colony,[7] directly contrary to our

---

  [6] The usual meaning of the word *lademaker* is that of a man who makes *geweerladen*, or gunstocks, *i. e.* a gunstock maker. Occasionally, however, the word occurs in the sense of a man who makes chests of drawers, in other words, a cabinet maker.

  [7] The authorities of the colony of Rensselaerswyck.

instructions, intended to make improvements to their building,[8] it is resolved to have the court messenger, Pieter Ryverdingh, serve our order on them in writing, as may be read therein at length.

[27] Extraordinary Session, October 28, 1652

Present:

    J: Dyckman   V: Jansz   C: T: van Westbroeck
    R: Jacobsz   A: Herpertsz

The court having examined the written request made of the court of the colony, and also the protest and prohibition to repair the building erected in spite of our protest which they thus far occupy and reside in by sufferance, and being informed that they intend to proceed with the repairs, it is, after mature deliberation, in view of the friendly request, protest and prohibition that have been made and pending the reciept of an answer to the letter written by the president to the Hon. General, resolved to leave the matter for the present in *statu quo,* until further order.

Whereas the president and the court messenger have informed the court that the Hon. Jan Labatie, appointed magistrate of this court, is going to live in the colony on the farm of Cornelis Theunesz van Breuckelen and therefore resigns from the office of magistrate, it is resolved to proceed anew to the nomination and election of an extraordinary magistrate. The Hon. Pieter Hertgers was elected by a plurality of votes and after the aforesaid Hon. Jan Labatie is duly released from his oath he will be installed in the office of extraordinary magistrate of this court and take the oath prescribed by our instructions.

                                    JOANNES DYCKMAN
                                    RUTGER JACOBSZ
                                    VOLCKART JANSZ
                                    ANDRIES HERBERTS
                                    CORNELUS TONISEN

---

[8] *Logement.*

[28] Ordinary Session, November 5, 1652

Present:

J: Dyckman   A: Herpertsz   C: Theu: v: Westbroeck

Evert Noldingh, plaintiff, against Jan van Breemen, defendant, for wages earned according to the contract, amounting to fl. 56:16.

The court orders defendant to pay plaintiff the aforesaid sum of fifty-six guilders, sixteen stivers, within the space of fourteen days, on pain of execution.

Pieter Bronck, plaintiff, against Jan van Bremen, defendant, for fifty guilders which he owes plaintiff.

The court having examined the circumstances of the case, order the defendant within fourteen days to present his evidence, showing what damage he suffered as to the plowshare and the gun, in order to pronounce and render judgment in accordance with the decision of the 22d of the preceding month.

Adriaen Jansz from Leyden, plaintiff, against Jan van Bremen, defendant, for fl.63:8:–, which he owes plaintiff for merchandise received according to the account submitted.

The court orders defendant to pay plaintiff the aforesaid sum of fl.63:8:–, within the space of six weeks, on pain of execution.

JOANNES DYCKMAN
ANDRIES HERBERTS
CORNELUS TONISEN

[29] Extraordinary Session, November 16, 1652

Present:

J: Dyckman   A: Herpertsz   C: Theunisz van Westbroeck

Commissary Dyckman, plaintiff, against Willem Albertsz from Monickendam, defendant, on account of the defendant's offensive conduct toward the person of Mr de Hooges, secretary of the colony of Rensselaerswyck, and his wife, according to the deposition and the testimony of Joost Theunisz, the baker, and the extract from a letter of the Rev. Domine Megapolensis. All of which papers, together with the sentence in the case passed by this court on the 4th of September last, [having been examined], it is decided, in view of the fact that there is no quorum present on the bench, to adjourn the case until the return of the magistrates who are absent, when final decision and sentence will be pronounced.

Meanwhile, the defendant is placed under arrest [with order] not to depart before further decision in the matter is made, unless released on bail.

JOANNES DYCKMAN
ANDRIES HERBERTS
CORNELUS TONISEN

Ordinary Session, December 3, 1652

Present:

Omnes

Received, a letter from the Hon. General Petrus Stuyvesant, dated the 26th of November 1652, and with it two ordinances, one of which, prohibiting the use of grain for brewing, is unanimously approved by all the magistrates for publication and for being posted. As to the other, regarding the tapsters' excise, the Hon. Rutger Jacopsz and Volckert Jansz declare themselves personally in favor of further communication [with the Director General], as [30] they have objections to its being published and posted.

Evert Nolden, tailor, requests to have a lot between the road near Annetgen Bogardus and Machiel, the lademaker.[9] The Hon. Volckert Jansz and Cornelis Theunisz van Westbroeck are appointed a committee to lay out and convey the said lot and road.

---

[9] *tusschen den wegh van omtrent annetgen Bogardus ende Machiel de lademaker;* literally, "between the road, from about Annetgen Bogardus and Machiel, the *lademaker.*"

Pieter Adriaensz, commonly called *Gemackelijck*, a resident of the fort, is upon the verbal report of Jacob Jansz Hap provisionally given permission to tap, on condition that in tapping and entertaining company he shall act quietly, in accordance with the provisions of the ordinance issued for that purpose.

Merten, the mason, is at his request granted the lot behind his place, on condition that if within six weeks he does not begin to build and gradually proceed with the work until it is finished, he shall be deprived thereof.

Hendrick Cassersz from Oldenborgh requesting a lot for a plantation near Wouter Aertsz van Petten, wheelwright, and a small hop yard, he is granted the same on condition that if he does not commence his plantation in the spring, he shall be deprived thereof, and that he must leave alone the lot of the aforesaid Wouter Aertsz and the necessary road or roads thereabouts.

JOANNES DYCKMAN
ABRAM STAES
RUTGER JACOBSZ
JAN LABATIE
VOLCKART JANSZ
ANDRIES HERBERTS
CORNELUS TONISEN

[31] Extraordinary Session, December 6, 1652

The lot granted heretofore to Philip Pietersz Scheuler, to the east, say to the west, of Marten, the mason, is approved and definitely entered as granted to him.

JOANNES DYCKMAN
ABRAM STAES
RUTGER JACOBSZ
JAN LABATIE
VOLCKART JANSZ
ANDRIES HERBERTS
CORNELUS TONISEN

Extraordinary Session, December 28, 1652

Present:

    J: Dyckman   V: Jansz   C: Theu: v: Westbroeck
    A: Staets   A: Herpertsz J: Labatie
    R: Jacopsz

On the date hereof, Evert Brantsen from Amersfoort, a soldier, is released by Commissary Dyckmans from his oath to the company taken as a soldier and engaged by this court as under-sheriff provisionally until next May, at wages of fl.18 a month and fl.100 for board, whereupon he has taken the oath of fidelity as under-sheriff.

Herman Bastiaensen, an inhabitant of Beverwyck, under arrest for misdemeanors committed by him regarding which evidence has been gathered, being arraigned before this court, has made confession and denial as set forth at length in the documents thereof. Therefore, the commissary is requested, if possible, to secure further evidence to be presented at the next session of the court, which he has undertaken to do. At the request [of the delinquent] [32] to be released on bail, this is for certain reasons granted upon severe conditions specified in the bail bond, whereupon Willem Fredrixsz, commonly called Bout, an inhabitant of Beverwyck, has appeared and after the bail bond was read to him, signed the bond as it stood before this court.

                      JOANNES DYCKMAN
                      ABRAM STAES
                      RUT JACOBSZ
                      JAN LABATIE
                      VOLCKART JANSZ
                      ANDRIES HERBERTS
                      CORNELUS TONISEN

Ordinary Session, January 7, 1653

Present:

J: Dyckman   R: Jacopsz   V: Jansz
A: Staets   J: Labatie

The commissary having submitted and complained to this court that in spite of the contract made with Herman Bastiaensen, carpenter, the Hon. Company's house is not being finished, notwithstanding the protest, friendly request and threats made, so that the company's house remains unfinished, to the great loss, prejudice and damage, not only of the company, but also of him, the commissary, and even of this court, it is after mature deliberation resolved and decided to order the aforesaid Herman Bastiaensz, as this court does hereby, to finish the work on the Hon. Company's house without any delay and not to let any good and suitable weather go by without working, on pain of having the aforesaid work executed and carried to completion by others [33] at the expense of the said Herman Bastiaensen, who is hereby ordered promptly to regulate himself accordingly. An extract herefrom shall be sent to him by the court messenger to regulate himself accordingly.

Jochem Becker, plaintiff, against Jan van Hoesem, defendant, for having hired of Willem Juriaensen the house standing on the plaintiff's lot, which he was prohibited from occupying.

Upon examination of the resolution concerning the lot passed by this court on the 30th of April last, it is decided that as long as Willem Juriaensz lives he shall be free to lease his aforesaid dwellinghouse to whomsoever he pleases.

Secondly, Jochem Becker, plaintiff, has exhibited a certain written contract made with Jan van Hoesem and Willem Juriaensen concerning the aforesaid lot, his furniture and baker's trade, which being read, Jan van Hoesem has requested a copy of the aforesaid contract, which request is granted on condition that Jan van Hoesem shall be bound to file his answer before the next session of the court.

Jan Claesz Brant, appearing before the court, requests a lot in Beverwyck, across the first kill, for the purpose of building thereon. After deliberation it is resolved and decided to request and appoint the Hon. Rutger Jacopsz and Volckert Jansz to lay out for him a lot near Willem Hap on the line.

The Hon. Abraham Staets having requested that the [description] [34] of the lot heretofore granted to him might be entered here, this is granted and it is situated as follows: Adjoining on the east side Rut Jacopsz, between [whose lot and his] there is a path five feet wide, reaching across the first kill; on the west side the hill, [length] six rods, two feet; southwards eight rods, on the north side the common wood road, twenty-five rods; again southward to the first kill, eight rods, and further along the boundary line of the said kill to the aforesaid five foot path.

JOANNES DYCKMAN
ABRAM STAES
RUTGER JACOBSZ
JAN LABATIE
VOLCKART JANSZ

Ordinary Session, Tuesday, January 14, 1653

Present:

J: Dyckman   J: Labatie   A: Herpertsz
A: Staets   V: Jansz   C: Th: v: Westbroeck
R: Jacobsz

Upon the request of the Hon. Jan Labatie for permission to take possession for his own use of the garden heretofore given to Jan Martensz, behind this fort, marked W 7, said permission is hereby granted him on condition that he obtain a patent from the Hon. General.

The president having stated that Jochem, the baker, according to the judgment of the court dated the 26th of August,[10]

---
[10] Not entered in the minutes.

owes him fl.50 on account of a dispute and that these have not yet been paid, the court decides that he must pay within fourteen days on pain of execution, which the officer is hereby authorized to levy.

[35] Jochem Becker, plaintiff, against Jan van Hoesem, defendant.

The defendant having appeared, requests that a member of this court proceed in his name against the plaintiff in the matter of the lot in issue between Jan van Hoesem and Willem Juriaensz, for which Jan van Hoesem received the patent.

The Hon. Rutger Jacopsz is unanimously chosen for this purpose, the present entry taking the place of a power of attorney.

Plaintiff says that the lot belongs to Willem Juriaensz.

Rutger Jacopsz, appearing for the defendant, demands security for the judgment.

Parties are ordered to give security for the judgment and to produce their evidence on the next court day when judgment will be pronounced.

Jochem Becker is notified and ordered to remove his lumber lying in the public road within twenty-four hours, on pain of forfeiting fifty guilders, of twice the amount on second notice, and of arbitrary correction on third notice.

On the side of Jan van Hoesem, Andries Herpertsz and Cornelis Theunisz van Westbroeck have become sureties for the judgment at the termination of the suit.

[36] This day, Arent Andriesz has taken the oath of burgher of Beverwyck before this court.

JOANNES DYCKMAN
ABRAM STAAS
RUTGER JACOBSZ
JAN LABATIE
VOLCKART JANSZ
ANDRIES HERBERTS

Ordinary Session, January 22, 1652

Present:

J: Dyckman R: Jacobsz V: Jansz
A: Staets J: Labatie

Volckert Jansz, plaintiff, against Pieter Bronck, defendant, for payment of fl.50 for Joost Theunisz, the baker.

The court having taken into consideration the judgment rendered by it, orders by virtue thereof prompt payment or execution.

Pieter Bronck, plaintiff, against Jan van Bremen, defendant, for the recovery of fifty guilders according the above written judgment given against the defendant.

The court order defendant to pay plaintiff within twenty-four hours, on pain of execution.

Barent Cramer, plaintiff, against Jan van Bremen, defendant, for the sum of fl.56:16, according to the judgment heretofore rendered.

Defendant says that he does not want to fulfil the contract because he was drunk when he signed it.

The court orders that defendant shall remain under arrest and imprisoned for debt until he has paid the aforesaid sum to the plaintiff, or gives security to the satisfaction of the plaintiff.

J. DYCKMAN
ABRAM STAAS
JAN LABATIE
RUTGER JACOBSZ
VOLCKART JANSZ

[37] There was read a petition from Goosen Gerritsz, burgher and inhabitant of Beverwyck, praying for a building lot, situated close to the third kill, on this side, with the thicket or swamp lying close to it. Resolved to note in the margin that the Hon. court is favorably disposed to accommodate the petitioner with a lot, but as to the other [ground], as it is considered best to keep this for common use, the request can not be granted.

JOANNES DYCKMAN
ABRAM STAAS
JAN LABATIE
RUTGER JACOBSZ
VOLCKART JANSZ

Ordinary Session, Tuesday, January 28, 1653

Present:

J: Dyckman   J: Labatie   A: Herpertsz
R: Jacopsz   V: Jansz   C: Theu: v: Westb:

Jochem Keteluyn having requested permission to have a lot next to Jan Claes Brant, on the north side, the same is granted and the Hon. Rutger Jacopsz and Volckert Jansz are requested to indicate the bounds of the lot, in order that he may obtain his ground brief in connection with his permit to build.

Commissary Dyckmans, plaintiff, against Pieter Adriaensen, innkeeper, defendant, on account of having tapped after commencement of divine service.

Defendant acknowledges that on the 19th of this month he was fined by the under-sheriff and that he used abusive language when fined.

The court orders him to pay the officer the sum of six guilders as a fine and if he is hereafter caught again, the double amount.

[38] A petition was read of Willem Fredrixsz, praying for permission to erect a horse mill in Beverwyck and to have the exclusive right to operate it for some time. Resolved to note in the margin that the petitioner must first indicate to this court

where he intends to put this mill and that then the matter will be taken under further consideration.

Jacob Hap and Jan de Visscher being called, the second default is taken against them.

Rutger Jacopsz, plaintiff, against Jochem Becker, defendant.

Plaintiff wants to know, first, whether the defendant still claims that the lot of Jan van Hoesem according to the ground brief belongs to Willem Juriaensz, and what proof he has thereof?

Secondly, plaintiff demands that the defendant, pursuant to the order of the court, give security for the judgment.

The defendant says that before the coming of the Hon. General to Beverwyck, no one had any ground of his own. The defendant refuses to give security or to bind himself for some one else and prefers to discontinue the suit.

The court orders the parties to live henceforth in peace and not to molest one another about the lot, on pain of being dealt with by this court as it may see fit; but with this provision, that the Hon. Magistrates Abraham Staets and Volckert Jansz are appointed to show the old captain [11] a place on the aforesaid lot where he may pile up his fire-wood, or to indicate to him how far he may use the lot, in order that the aforesaid Jan van Hoesem may properly fence off [39] his lot to suit his convenience.

On the complaint of Jochem Becker that Jan van Hoesem or his family were throwing hot ashes or embers against his clabboards, which he fears may some day cause a fire to the great detriment of himself and his neighbors, it is resolved to have the court messenger, Pieter Ryverdingh, enjoin the said van Hoesem in the name of this court from doing so in the future.

JOANNES DYCKMAN
RUTGER JACOBSZ
VOLCKART JANSZ
JAN LABATIE
CORNELUS TONISEN
ANDRIES HERBERTS

---

[11] Willem Juriaensz.

Ordinary Session, February 11, 1653

Present:

J: Dyckman   Jan Labatie   A: Herpertsz
A: Staets   V: Jansz

Goosen Gerritsz, plaintiff, against Rut Arentsz.
Both parties in default.

Herman Bastiaensz against Cornelis Hendrixsz, defendant.
First default of both parties.

Jacob Jansz Schermerhooren, plaintiff, against Adriaen Jansz from Leyden, about a certain lot situated next to the lot of the plaintiff, near the hill, marked No. 4, drawn by him last year, but afterwards promised to the plaintiff, or to Lysbet Cornelis, wife of Gisbert Cornelisz, whereof sufficient evidence has been shown to this court.

The Hon. Magistrate Jan Labatie, [40] appearing for the defendant to answer the plaintiff's demand, says that the defendant had no power to give away the lot, for if he did not wish to take possession of it, it reverted to this court.

The court having heard both sides, assign the lot from now on to Lysbet Cornelis, on condition that she must secure a ground brief therefor and that the defendant may take possession of the lot drawn by her on the conditions agreed to.

Goosen Gerritsen, plaintiff, against Rut Arentsz, tailor, defendant, for beer furnished and money due, amounting to fl.86:—

Defendant admits the debt.

The court orders defendant to pay plaintiff the aforesaid sum of fl.86:— or thereabouts, within the space of six weeks, on pain of execution.

Willem Fredrixsz having requested on January 28, last past, permission to erect a horse mill for the convenience of the burghers, it is after deliberation resolved to grant him permission to do so on his own lot, on condition that he keep within the street line; but as to his request for exclusive privilege, he is referred to the Hon. General and Council of the province at the Manhatans.

Received and read a letter from the Hon. General, dated the first of this month, giving notice of and inclosing an ordinance prohibiting the baking and sale to the Indians [41] of white bread and cake and the malting of hard grain, whereupon it is resolved to cause the same to be published.

On receipt of a letter from the Hon. General about the nonimposition of the tapsters' excise on beer and wines for a time, it is upon reconsideration of the matter resolved to give public notice that innkeepers shall hereafter not be allowed to ask more than 8 stivers for a *mutsje* of brandy and nine stivers for a can of beer, on pain of forfeiting for the first violation one hundred guilders, the second time twice as much and of receiving arbitrary punishment the third time.

JOANNES DYCKMAN
ABRAM STAES
JAN LABATIE
VOLCKART JANSZ
ANDRIES HERBERTS
CORNELUS TONISEN

Ordinary Session, Tuesday, February 18, 1653

Present:

J: Dyckman   V: Jansz   A: Herperts
A: Staets   J: Labatie   C: Theu: v: Westb:
R: Jacopsz

Rut Arentsz, plaintiff, against Aert Jacopsz, defendant.
Parties' first default.

Herman Bastiaensz, plaintiff, against Dirrick Jansz, defendant, about some disputed accounts outstanding between them.

The arguments on both sides having been heard by the court, it is decided that the plaintiff shall on demand promptly pay to the defendant what he is found to have received more than his share of the common account.

[42] [Plaintiff] also [demands] the sum of fl.211:–, for some gunstocks [12] made together. At the request of the defendant the case is put over to the next court day.

Steven Jansz, plaintiff, against Marten, the brewer, defendant, for carpenter's wages, moneys advanced and goods.

Defendant admits the debt.

The court orders defendant to pay plaintiff in accordance with the terms of the contract made together, within eight weeks, on pain of execution.

Commissary Dyckman, plaintiff, against Jochem Becker, defendant, for baking cake and white bread contrary to the ordinance.

Defendant says that he has not baked since the publication of the ordinance.

Jan van Hoesem, or Rut Jacobsz, as attorney, plaintiff, against Jochem Becker, defendant, about the accounts of the expenses incurred by the parties during the suit about the lot of Jan van Hoesem, claimed by the old captain, Willem Juriaensen. The court orders parties on both sides to pay the costs of the suit, and in case they are not satisfied with the judgment pronounced on the 28th of the preceding month and find themselves aggrieved by it, they are given the right to appeal to the Hon. General and Council of New Netherland. The court having heard the report made on the aforesaid date by the Hon. Abraham Staets and Volckert Jansz, the same is approved as to its provision that the old captain, Willem Juriaensen, may possess the aforesaid lot as long as he lives.

[43] Jan Smit, plaintiff, against Jan Gauw, defendant, for wounds inflicted on plaintiff by defendant. Plaintiff claims damages for pain and injury suffered and also payment of the surgeon's fees.

Defendant states that it was plaintiff's fault and that he pushed him and claims damages for lost time.

The court orders parties on both sides to present their evidence on the next court day.

---

[12] *Laaden.*

Commissary Dyckman, plaintiff, against Jacob Flodder, defendant, for fighting last Sunday with a hoe against Ellert, at the house of Pieter Bronck.

Commissary Dyckman, plaintiff, against Elbert Gerbertsz, defendant, for drawing his knife against Jacob last Sunday at the house of Pieter Bronck.

Defendant denies at first.

Pieter Bronck being questioned on oath says, Yes. Likewise the under-sheriff.

The court orders defendant to pay plaintiff at once a fine of twenty-five guilders and a like sum of twenty-five guilders to the poor, with the proviso that he shall remain in custody until the aforesaid payments are made.

Commissary Dyckman, plaintiff, against Rut Adriaensz, tailor, defendant, and Lysbet Rosekrans, on account of carnal conversation, committed according to mutual [44] confession on the seventh of this month at the house of the said Rut Arentsz.

Rut Arents declares that she, the said Lysbet Rosekrans, is and will remain a whore and that he does not want to marry her.

The aforesaid Rut Arentsz and Lysbet Rosekrans are ordered to appear on the next court day to hear the sentence of the court.

JOANNES DYCKMAN

Upon the request of the Hon. Magistrate Jan Labatie for permission to build on the corner of the first kill and to have the lot between the kill and the lot provisionally inclosed by Sander Leendertsen, said request is granted, the lot to be properly surveyed and the lines indicated to him.

JOANNES DYCKMAN
ABRAM STAAS
RUT JACOBSZ
JAN LABATIE
VOLCKART JANSZ
ANDRIES HERBERTS
CORNELUS TONISEN

Ordinary Session, Tuesday, March 4, 1653

Present:
J: Dyckman   R: Jacobsz   V: Jansz
A: Staets   J: Labatie   A: Herpertsz

Jan Smit, plaintiff, against Jan Gauw, defendant, for wounds inflicted by defendant on plaintiff's hand.

The court having heard the arguments on both sides and considered what took place at the last session, decides and orders, as it does hereby, that defendant shall pay plaintiff immediately the surgeon's fees, without the plaintiff having anything to claim on account of permanent injuries.

[45] The written complaint and demand being read of the president, ex officio, against Herman Bastiaensz, for cutting down the street line post, and the court having considered the serious consequences which in future might result therefrom, but being in hopes that he will behave better in the future, he is ordered by this court to pay the commissary, in his capacity as prosecuting officer, a fine of fifty guilders, and in addition to make promise of better behavior.

Dirrick Jansz Kroon, plaintiff, against Herman Bastiaensz, defendant, on account of a dispute about former accounts.

First, as to the collecting of the money, they are referred to the judgment heretofore rendered.

Secondly, as to the gunstock making, they are referred to Ariaen Jansz from Leyden and Master Ariaen van Ilpendam, arbitrators and referees, in order to come to an agreement if they can, of which a report is to be made to this court.

Giertgen Nannix, being cited before the court, declares at the request of Commissary Dyckman that Rut Arentsz before going home [promised that he would] legally marry her and that to that end he would give her a ring as a pledge of marriage before sleeping with her.

Commissary Dyckman, plaintiff, against Elbert Gerbertsz and Jacob, the carpenter, defendants, for having wounded each other in the neck and caused the blood to flow.

The parties are ordered to present their evidence at the next session of the court.

Pieter Bronck has become bail for the appearance of Elbert Gerbertsz on the next court day.

[46] A petition was read from the respective bakers in Beverwyck, requesting mitigation of the ordinance concerning the baking of white bread, pretzel and cookies to be sold to the Indians. Resolved to refer the petitioners to the ordinance.

JOANNES DYCKMAN
ABRAM STAAS
RUTGER JACOBSZ
JAN LABATIE
VOLCKART JANSZ
ANDRIES HERBERTS

Ordinary Session, Tuesday, March 18, 1653

Present:

  J: Dyckman   R: Jacobsz   V: Jansz

Jan van Hoesem, plaintiff, against Merten, the mason, defendant.

Parties' first default.

Jan de Visser, plaintiff, against Merten, the mason, defendant.

Defendant's first default.

Dirrick Bensingh, plaintiff, against Merten, the mason, defendant.

Jan Labatie, plaintiff, against Jochem Becker, defendant.

Defendant's first default.

Commissary Dyckman, plaintiff, against Abraham Pietersz Vosburgh, defendant, for fl.16, which he must pay to Arent Schapenbout and which the commissary desires shall be paid to him on account of a fine.

Resolved, that the same shall for the present remain attached; also the money which is due to him from Merten, the brewer, wherefore the court messenger is ordered to attach the one and the other anew until such time as this court shall make a further decision in the matter.

[47] Pieter Ryverdingh, plaintiff, against Jacob Luyersz and Jan Machielsz, defendants, for messenger fees amounting to fl.18:15:—

Defendants say that Sander Leendertsen must pay the same according to the judgment previously rendered by this court.

Ordered that the plaintiff may cite the parties or Sander Leendertsen to appear on the next court day.

Jan Labatie, plaintiff, against Jacob Hap, defendant, on account of fighting and a blow with the fist.

Plaintiff's first default.

A petition having been read from the respective bakers residing in Beverwyck, whereby they request permission to sell some white bread for the Indians, especially cake, for reasons more fully set forth in the petition, it is decided that as the president and some of the members of this court are to leave for the Manhatans, they may discuss the matter with the Hon. General, the report whereof shall be awaited. Until such time the petitioners must have patience and shall not be allowed to sell either stuff to the Indians.

JOANNES DYCKMAN
RUTGER JACOBSZ
VOLCKART JANSZ

Extraordinary Session, Saturday, April 5, 1653

Present:

The Hon. Fiscal Thienhoven	J: Dyckman	A: Staets
C: Theunisz van Westbroeck	Paulus Leendertsz	J: Labatie
Maximiliaen van Geel	A: Herpertsz	V: Jansz

The honorable fiscal and the delegates from the city of New Amsterdam have in the presence of the commissaries of this inferior court of justice verbally and in writing set forth and explained the reasons which have induced the Hon. Director General and Council of New Netherland to send the aforesaid delegates hither, said reasons being in the main twofold, namely:

First, that the ordinances heretofore issued concerning the malting and using of hard grain for brewing purposes have been duly published by this court and observed [48] as far as practicable, in connection with which the honorable delegates in the name of the Hon. Director General and Council of New Netherland thank the commissary and members of this court for the timely warning in regard to the consumption [of beer] as aforesaid, but that the court of the colony of Rensselaerswyck has thus far failed to put into execution the orders regarding the publication, posting and observance of the aforesaid well-meant and necessary ordinances. For this reason the honorable fiscal, together with the Hon. Paulus Leendertsen and Maximiliaen van Geel, were sent in order that they, with Commissary Dyckman and two members of this court, whereto after deliberation were chosen Abraham Staets and Jan Labatie, might request them, namely those of the court of Rensselaerswyck aforesaid, once more and finally, to publish and post the same. For which purpose the court messenger, Pieter Reverdingh, was sent to the director of the colony, Jan Baptista van Rensselaer, to inquire when it would be convenient for his honor to have their honors call upon him, whereupon the court messenger reported that he received for answer that his honor would let them know in the afternoon.

Secondly, the honorable fiscal and the delegates aforesaid have exhibited an order for a day of fasting and prayer to be held on the 9th of this month, being Wednesday, and thereafter on the first Wednesday of each succeeding month, which it resolved to communicate to the court of the aforesaid colony and subsequently to the Reverend Domine Gideon Schaets, in order that it may thus be observed and punctually carried out in accordance with the good intention and meaning of the Hon. General and Council of New Netherland.

[49] Extraordinary Session, Thursday, April 10, 1653

Present:

The honorable fiscal Maximiliaen van Geel J: Verbeeck
Paulus Leendertsz   J: Dyckman   J: Thomasz

For the accommodation of the good inhabitants here, surveyors have been summoned to lay out some lots beyond Gysbert Cornelisz, from his lot to the palisades of the land in use by Thomas Jansz, which surveyors having reported that eight lots, each forty feet wide, may be conveniently laid out, the first lot is given to Commissary Dyckman, the second to Domine Gideon Schaets, the third to Abraham Staets, the fourth to Jan Labatie, the fifth to Adriaen Jansz from Leyden, and the sixth to Pieter Ryverdinck, the other [two] lots to be granted later when there is occasion for it.

COR: VAN TIENHOUEN
JOANNES DYCKMAN

Extraordinary Session, Saturday, April 12, 1653

Present:

The honorable fiscal R: Jacopsz   J: J: Schermerhooren
Paulus Leendertsen   A: Herpertsz   C: Theunisz
M: van Geel   J: Verbeeck   Jan Thomasz
J: Dyckman

Commissary Dyckman having submitted to the court that yesterday, with the consent and order of the honorable fiscal, he had caused Jochem Becker, the baker, to be summoned by Pieter Reverdingh, the court messenger, because in violation of the ordinance he had in the absence of the commissary publicly blown the horn to sell white bread, directly contrary to the tenor of the ordinance of the Hon. Director General, and in addition given out and stated to the Hon. Abraham Staets that he had permission thereto from the aforesaid commissary, he has appeared before the court and persisted in his statements, and appealed to Hendrick Jansz Westerkamp, also a baker in Beverwyck as a witness, who being also summoned to appear by order of this court, was asked whether he, Westerkamp, had any knowledge thereof, whereupon he declared, No, so that the statement is found to be untruthful. The court having considered the evil consequences and results which might arise if no proper provision were made, especially at this juncture of time, [50] in the matter of disregard of the well-meant ordinances of the Hon. Director General and Council of New Netherland and false accusation of the commissary, therefore condemn the aforesaid Becker, as they do hereby, to pay a fine of fifty guilders within twenty-four hours, on pain of execution, one-third to go the poor.

This court having seen and read the written complaint and demand of the Hon. Fiscal Cornelis van Thienhooven against Jochem Becker, baker in Beverwyck, and the proper evidence in the case, showing contempt of this court and that some time ago he not only slandered the Hon. Magistrate Volckart Jansz and called him names, but also wanted to attack him by force with the sword which he had put on, demanding that his honor should go outdoors and intending to cut him; also that he has failed to show proper respect for this court and has refused to move the pigpens according to the order of this court which to the annoyance and detriment of his neighbor he had erected in front of the door; furthermore that he has unjustly accused the honorable magistrates, namely, by stating that when they came out of court they reported what had taken place at the house of Jan van Hoesem; and that he has falsely charged Commissary Dyckman with having offered to Jan van Hoesem to deliver to him the lot of Willem Juriaensen for three beavers, all according to his own confession made before this court; all of which are matters of very serious consequence; therefore, this court have unanimously decided, as they do hereby, to condemn him, on promise and in hopes of better behavior, to pay a fine of one hundred guilders, to be paid within twenty-four hous, on pain of peremptory execution, or the double amount within forty-eight hours, and so on in succession, whereof one-third is to go to the poor, one-third to this court and one-third to the prosecuting officer. Also that he shall immediately tear down and remove the pigpens, or that they shall be immediately torn down by order of this court.

[51] Extraordinary Session, Post meridiem, April 12, 1653

Present:
The honorable fiscal J: Dyckman   J: Thomasz
Paulus Leendersen   R: Jacopsen   C: Theunisz van Westb^r.
Maximiliaen van Geel A: Herpertsen

Before this court appeared Jan van Hoesem and Willem Juriaensen and exhibited a certain contract made between them under date of the 30th of January 1650.

Parties on both sides having been heard and the matter being duly considered, it is decided and ordered by the court that the aforesaid contract shall in all its parts and according to the tenor thereof be completely observed and carried out by the parties on both sides, with the understanding that the property mentioned in the contract shall be placed in the hands of Jan van Hoesem to have the use thereof according to the terms of the said contract. Furthermore, to prevent all further disputes and differences, it is ordered that Willem Juriaensen shall have to comport himself as a decent old man should and at noon and in the evening come to meals at regular hours as is proper and shall also have to be satisfied with the ordinary food which Jan van Hoesem daily provides for himself and his family; therefore, that Jan van Housem is not bound to supply Willem Juriaensen outside of his own house with food, or drink, or money for board.

Ordinary Session, Tuesday, April 29, 1653

Present:

J: Dyckman J: Verbeeck   Cor: Theunisz van Westbroeck
R: Jacopsz   J: J: Schermerhoorn   Jan Thomasz
A: Herpertsz

Jan Barentsz Poest, plaintiff, against Marten, the brewer, defendant, for two thousand brick delivered by plaintiff to the defendant.

Defendant admits that he is indebted for the brick and that he built his oven with them.

Plaintiff says that he heard Hendrick *de Moff* [13] say that the defendant broke his contract first.

The court orders the plaintiff to produce at the first opportunity the evidence which he claims to have of the breaking of their contract, when this court will consider the matter further and take a decision.

The Reverend Domine Gideon Schaets having appeared before the court requests to have a garden heretofore drawn by lot by Dirrick Bensingh, [marked] No. 24.

[52] The said Dirrick Bensingh having appeared, has offered to relinquish the same and it is therefore given to his Reverence.

Dirrick Bensinck is granted a garden behind the fort, No. 11, with the consent of the Hon. Jacob Jansz Schermerhoren, who gets No. 16 in place thereof.

The garden heretofore provisionally given to Dirrick Bensingh, next to Ariaen from Alckmaer, it is decided to give to Hendrick Jochemsz, upon condition that he, Hendrick Jochemsz, shall compensate Dirrick Bensinck for the palisades, carting of brick, etc., it being left to the discretion of the Hon. Andries Herpertsz and the Hon. Jan Verbeeck to indicate to said Bensingh how much he is entitled to claim therefor.

Steeven Jansz, plaintiff, against Merten, the brewer, defendant, for 187 guilders due by defendant to plaintiff for wages

---

[13] A contemptuous expression applied to a German.

earned by him, in regard to which judgment has been given before.

Defendant promises to do his best to pay within 8 or 14 days at the longest fl.50; another fl. 50 a month later and the rest at the first opportunity.

Dirrick Bensingh, plaintiff, against Merten, the mason, defendant, for fl.104:— for goods delivered.

Defendant admits the debt.

The court orders defendant to pay plaintiff the aforesaid sum of fl. 104:— on the first of August next ensuing, on pain of execution.

Jochem Becker, plaintiff, against Jan van Hoesem, defendant, for throwing dirty water and dirt on plaintiff's [53] lot.

Defendant and his family are ordered by the court to refrain therefrom, on pain of [forfeiting] the first time twelve guilders, the second time twenty-four guilders, and [of being subjected] the third time to arbitrary correction.

Upon the request of the Hon. Jan Labatie that the case between Rut Arent and Lyssbet Rosekrans pending before this court might be disposed of, the officer is requested and ordered to have the complaint and demand ready at the next session of the court.

There was read a petition of Thomas Sanderts and Master Ariaen van Ilpendam, praying for extension of time in which to fence in their garden heretofore granted to them. Time is given them until the first of October next.

There was read a petition from Abraham Pietersz Vosburgh, praying for permission to tap now and then beer by the can for home consumption. As the same is contrary to the ordinance, the request is denied.

JOANNES DYCKMAN
RUTGER JACOBSZ
ANDRIES HERBERTS
JAN VERBEECK
JAN THOMASZ
CORNELUS TONISEN
JACOB JANSEN SCHERMERHOOREN

Ordinary Session, May 13, 1653

Present:

Rut Jacopsz J: J: Schermerhoorn J: Thomasz
An: Herpertsz C: T: van Westbroeck J: Dyckman
J: Verbeeck

Dirrick Jansz, ensign, being asked whether he was willing to work yonder on the gristmill, or not, says, No, and is guilty therefore of contempt of the order of both courts.

Pieter Hartgers declares that he does not recognize in this matter the order of the magistrates, but only of the Hon. General.

Goosen Gerretsen declares that if the Hon. General orders it, he will work.

Volckert Jansz declares that if it were erected between the boundary posts, he would do so, otherwise not.

[54] Jochem Becker being summoned to appear, is notified that he must this day pay the fines heretofore imposed on him, amounting to fl.250:— on pain of forfeiting fl.12 additional for each day that he delays to pay.

Rut Jacopsz, plaintiff, against Jacob Clomp, defendant, for the balance of a *last* of wheat which defendant promised to deliver to plaintiff according to contract and of which 12 schepels have been delivered.

Parties are ordered to produce their documents and proofs on the next court day.

Jan Barentsz Poest, plaintiff, against Merten, the brewer, defendant, for 2000 brick and payment.

Parties satisfied.

Philip Pietersz, plaintiff, against Willem Albertsz, defendant. Defendant's first default.

There was read a writing from the Hon. Cornelis van Thienhooven, fiscal, in the name of the Hon. General, besides Mr Rensselaers and Domine Schaets. Resolved to write about it to the Hon. General.

Frans Barents, Jacob Jansz Schermerhoren and Symon Volckertsz, having appeared, request that they may be excused from paying the fines for not yet having fenced in their gardens.

Granted in view of the fact that they have already taken possession of the said gardens.

Willem Juriaensen having appeared before the court and protested that he is still willing to fulfil the contract made between him and Jan van Hoesem, he is informed that he can have his opponent summoned to appear on the next court day.

JOANNES DYCKMAN
RUTGER JACOBSZ
ANDRIES HERBERTS
JAN VERBEECK
JACOB SCHERMERHOOREN
CORNELUS TONISEN
JAN THOMASZ

[55] Extraordinary Session, June 6, 1653

Present:

J: Dyckman J: Verbeeck   C: Thuenisz van Westbroeck
R: Jacobsz J: J: Schermerhoorn Jan Thomasz
A: Herpertsz

Philip Pietersz Scheuler, plaintiff, against Willem Albertsz from Monickendam, defendant, for contempt of this court in escaping on the 13th and going away on the 14th of May last with his yacht which the plaintiff had attached and for some insults offered to the president in person which on trial the defendant could neither prove nor make good.

The witnesses being heard and everything being considered that pertains to the case, the defendant is ordered to pay to the officer of this bench the sum of forty guilders, in addition to the costs of the extraordinary session and messenger fees, the defendant being ordered to pay the said sum within twenty-four hours and to declare, as he has done, that he has nothing to say about the officer, nor about the plaintiff, Philip Pietersz, but what is fair and honorable.

Fines	fl. 40:–
Messenger fees	7:[10]
Extraordinary session, two days	32:–
Total	fl. 79:10

JOANNES DYCKMAN
RUTGER JACOBSZ
ANDRIES HERBERTS
JAN VERBEECK
JACOB SCHERMERHOOR[EN]
CORNELUS TONISEN

Ordinary Session, June 10, 1653

Present:

Dyckman   A: Herpertsz   J: J: Schermerhoorn
R: Jacopsz   J: Verbeeck   C: Theunisz van Westbroeck

Evert Pels, plaintiff, against Rut Arentsz, defendant.
Defendant's first default.

Claes Jacobsz, plaintiff, against Claes Cornelisz Croon, defendant, for a year's rent of a house standing at the Manhatans, hired by defendant, Claes Rips and Frans . . . ,[14] for the sum of one hundred guilders, to be paid by them [jointly and] severally, and due on the 27th day of March 1652.

The court orders defendant to pay plaintiff the sum of one hundred guilders within the space of three weeks, on pain of execution.

Steven Jansz, plaintiff, against Rut Arentsz, defendant.
Defendant's first default.

---

[14] Blank in the original record.

[55a] Willem Fredrixsz, plaintiff, [against] Juriaen Theunisz, defendant, for fl.57 due to plaintiff.

The court orders defendant to pay plaintiff the aforesaid sum of fl.57 within the space of six weeks.

Commissary Dyckman, plaintiff, against Jacob Clomp, defendant, for having sold some brandy or strong drink to the savages, according to the deposition.

The court orders that his person and yacht shall remain attached until the witnesses who made the aforesaid deposition shall have been further examined under oath and the court have further investigated the case.

Resolved, to post an order prohibiting [people from letting] chickens, hogs, or other animals come on the bastions of the fort and requiring said bastions to remain properly closed, on pain of forfeiture [of said animals] at the discretion of the court.

JOANNES DYCKMAN
RUTGER JACOBSZ
ANDRIES HERBERTS
JAN VERBEECK
JACOB SCHERMERHOOR[EN]
JAN THOMASZ

Ordinary Session, June 17, 1653

Present:

| J: Dyckman | A: Herpertsz | Jan Verbeeck |
| R: Jacobsz | J: J: Schermerhooren | Jan Thomasz |

Andries de Vos, appearing before the court, requests that inasmuch as Jan Labatie has conveyed to him his lot No. 4, past Thysen's, he be granted the ownership thereof on the usual conditions and writing. Whereupon Labatie, being summoned, has approved the same and the request is granted.

Commissary Dyckman, plaintiff, against Albert Gerritsz, defendant, for fighting with Lambert Cornelisz, on the second of June last, [55b] in the company's garden.

The deposition about the fight being examined and the defendant being found guilty according to the contents of the deposition, the defendant is ordered to pay the plaintiff within three days the sum of forty guilders, with costs.

JOANNES DYCKMAN
RUTGER JACOBSZ
ANDRIES HERBERTS
JAN VERBEECK
JACOB SCHERMERHOOREN
JAN THOMASZ

Extraordinary Session, June 19, 1653

Present:

J: Dyckman	A: Herpertsz	C: Theu: v: Westbroeck
R: Jacobsz	J: Verbeeck	J: J: Schermerhooren

Gillis Douwesz Fonda, plaintiff, against Jan Dirrixsz van Bremen, defendant, for delivery of a hog, for which he delivered a half anker of brandy and [paid] some incidental expenses, amounting to about fl.30:–, for the payment of which the Hon. Rut Jacopsz has become surety.

Aert Aertsz, plaintiff, against Jan Dirrixsz van Bremen, defendant, on account of fl.10 for some stockings, which the defendant is alleged to owe the plaintiff.

The plaintiff declares that he does not know whether they were charged or not when they settled their accounts.

The defendant refers to his account.

The parties are ordered to examine the account and if not paid, [the defendant is] to satisfy [the plaintiff].

Jan Dirrixsz van Bremen declares under solemn oath that Jacob Symonsz Clomp, skipper, lately sold brandy in a kettle to the savages at Catskill. Furthermore, in the form of an ordinary declaration, that some beavers' worth of brandy was sold by Jacob Clomp to the savages at the Esopus, according [56] to the complaint made to him by some inhabitants of the Esopus, who declared that they suffered great annoyance from them in consequence thereof. And as to Katskill, that the trouble and difficulties which have arisen are the result thereof and are also due to Kit Davitsz.

This day, Jacobus Theunisz from Naerden has by solemn oath confirmed the above deposition concerning the sale of brandy by Jacob Clomp, as shown by his signature.

Willem Fredrixsz has become bail for Jacob Symonsz Clomp on account of the selling of strong drink to the savages in the sum of ten hundred guilders and signed [the bond] with his own hand.

Jacob Clomp is granted permission to sail for the Manhatans, on condition that he take on board or with him as much grain as he can get to be delivered at the Manhatans.

Jacob Clomp has admitted before this court that he sold a kettle to the savages and that after the payment was made, there being 8 or 9 stivers too much, he gave the savages brandy therefor.

JOANNES DYCKMAN
RUTGER JACOBSZ
ANDRIES HERBERTS
JACOB SCHERMERHOOREN

[57] Ordinary Session, Tuesday, July 5, 1653

Present:

    J: Dyckman   R: Jacopsz   J: J: Schermerhooren

Evert Pels, plaintiff, against Rut Arentsz, tailor, defendant, for the sum of fl.134:5, for cloth furnished to him.

Defendant's third default.

The court orders the defendant to pay the plaintiff the abovementioned sum of fl.134:5, within the space of three weeks, on pain of execution.

Elmerhuysen Kleyn, plaintiff, against Thomas Jansz, defendant, about the purchase of 34 schepels of maize, @ 30 stivers.

Parties appeal to Dirrick Bensinck. Case adjourned until the next court day.

Pieter Bronck, plaintiff, against Jan Machielsz, defendant. Defendant's first default

JOANNES DYCKMAN
RUTGER JACOBSZ
ANDRIES HERBERTS
JACOB JANSEN SCHERMERHOOREN

Ordinary Session, July 8, 1653

[*Present:*]

J: Dyckman
A: Herpertsz
J: Verbeeck
C: Theu: Wesbroeck

Pieter Bronck, plaintiff, against Jan Machielsz, defendant, for the sum of fl.78:— which defendant owes plaintiff and for which the president became surety.

Ordered that the defendant shall pay the plaintiff within the space of three weeks, or else that the surety shall be bound to do so.

Pieter Winnen, plaintiff, against Jacob Adriaensz, wheelwright, defendant, on account of the making of a wagon for the harvest, one-half of the payment for which he has already received, but which he fails to deliver.

The court orders the defendant to finish the wagon at the earliest opportunity [58] and to deliver it to the plaintiff, or, if he remains in default, to compensate the plaintiff for his loss, the plaintiff being authorized to recover such loss from the defendant where and in such a way as he shall see fit.

Herman Bastiaensz, plaintiff, against Dirrick Jansz Croon, defendant, in regard to disputed accounts.

Decided that Herman Bastiaensz shall return first three

beavers and thereafter the half of the money of Goosen Gerritsen, whereupon receipts signed by both parties shall be exchanged and parties must be satisfied.

JOANNES DYCKMAN
ANDRIES HERBERTS
JAN VERBEECK
CORNELUS TONISEN

Ordinary Session, July 15, 1653

Present:

| J: Dyckman | J: Verbeeck | J: Thomasz |
| R: Jacobsz | A: Herpertsz | C: T: v: Westbr: |

Paulus Schrick, plaintiff, [against] Femmetgen Albertsz, defendant, for fl.100 or 12½ beavers, according to obligation.

The court orders the defendant to pay the aforesaid sum of one hundred guilders to the plaintiff before the departure of the ships for *patria*, on pain of execution, the house to be plaintiff's security and he to be preferred to others.

Mariken ten Haer, plaintiff, against Jochem Becker, plaintiff being charged with having beaten her at the house of Hendrick Jansz Westerkamp and thrown her goods into the street, according to the declaration of Hendrick Jansz Westerkamp.

Defendant's first default.

Jacob Clomp, plaintiff, against Jan Dirrixsz van Bremen, defendant, for two hundred and twenty-seven guilders which defendant is alleged to owe plaintiff.

Plaintiff swears to the correctness of his book, showing that so much is due him by balance of accounts and confirms the debt by oath.

[59] The court orders the defendant to pay the plaintiff the above-mentioned sum of two hundred and twenty-seven guilders and not to depart without having given security for the payment to the satisfaction of the plaintiff.

Marten Marttensz declares that by order of Jacob Symonsz

Klomp he passed a little brandy in a kettle over the side of the bark to the savages at Katskill.

The court having seen the written complaint and demand of Commissary Dyckmans, plaintiff ex officio against Jacob Symonsz Clomp, defendant, for having sold brandy to the savages, and having examined the sworn testimony and all further evidence in the case, the honorable members of this court therefore condemn the defendant to pay immediately a fine of two hundred and fifty guilders, two-thirds to go to the officer here and one-third to the bench, on condition that if further evidence be found that he has done so, he shall be punished at the discretion of the court.

JOANNES DYCKMAN
RUTGER JACOBSZ
ANDRIES HERBERTS
JAN VERBEECK
CORNELUS THONISEN
JAN THOMASZ

Extraordinary Session, July 25, 1653

Present:
  J: Dyckman   An: Herpertsz   J: J: Schermerhooren
  Rut Jacopsz   Cor: Theunisz   J: Thomasz

Merten Ottsen, plaintiff, against Willem Albertsz from Monickendam, defendant, for 34 beavers and fl. 2:–, which the plaintiff claims the defendant owes him for the purchase of a yacht called the *Gloeyende Oven* (Glowing Oven), sold by the plaintiff to the defendant according to the bill of sale.

The court, having examined both parties and duly considered the case, orders the defendant to pay the plaintiff the abovementioned sum of 34 beavers and fl. 2:– before sundown and to bring it here into court, [60] provided that the defendant shall also be bound to pay the costs of the trial and to appear here before the court with the beavers, on pain of execution.

JOANNES DYCKMAN

Ordinary Session, August 19, 1653

Present:

    Rut Jacopsz   Cor: Theunisz   Jacob Schermerhooren
    An: Herpertsz

Jan Lamontagne, plaintiff, against Adriaen van Ilpendam, defendant, for fl. 64, which the defendant owes A: Keyser on account of the defendant's father's estate, as shown by said Keyser's account.

The defendant states that he has not had so much, but only [goods to the value] of fl. 55:5, as may be seen by his note.

The arguments on both sides having been heard, the honorable court orders A. Keyser to present further evidence against the defendant, to which reference is made by him in his letter.

Furthermore, the plaintiff, as attorney in the name of his honorable father,[15] demands of the defendant the sum of fl. 88;— earned by the plaintiff in curing the defendant's wife. As the defendant says that to the best of his knowledge fl. 51:15— was paid to the plaintiff, the court orders the defendant to pay the attorney, as plaintiff, the remaining sum of fl. 36:5, before the plaintiff's departure from here. In case the attorney finds afterwards that the aforesaid money was not paid and feels himself aggrieved, he may further seek to recover the aforesaid fl. 51:15 from the defendant.

[61] Ordinary Session, October 14, 1653

Present:

    J: Dyckman   An: Herpertsz   J: J: Schermerhooren
    Rut Jacopsz   J: Verbeeck   Cor: Theunisz

Commissary Dyckman, plaintiff, against Hendrick Jochem and Lourens Jansz, defendants, on account of fighting and wounding of the person of Lourens Jansz, and against Lourens Jansz on account of assault in Hendrick Jochem's house and beating Hendrick Jochem's wife.

---

[15] Doctor Johannes de la Montagne.

The court having examined all the evidence in the case, condemn the defendants to pay fines, to wit, Hendrick Jochems in the sum of forty guilders and Lourens Jansz in the sum of thirty guilders, with the stipulation that they must henceforth leave each other unmolested and in peace, on pain of further action by the court.

Commissary Dyckman, ex officio plaintiff, against Jacob Luyersz, defendant, on account of an assault committed on the 9th of this month on the public street upon the plaintiff and Mr Slechtenhorst.

Case adjourned until the next court day. Meanwhile the plaintiff is requested to present his written complaint and demand, the defendant being sent home to file his answer on the next court day.

JOANNES DYCKMAN
RUTGER JACOBSZ
ANDRIES HERBERTS
JAN VERBEECK
CORNELUS THONISZ

Monday, October 21, 1653

Present:

The Hon. General   An: Herpertsz   J: J: Schermerhoren
J: Dyckman   Jan Verbeeck   Cor: Theunisz
R: Jacopsz

Whereas some extraordinary expenses have been incurred in repairing the fort, building the guardhouse and executing other works, and some other work still remains to be done, such as making necessary repairs to the bridge in the village of Beverwyck, which make it necessary to raise funds out of which the expenses incurred or still to be incurred for necessary [62] repairs may be defrayed; Therefore, the Honorable General and the Honorable Magistrates of the aforesaid Fort Orange and the village of Beverwyck having made a general calculation of the expenses incurred and still to be incurred, the said Honorable General and the Honorable Magistrates have for the present time not been able to find a more expedient or suitable means [of paying these] than by levying a general tax on the houses, lots and single persons trading here, as follows:

A dwelling house with interior finishing shall pay fifteen guilders, and if the house is leased, the tenant and the owner shall each pay one-half.

A vacant lot or garden, half as much; and

A single person, not having any house or lot, one pound Flemish.

And the worthy Abraham Staets, captain of the burgher guard, and Sander Leendertsz are hereby authorized to collect the aforesaid moneys once for all, and after collection, to make payment to the creditors in the presence of the aforesaid court, in the absense of the Honorable General, and as treasurers to take care of the surplus, to be used and employed on other occasions as the needs of the aforesaid village and Fort Orange may require.

Thus done and ratified on the 21st of October and taken up again on the 22d of October 1653, in Fort Orange in N: Netherland.

       P. STUYVESANT
       J: DYCKMAN
       RUTGER JACOBSZ
       ANDRIES HERBERTS
       JAN VERBEECK
       JACOB SCHERMERHOOREN
       CORNELUS THONISEN

[63] Wednesday, October 22, Anno 1653

By the Hon. General and the magistrates of Fort Orange and the village of Beverwyck have been examined and inspected the documents in the suit between Willem Juryaensen and Jan Fransen van Hoesem, growing out of a contract made and entered into by them on the 30th of January 1650, which said contract the parties on both sides have failed to fulfil, especially the plaintiff, Willem Juryaensen, as shown by his categorical answer made on the 30th of November 1651 before the court of the colony, as follows: "Willem Juryaensen, being asked by the court whether he is willing to fulfil the contract entered into on the 30th of January 1650 with Jan van Hoesem, answers, No. Agrees with the record, Anthony d'Hooges." By which answer the defendant, Jan van Hoesem, claims and maintains that the contract has been broken by the plaintiff himself and that therefore he is not bound by it.

The defendant further says and maintains that the plaintiff, Willem Juryaensen, has broken the aforesaid contract not only by words, but also by deeds, in failing to perform or carry out the stipulations of the contract, namely, to serve the defendant and to teach him to bake, and by removing the baking utensils to prevent the defendant from baking and make it impossible for him to do so.

The court, therefore, finds that according to the foregoing statements the contract was violated and annulled by the plaintiff himself and that under the rule of law the defendant might be relieved of the necessity of pleading and the plaintiff's claim and demand be denied. However, in view of a subsequent judgment given by the aforesaid court and also considering the needy circumstances of the plaintiff and the fact that the defendant by virtue of the contract has built upon a part of the lot claimed by the plaintiff, and that the parties can not live together, the Hon. General and the magistrates order that the plaintiff shall as long as he lives stay in the old bake house, have the use of the bake oven and the utensils belonging thereto, together with his own furniture and household goods, and be free to dispose of them as he shall see fit. As to the claim of the lot, which by virtue of the contract was partly built upon by the defendant, the plaintiff, Willem Juriaensen, occupies the same only by sufferance and is not entitled thereto by any patent or conveyance; consequently, he is not able or competent to dispose thereof as he might do of his own property. However, in view of the plaintiff's poverty and the fact that he has resided for a considerable time on the aforesaid lot and used it as a garden, the Director General and [64] the magistrates aforesaid order and decide that the defendant, Jan van Hoesem, shall pay the plaintiff for improvements the sum of one hundred and twenty-five guilders, in three instalments, to wit, one-third cash, one-third a year from this date and the last third within two years, the parties respectively being ordered to acquiesce herein on pain of being fined twenty pounds Flemish, to be applied at the discretion of the court. And in case it should hereafter be found that the plaintiff, Willem Juryaensen, according to his wont, should continue to blaspheme and abuse the name of God or His service, or any of the magistrates of the court, whether in general or in particular, he shall without exception be corrected by the court, either by the infliction of banishment or corporal punishment, as the case may require.

Thus done and decided, this 22d of October 1653, by the court of Fort Orange.

The Hon. Director General has engaged as surveyor, for the service of the court and the burghers here, Harmen Bastiaensz, carpenter, who has taken the following oath before the Hon. Director General:

I, Harmen Bastiaensen, promise before the Hon. Director General that in the office of surveyor I shall conduct myself uprightly, without making any false returns either in favor or to the prejudice of any one. So, help me God Almighty.

[65] Tuesday, November 25, 1653

Present:

J: Dyckman A: Herpertsz J: J: Schermerhoren
R: Jacobsz J: Verbeeck C: Theunisz van Westbroeck

Pursuant to the judgment rendered on the 12th of the preceding month, Volckgen Jans, in the stead of her husband, Jan Fransz van Hoesem, who is absent, has in accordance with the aforesaid judgment brought into court forty guilders, being the first payment or instalment which he, Jan van Hoesem, is to pay to Willem Juryaensen, thereby complying thus far on her part with the aforesaid judgment, which forty guilders have been handed to the collector, Pieter Reverdingh, to be turned over to Willem Juriaensz, and in case he, Willem Juriaensen, refuses to accept and receive them, the said Reverdingh shall report the circumstances on the next court day.

In order to stop and prevent the excise frauds of beer and wine as much as possible in the future, it is decided to have the following notice posted, in order that every burgher and inhabitant of this jurisdiction may govern himself accordingly and at the same time to give the president in his capacity of officer power to inspect the houses and cellars of all tapsters when there is occasion for it or necessity may demand it.

Notice

Whereas in the presence and with the approval of the Hon. Director General it has been decided by this court that, in order to stop and prevent as far as possible all frauds of the excise of beer and wine, every burgher and inhabitant of this jurisdiction, as well as the tapsters, before having their purchased heavy beer and wines carried into their houses and cellars, shall be bound to obtain, or cause to be obtained, a proper certificate from the collector, Pieter Reverdingh, without paying however any excise, but only a fee of two stivers for the writing of the certificate of delivery, [66] on pain of forfeiture of the beer, wines, or distilled liquors, and in addition of paying the requisite fine; therefore, this is hereby brought to the notice of the community, in order that every one may in the future govern himself accordingly and prevent his suffering any loss, notwithstanding it has heretofore been ordered and proclaimed that no sloops coming from the Manathans may unload before they have obtained consent or the officer has been on board to make a proper inspection, on pain of incurring the penalty provided therefor.

Thus done at the session of this court, in Fort Orange, on the date above written.

> Warrant for the president, in his capacity of officer, to inspect the houses and cellars of all the tapsters living within this jurisdiction

The commissary, Joannes Dyckman, is hereby authorized by this court to inspect on occasion, as often and repeatedly as it will suit his convenience or circumstances may require it, the houses of all tapsters belonging to this jurisdiction, and in case he finds any heavy beer, or wines, or distilled liquors which have not been entered, to seize these and to do therewith as is proper, and whoever is found to oppose this shall be dealt with according to the exigency of the case. In witness whereof this is signed in Fort Orange, on the date above written, and was signed: Rutger Jacobsz, Andries Herpertsz, Jan Verbeeck, Jacob Schermerhooren, Cornelis Thonisz, Jan Thomasz.

JOANNES DYCKMAN
RUTGER JACOBSZ
ANDRIES HERBERTS
JAN VERBEECK
JACOB SCHERMERHO[OREN]
JAN THOMASZ
CORNELUS THONISEN

[67] Tuesday, November 9, 1653

Present:

J: Dyckman
R: Jacopsz
A: Herpertsz
J: Verbeeck
J: Schermerhoren
Cor: Theunisz
Jan Thomasz

The collector, Pieter Reverdingh, reports to the court that by order of the court he has offered to Willem Juriaensen the forty guilders in seawan, being the first payment or instalment which he was to hand said Willem Juriaensz in the name of this court, but that he, Willem Juriaensen, has refused to accept said money. Whereupon it is decided that this money shall for the present remain in the hands of the collector aforesaid, until further order of this court.

Rem Jansz, smith, by virtue of a power of attorney from Jan Jansz from Gottenborgh, shown to this court, demands in his, Gottenborgh's, name of Merten Herpertsz, mason, [payment] according to a bond executed before schepens on the 8th of October 1651, in the sum of fifty-eight beavers, which he agreed to pay even before the departure of the ships and which is not yet paid, [praying that] in case of longer delay he may proceed to execution and in that way secure payment.

Resolved, that the defendant, Merten, the mason, shall be bound to satisfy plaintiff within the space of six weeks, on pain of peremptory execution, according to law.

Commissary Dyckman, plaintiff, against the following persons, on account of their not having built upon or fenced in their lots or garden assigned and granted to them within the specified time granted to each, on pain of being fined fl.25, and whose time has long since expired.

Adriaen Jansz from Leyden has adduced reasons for excuse which are so far-fetched that he, the defendant, or the person who claims the title to the lot, shall at the first opportunity have to tender and pay the required twenty-five guilders to the officer.

Gabriel Leendertsen, about inclosing his garden, although he has not built on any lot, according to the order. He offers excuses which are so far-fetched that he must build in the spring at the latest on a lot to be requested by, and assigned to, him, on pain of being deprived of the garden and of paying immediately to the officer a fine of fl.25 and fl.3 for having used abusive language before this court, total fl.28, in case he fails to build.

[68] The commissary, for reasons above written:

Master Adriaen van Ilpendam, schoolmaster, who has offered excuses which are accepted as sufficient.

The excuses of Rem Jansz, smith, being heard, but not judged sufficient, he is ordered to pay at the first opportunity the sum of twenty-five guilders.

Machiel, the *lademaker*, condemned likewise in the sum of fl.25.

Pieter Bronck, as above, fl.25.

Goosen Gerritsz likewise in the sum of fl.25.

Pieter Hertgers for not inclosing his two gardens, one of himself and the other of Annetgen Bogardus, @ fl.25:– each, is condemned in a fine of fl.50.

Merten, the mason, in the sum of fl.25, for not having built on his lot behind his house.

Lourens Jansz absent, and his first default.

Jacob Clomp and Willem Bout. Parties' first default.

Jochem Ketelhuyn, on account of the garden. First default.

Ellert Gerritsz. First default.

Jacob Luyersz, being summoned and informed of the complaint and demand of the officer, ex officio, on account of the assault committed in the street, appeals [for his defence] to the personal appearance of Mr Slichtenhorst before this court.

Resolved, to request Mr Slichtenhorst to consent to appear on the next court day, in order to proceed upon a surer foundation.

Hendrick Jochemsz, innkeeper, for smuggling a half barrel of good beer, laid in last Saturday.

Defendant acknowledges the fact but states that he has not been able to enter the same on account of the inconvenience of his wife's being in childbed.

Resolved, this first time to overlook the matter, he to pay the excise without any fine, but that in the future he shall have to guard himself against repeating the offense, on pain of paying the full fine provided in such cases.

Elmerhuysen Kleyn and Jan, the soldier, being summoned to appear, they are notified that they must henceforth perform the company's service as required, whereupon Elmerhuysen has answered that he was out of the service. Resolved, that the commissary shall inform the Hon. General hereof by letter.

[69] Albert, the carpenter, being cited to appear on account of the inclosing of his garden, first default [is entered against him].

The collector, Pieter Reverdingh, reports to the court that Herman Bastiaensz, Hendrick Jochemsz and Willem Bout bought some goods of the persons who perished, which until now they have not paid for. They are ordered to pay the collector without delay for what they have received, on condition that they are to share pro rata with the other creditors in the distribution and shall receive what is proper.

JOANNES DYCKMAN
RUTGER JACOBSZ
ANDRIES HERBERTS
JAN VERBEECK
JACOB SCHERMERHOOREN
JAN THOMASZ

Tuesday, December 23, 1653

Present:
J: Dyckman   A: Herpertsz   Jan Thomasz
R: Jacopsz   J: J: Schermerhoren

Pieter Bronck, plaintiff, against Merten Herpertsz, mason, defendant, for fl.358:14–, which defendant owes plaintiff. Requests payment, or in default thereof a bond executed before this court.

Defendant's first default.

Jacob Jansz Schermerhoren, plaintiff, against Merten Herpertsz, mason, defendant, for what is due by defendant to plaintiff according to his account for goods delivered a long time ago, amounting to fl.247:– and also for upsetting a canoe, in which were about 30 schepels of maize and a *mudde* of beans, which were thereby spoiled and perished through his carelessness.

Defendant's first default.

Albert Gerritsz, plaintiff, against Merten Herpertsz, mason, defendant, for 32 beavers which defendant [70] owes plaintiff, according to a bond in which he specially binds and mortgages his house, arising from wages earned in building his house and goods delivered to him, upon which the defendant has paid six beavers on account.

Defendant's first default.

Albert Gerritsz, plaintiff, against Rut Arentsz, tailor, defendant.

Defendant's first default.

Commissary Dyckman, plaintiff ex officio, against Jacob Symontsz Clomp, defendant, for payment of a fine of fl.250:– imposed by sentence of the 15th of July last.

Defendant is again ordered by the court to bring this money and to deposit it within twenty-four hours in the hands of the collector, Pieter Reverdingh, on pain of peremptory execution, but with this reservation that in case he has hereafter any charges to bring against the officer in regard to any words passed at the house of Willem Fredrixsz, according to the deposition exhibited [to the court], he, the defendant, can do so, but that meanwhile he must comply with the sentence.

This being brought to the defendant's notice, he declares that he is not willing to do so and refuses to satisfy the judgment.

Commissary Dyckman, ex officio plaintiff, against Willem Fredrixsz Bout, defendant, on account of slander, abusive language and assault committed on the plaintiff when the honorable court on the 9th instant was sitting at the house of Pieter Bronck to settle the accounts of the persons who perished, namely Frans Borremans, Jurgen Evertsz and Abraham Jacobsz, carpenter, when, as set forth in the complaint and demand of the president and officer, he dared to villify the honorable court there; wherefore it is resolved [71] to insert the same here as follows, to wit:

Commissary Dyckman, in his capacity of officer ex officio plaintiff, against Willem Fredrixsz Bout, defendant.

Whereas this day two weeks ago, being the 9th day of this month of December, the plaintiff was sitting with the members of the court here in the house of Pieter Bronck, innkeeper, to make an estimate of the goods left behind and sold by the persons who perished, namely, Frans Forremans from Veuren, Jurgen Evertsz from Rencum and Abram Jacopsz, carpenter, and of what might be due by and to the joint creditors and debtors, in order to do justice to every one according to law and to give satisfaction as far as [the money] will go; it happened that the defendant, while the plaintiff sat at the table with some members of the court to make the aforesaid calculation and consider the matter, has dared to assault the plaintiff without a word of warning or reply and in the presence of the court has almost pushed him off the bench on which he sat, so that the honorable court, on account of the confusion which arose from the defendant's attack, were forced to suspend the business commenced. Yes, what is more, after the plaintiff had arisen, he not only threatened to beat him, but in addition often and repeatedly called him an unfaithful man and a rascal and that he had shown himself as such to the defendant, repeating the same statement many times, and whereas this took place publicly and in the presence of the court as aforesaid, it is not necessary to have any further proof that the common and honest testimony which may be secured from the bystanders if necessary.

The plaintiff, therefore, in the capacity aforesaid, demands that the defendant, *in vinculis*, as a criminal and malefactor, [72] shall have to answer for his deeds and in case the court here, contrary to the plaintiff's rightful expectations, refuses to do justice in the matter, he requests that the defendant may meanwhile remain *in vinculis* until the river is open, in order to be sent in irons to the Hon. General and Council of New Netherland at the Manathans to answer there before their honors for his crimes if he can; and otherwise, that he be punished here as an example to others, justice having been made an object of derision, as far as it lay in his power. As the plaintiff trusts that his demand for imprisonment will not be denied, he awaits an order thereon from this court. This 23d of December 1653, in Fort Orange, and was signed: Joannes Dyckman.

Which complaint and demand having been read and examined by this court, it is resolved by their honors that a copy thereof shall be served on the defendant at his house, with order to deliver his written defense on the next court day, when the further complaint and demand of the officer are to follow.

Maximiliaen de Winter, appearing before the court, requests, in accordance with the recommendation of the Hon. General, that he be permitted to dwell in the company's little house, [the same to serve for the accommodation] of himself as well as of the court messenger, Pieter Reverdingh.

The matter being taken into consideration it is resolved and decided that as the clerk urgently needs a small place to write in and to keep his writings and papers, the same shall be kept therefor in the future, but that for the present the said de Winter shall also be allowed to reside there until further order.

The collector, Pieter Reverdingh, has presented to the court his account [73] of the receipts and disbursements of the persons who perished, Abraham Jacopsz, carpenter, Jurgen Evertsz from Rencum and Frans Bormans from Veuren, which is accepted and approved.

Commissary Dyckman, ex officio plaintiff, against Lourens Jansz, defendant, to reply to the following interrogatories:

Interogatories on which this court is to examine Lourens Jansz, burgher and inhabitant of Beverwyck

1 How old he is and where born? — Answers, 48 years and born at *Hoesem*.[16]

2 Whether about four months ago he was not in the Esopus with Commissary Dyckman? — Answers, Yes.

3 Whether, when there, he did not understand and hear Christoffel Davits say, in presence of the commissary, that he, Christoffel, had sold to the savages at one time 22 *mutsgens* of brandy and afterwards also a half anker of brandy? — Answers, Yes.

4 Whether he did not understand and hear Marcelis, the servant of Mr de Hulter, say that he, Christoffel Davits, now and then had sold not one, but several ankers of brandy to the savages, which he, Marcelis, had noticed and seen [74] while he lived there at the house of Christoffel Davits? — Answers, Yes, and that Christoffel Davits himself said that the *sackemaas* of the savages themselves had been to see him, Kit Davits, and begged him not to sell any more brandy to the savages, as through it they got into serious fights with each other and made trouble.

---

[16] Husum, in Schleswig.

Which interrogatories, the questions as well as the answers, were sworn to by the defendant before the officer.

> JOANNES DYCKMAN
> RUTGER JACOBSZ
> ANDRIES HERBERTS
> JACOB SCHERMEHOOREN
> JAN THOMASZ

Extraordinary Session, Wednesday, December 25, 1653

Present:
All, with the exception of Jan Verbeeck

Pieter Bronck, plaintiff, against Poulus Thomasz, defendant, for fl.126:15st. which are due to plaintiff by defendant.

The defendant being heard, admits that he owes plaintiff fl.109:–.

The plaintiff offers to swear that the entire sum aforesaid is due to him.

The defendant is ordered by this court not to leave this jurisdiction without having satisfied the plaintiff, either by paying him, or by giving good security. Furthermore, the defendant is condemned to pay the costs of the suit, provided that the plaintiff shall advance the money and have a claim on the defendant for the return and restitution thereof. And in case the plaintiff swears that according to his book he is entitled to the entire amount aforesaid, the defendant shall have to pay and satisfy the plaintiff.

It is decided and resolved to have the court messenger summon Jan Barentsz Wemp [75] to appear on the next court day, provided that he, Wemp, bring with him the order he may have from the Hon. General as to inclosing the lot next to that of Gysbert Cornelisz, deceased.

Propositions made this day by Stick Stiggery and others in the name and on the part of the Maquas

First, that this court would write to the French authorities in Canada that the peace concluded between the Maquas and the aforesaid French was agreeable to us and that we or the Christians were well pleased with it. To which was answered, Yes, and that at the first opportunity we should communicate the matter to the Hon. General.

The Maquas further requested that this court would write to the French nation there that in case they had any difficulties and again got involved in war with the French savages, that the French should keep out of it. Whereupon the Maquas were given for answer that this would be written by this court alone.

Which propositions and answers were made in the presence of two French delegates, whereupon it was resolved to send the following letters in French or Latin to Messrs de Loison and Boucher, the contents of which are as follows:

To Monsr Johan de Loison,[16a] governor in Quebec and Pierre Boucher, commander on the three rivers.

To Monsr Loison

Honorable, etc.

We have duly received your honor's agreeable letter of the 19th of the past month of November and learned both from this letter and the report made by the two Frenchmen who were sent to us and some Maquas Indians of the treaty of peace made between your honor's nation and the Maquas, in which we rejoice not a little with your honor, seeing that this sad war has to our deep sorrow been carried on for so long between [76] your honor and the said Indians, which we should have liked to have ended sooner, but which it seems could not be brought

---

[16a] Jean de Lauson, governor of Canada, 1651–56.

about. We, on our side, hope that the same may continue for a long time, for the best of your honor and ourselves. On our side we have never failed to ransom the Christian prisoners of your nation out of the hands of these cruel people, as far as it was possible, which by nature and God's command we found it our duty to do and which we therefore did gladly, even at a considerable sacrifice and expense to the community here, as your honor can readily understand yourself. This nation of the Maquas has even this day promised us that as far as it is in their power they will observe and carry out the [terms of] peace concluded [with them] and they have requested us to ask your honor that the same might be done on your side, which we doubt not, provided there be no shortcoming on their side.

Furthermore, if they, the Maquas, should become involved in any war or trouble with your honor's savages, they request that your honor and your honor's nation would not interfere, which we could not do otherwise than promise them [to write] and which we therefore do hereby, and which we shall also at the first opportunity communicate by letter to the Hon. General, at the Manathans.

On our part we shall not fail to make every effort in our power to keep the Maquas disposed to continue the recently concluded peace, much innocent Christian blood of this nation having been shed to our great sorrow. We doubt not of your honor's good disposition and earnest inclinations toward us, such as we, by reason of the close alliance between our respective principals, also bear toward your honor and your nation and which on all occasions that may arise, as has been shown heretofore and as behooves close allies, [77] shall not be lacking on our part. Meanwhile, after greetings, we commend your honor and all the good friends there to [the protection of] God.

Canaqueese, the bearer hereof, a savage who is much beloved by the Maquas, has requested of us a letter of recommendation to your honor, in order that he may be well treated there and be allowed to go and come freely, which we request hereby.

Depending thereon, we remain,

Your honor's willing servants, the president and magistrates of the court of Fort Orange and Beverwyck.

And was signed in the name and by order of the aforesaid court,

JOANNES DYCKMAN

Fort Orange, December 25, 1653

Mutatis mutandis a letter was sent the same day to Monsr Pieter Boucher, governor on the three rivers, except [that it was stated therein] that we had received his honor's letter of the eleventh of November aforesaid.

JOANNES DYCKMAN
RUTGER JACOBSZ
ANDRIES HERBERTS
JACOB SCHERMERHOOREN
CORNELUS THONISEN
JAN THOMASZ

[78] Tuesday, January 6, 1654

Present:

All, except Jan Verbeeck

Pieter Bronck, plaintiff, against Merten Herpertsz, defendant, for fl.358:— which the defendant admits he owes to the plaintiff according to a note signed on the 10th of December last past.

The court orders defendant to pay plaintiff the aforesaid sum of fl.358:— within six weeks, on pain of execution.

Jacob Jansz Schermerhoren, plaintiff, against Merten Herpertsz, defendant, for fl.247:— which the defendant owes plaintiff and further for 30 schepels of maize and a *mudde* of beans which were lost through the defendant's carelessness, as shown by the affidavit of Christoffel Davits.

The court orders the defendant to pay the plaintiff the aforesaid fl.247:— within six weeks, on pain of execution. As to the maize and beans, parties are referred by this court to Rem Jansz, the smith, and Adriaen Jansz from Leyden, as referees, who are to bring about an agreement if they can and to report their findings to this court.

Lysbet Cornelis' daughter, plaintiff, against Merten Herpertsz, defendant, for fl.174:— which defendant owes plaintiff according to the account handed in.

The defendant admits the debt.

The court orders defendant to pay plaintiff the aforesaid fl.174:— within six weeks, on pain of execution.

[79] Albert Gerritsz, plaintiff, against Merten Herpertsz, defendant, for fl.208:— or 26 beavers, which are due to the plaintiff from the defendant for wages earned and for what he furnished the defendant according to the defendant's own confession.

The court orders the defendant to pay the plaintiff the aforesaid sum of fl.208:— within six weeks, on pain of execution.

Albert Gerretsz, plaintiff, against Rut Arentsz, tailor, defendant.

Defendant's first, that is to say, second default.

Jacob Jansz Flodder, plaintiff, against Dirrick Bensingh, defendant, on account of the purchase of a half interest in a yacht called the *Princess Royale*, according to the bill of sale executed before Commissary Dyckman on the first of this month, bought by the defendant of Jacob Jansz Stoll.

The arguments on both sides having been heard, it is decided to refer parties to Volckert Hansz and Pieter Hertgers, referees, who are to bring about an agreement if they can and to report their findings to this court.

Steven Jansz, plaintiff, against Roeloff Jacopsz, innkeeper, defendant, about a *mudde* of wheat.

Defendant's first default.

Jacob Symontsz Clomp, appearing before the court, complains that Commissary Dyckman has attached some moneys in the hands [80] of Jan van Bremen at Katskill, and also about some abusive language used at the house of Willem Fredrixsz.

The court orders the attachment vacated whenever he, Clomp, delivers to this court the fl.250:— which he must pay pursuant to the sentence heretofore pronounced, which money he, Clomp, is to deliver into the hands of the Hon. Rutger Jacopsz, under the penalty provided.

Upon examination of the account of Goosen Gerritsen for beer delivered to the Hon. Company and to Commissary Dyckman, it is resolved at his request to give for apostil that he will be paid next spring, or that he must wait until the arrival of the Hon. General, when a decision will be made as to the payment of the aforesaid account.

At the request of Merten Herpertsz, mason, it is resolved that his house and garden will be sold by this court, for the purpose of paying his joint creditors out of the proceeds of the sale, at the house of Pieter Bronck, innkeeper, a week from the following Monday, being the 19th of this month of January, at two o'clock in the afternoon.

Commissary Dyckman and the collector, Pieter Reverdingh, are authorized by this court, this afternoon, at the house of Pieter Bronck, to make up the accounts of the persons who were lost and drowned, and in accordance therewith to settle with every one pro rata to the amount that is due him and draw bills of exchange on whom and for such amounts as may be necessary.

JOANNES DYCKMAN
RUTGER JACOBSZ
ANDRIES HERBERTS
JACOB SCHERMERHOOREN
CORNELUS THONISEN
JAN THOMASZ

[81] Tuesday, January 13, 1654

Present:
    Omnes dempto Rutger Jacopsz

Albert Andriesz, plaintiff, against Merten Herpertsz, defendant, about boards delivered to plaintiff by the defendant to the value of 27 beavers.

Defendant declares that he does not know how he can pay for them.

The court decides that the plaintiff may take back the boards delivered by him, notwithstanding the attachment issued against them, and in case there are any less than the full number delivered, he can afterwards make this known to the court, so as to recover damages for them if possible.

Cornelis Thomasz, plaintiff, against Merten Herpertsz, defendant, for fl.78:— which plaintiff claims for washing defendant's dirty linen.

Defendant admits the debt, and is ordered to pay plaintiff the fl.78:— within six weeks, on pain of execution.

Albert Gerritsz, plaintiff, against Rut Arentsz, tailor, defendant, for four beavers and fl.56 in seawan, for wages claimed by plaintiff of the defendant.

The court orders defendant to pay plaintiff the aforesaid amount with costs within six weeks, on pain of execution, and as to the complaint made by the defendant that the ground timbers of his house have not been properly laid and that the uprights are cut too short, parties are referred to the surveyors, who are to inspect the work and to report their findings to this court.

[82] Steven Jansz, plaintiff, against Roeloff Jacopsz, defendant, for fl.10, which defendant owes plaintiff.

Defendant's second default.

At the request of the Hon. Andries Herpertsz a garden is granted to him behind the fort among those that have not yet been allotted, for the benefit of his small house next to his residence, at the place to be hereafter indicated to his honor.

Hendrick Jochems, being summoned to testify in regard to what took place in his presence on the 10th instant between Jacob Jansz Stoll and Lourens Jansz, in the course of their fight at his house, declares as may be seen by his declaration. Whereupon Commissary Dyckmans is requested and ordered to prepare interrogatories for the further examination of the witness on the next court day. Likewise Rem Jansz, smith, being also summoned to appear, declared that he was not present at the fight, but only heard some contentious words out of the mouth of Lourens Jansz and that he went away to tend to his own affairs.

JOANNES DYCKMAN
ANDRIES HERPERTS
JAN VERBEECK
JACOB SCHERMERHOOREN
CORNELUS THONISEN
JAN THOMASZ

[83] Tuesday, January 20, 1654

Present:

Omnes dempto Jan Verbeeck

Jacob Adriaensen, wheelwright, plaintiff, against Jan Dirrixsz van Bremen, defendant, about five schepels of wheat which defendant is said to owe plaintiff.

Defendant's first default. The court, however, enjoins the defendant [not] to depart from here for Katskill unless he satisfies the plaintiff. Furthermore, with respect to the officer's complaint about some slanderous remarks uttered last November before the honorable court, the defendant must make amends to the court before his departure from here; likewise for having last year run away and escaped from the arrest caused to be made by Jacob Symentsz Klomp. And in case the defendant should venture to leave without permission, he shall with or against his consent be brought back from Katskill at his own expense. And in order that he may hereafter not plead ignorance hereof, a written extract from this order shall be served upon the defendant by the court messenger; all *cum expensis.*

Willem Fredrixsz, innkeeper, appearing before the court, requests the privilege of contracting in a lump sum for the excise on the beer which he may have occasion to tap in one year in his house, which in view of the fact that but few members of the court are present is laid aside until the next court day. Meanwhile he may provisionally lay in the beer that is to be received by him on obtaining a certificate from the collector, Pieter Reverdingh.

[84] Stoffel, the carpenter, has handed in a memorandum that there is due him by Merten Herpertsz, mason, according to his own admission, fl.31:4:–, which is entered here by way of memorandum and information.

Claes Gerritsz has requested a lot on the hill near [the lot of] Andries de Vos. Granted to him at the place hereafter to be indicated to him, together with a garden for his use.

There was read a petition of Andries de Vos, requesting permission to fence in a piece of land behind his lot, to the south of the third kill, into the woods, to be used as a pasture and meadow land.

Decided to note in the margin of his petition that as but few members are present at this meeting, he may present his request a week from today, when the court will take favorable action in the matter.

JOANNES DYCKMAN
RUTGER JACOBSZ
ANDRIES HERBERTS
JACOB SCHERMERHOOREN
CORNELUS THONISEN
JAN THOMASZ

[85] Extraordinary Session, Saturday, January 24, 1654

Present:

Omnes

Jacob Adriaensen, wheelwright, plaintiff, against Cornelis Segertsz, defendant, about the purchase of a house and lot and a garden belonging thereto.

The defendant says or declares that he is willing to accept the house in accordance with the contract of sale, upon proper security.

The court adjudges that the parties must at once have the contract entered into by them put in writing and that the grantor, when the first payment is made, must furnish two sufficient sureties for the delivery [of the property] free from all claims, the term of the security to extend from the date of the first payment until the delivery is completed. The first payment, of one hundred beavers, is to take place promptly on the first of May next and the successive payments according to the terms of the contract made and agreed upon by them and hereafter to be written. And the defendant is ordered to pay the costs of this [session of the] court, as he, the purchaser, upon offer of security, has refused to accept and take the aforesaid house and also been unwilling to have the contract put in writing and to forward the work.

JOANNES DYCKMAN
RUTGER JACOBSZ
ANDRIES HERBERTS
JAN VERBEECK
JAN THOMASZ

[86] Extraordinary Session, Sunday, January 25, 1654

This court having been reliably informed that the Rev. Domine Gidioni Schaets, at the close of the morning service, has announced from the pulpit that whoever had any charges to bring against the person of Brant van Slichtenhorst must do so at once, on pain of forever after keeping silent, it is after careful examination of the matter decided by this court to draw up a protest against it in writing and to have the commissary serve it orally at the close of the afternoon service, so as to be heard by the entire congregation, as follows:

Cry by the commissary:

Hear Ye, good inhabitants of Fort Orange and Beverwyck and all others who belong to the jurisdiction of the same!

I, Joannes Dyckman, commissary and vice director of Fort Orange in the service of the honorable West India Company, together with my associate councilors or magistrates of the court of the aforesaid Fort Orange and Beverwyck, in the name and on behalf of the Honorable Company aforesaid and the Honorable Director General Peter Stuyvesant and the Honorable Council of New Netherland, representing the supreme government of this country, are constrained to protest publicly in this place where it is customary to hold divine service, although disliking to do so, seeing that this place is not intended for the administration of justice, but only to be used for divine service.

The fact is, however, [87] that it has come to the attention of the commissary and the magistrates aforesaid — some of whom have even heard it themselves and therefore have certain knowledge thereof — that this forenoon, at the close of the morning service, it has pleased the Rev. Domine Gidioni Schaets, contrary to the order and opinion of this court and without its previous consent, to announce publicly from the pulpit that whoever had any charges to bring against Brant van Slichtenhorst, the former director of the colony of Rensselaerswyck, must do so forthwith, or hereafter remain silent.

Considering that the said Slichtenhorst has three times, or on three distinct court days, in April 1652, by several inhabitants of this place been legally cited to appear before the Hon. Director General and Council of Netherland to answer their complaints, presented in this fort in the form of petitions or otherwise, and on his third failure to appear been declared completely in default, notwithstanding due opportunity was afforded him to obtain right and justice, the same as every one else, upon presentation of proper proof in the matter — which would not have been refused him, Slichtenhorst, if he had appeared — the court of the aforesaid fort, and hence also of this place, feel that they can not sit idly by, but must notify this good community that in case he, Slichtenhorst, should make any further announcements (however, not there, which is judged improper, but rather by or before the judge or judges), the honorable magistrates of this court forbid all good inhabitants aforesaid, in spite of the announcement which has been made that all charges against his person must be brought before the court of the colony, [88] to do so, or to comply therewith, as it is considered illegal, since he can not be summoned to appear before that bench of justice, but only before the court of this place and the plaintiffs' own competent judges.

As what has been done or occurred herein and all similar practices are not only prejudicial to the Hon. Company and the good inhabitants aforesaid, but, as is claimed and presumable in such cases and by such means, also tend to make the good inhabitants disobedient and rebellious to their lawful superiors, this will serve therefore to inform every one that, pursuant to the orders issued by the supreme government and the proper authorities aforesaid, the honorable magistrates of this court prohibit such announcement, or announcements, from being made in the future, under [threat of] calling [the offender] further to account and [subjecting him to] heavy penalties, the honorable court declaring hereby the announcement which has been made to be *re infacta*, or null and void, and forbidding similar announcements from being made hereafter.

Served by the commissary in the presence of the attending congregation, on the date above written, at the close of the second service, while, or before, the people were leaving the church.

> Joannes Dyckman
> Rutger Jacobsz
> Jan Verbeeck
> Jacob Schermerhooren
> Cornelus Thonisen
> Jan Thomasz
> Andries Herberts

Tuesday, January 27, 1654

Present:
   Omnes dempto Andries Herpertsz

Jacob Symontsz Klomp, master of a bark, plaintiff, against Jan Dirrixsz van Bremen, defendant, for fl.102:8:— which the plaintiff claims is due him from the defendant by balance of account for various goods delivered.

The court orders the defendant to pay the aforesaid sum of one hundred and two guilders and eight stivers before his departure for Katskill, or in default thereof to give security for the prompt payment as soon as the river is open, under the penalty heretofore provided.

Lysbet Cornelis' daughter, plaintiff, against Merten Herpertsz, that is to say, Jacob Schermerhoren, defendant, for 30 schepels of maize and one *mudde* of beans of the plaintiff, which were lost through the defendant's fault.

The court, having duly examined and considered the documents, adjudges that the defendant must pay the plaintiff the sum of thirty-six guilders within the space of six weeks, on pain of execution.

Lysbet Cornelis, plaintiff, against Gerrit Jansz, defendant.

The plaintiff demands a perfect deed of conveyance of the house standing in the fort, adjoining on the south side the Hon. Company's newly built house and on the north side as the house and lot to all appearances stand and are situated, for which the plaintiff says the defendant was fully paid in the lifetime of her deceased husband, Gysbert Cornelisz.

The defendant admits that he was paid in full to his satisfaction according to the contract of sale and that the ground brief was also handed and delivered by him to the deceased[17] at the Manathans, to be entered in this record [90] because he promised to free the purchaser from all further claims in regard to the aforesaid house and lot for a year and a day, according to law; persisting once more that he delivered the ground brief to Gysbert Cornelisz, deceased, at the Manathans, which is entered here by way of memorandum to serve the purchaser and plaintiff in the future in the stead of a proper deed and conveyance, until such time as it shall be convenient [to execute the latter].

Claes Gerritsz, appearing before the court, requests permission to have a lot in Beverwyck to build thereon a house and in addition a garden for his use. The matter being considered, it is resolved and decided to appoint and authorize two magistrates to allot to him a lot and garden, the Hon. Rutgert Jacopsz and Andries Herpertsz, magistrates of this court, being appointed for that purpose and to make a report of their findings to this court.

Whereas the commissary and officer, Dyckman, complains that he is not yet fully paid the fine imposed by sentence on Arent Cornelisz Vogel, commonly called "Schapenbout,"[18] amounting to six guilders for himself and ten guilders for the poor here, and whereas this court is informed that the said Vogel has sixteen guilders coming to him from Abraham Pietersz Vos-

---

[17] The original record has: "was by the deceased delivered and handed to him."
[18] Meaning: Leg of mutton.

burgh, master carpenter, for nails delivered to him it is decided that the said Vosburgh shall pay the aforesaid sixteen guilders to both parties, each pro rata what is due to them, provided that the court shall free the said Vosburgh from all further claims on that account.

JOANNES DYCKMAN
RUTGER JACOBSZ
JACOB SCHERMERHOOREN
CORNELUS THONISEN
JAN THOMASZ

[91] Tuesday, February 3, 1653 [19]

Present:

All, except Jan Verbeeck

Various persons examined on interrogatories regarding the crimes committed by Jacob Jansz Stoll, of Amsterdam. In the first place, the person of Jochem Becker, baker.

How old he is and where born?	Answers, 38 years; at Jeveren.
Whether last summer he did not keep watch in this fort as corporal of the burgher guard?	Answers, Yes.
Whether, at one time, being on watch with his corporal's guard, he did not see Jacob Jansz Stoll come to the guard-house drunk and full, or at least quite intoxicated, after the men had gone on watch?	
About how long ago?	Answers, Yes.
	Declares that he has forgotten, or does not know very well, the exact time.

---

[19] This should be 1654.

What he, Hap, did there and whether he did not go to his house to get his sword, intending to clear out the guardhouse therewith?

Answers, Yes, and that he gave Adriaen, the schoolmaster, a handkerchief to fight against him with his sword and threatened to cut and hack at him, the corporal, with the sword, holding it unsheathed in front of said corporal's nose and saying: "I dare you to draw your colonel's rapier."

Whether he at that time did not strike Mr Adriaen van Ilpendam, clerk of the burgher guard, standing before the fire at the guardhouse?

Declares that he does not know exactly whether he did or not, but only saw that there was some trouble near the fire.

Whether he, Hap, having fetched his sword, did not by force try to fight with him, the corporal, life for life?

Declares, Yes, holding for that purpose the naked sword before said corporal's face.

Whether it was Jacob Hap's turn to do guard duty?

Answers, No.

Whether he, Hap, having thereafter come outside [92] the gate of this fort, wanted to assault the said Mr Adriaen, and not only him, but any other bystanders who wanted and were willing to fight?

Answers, Yes, and said to Mr Adriaen, "Draw your sword;" and wanted to attack him by force, which was prevented by the deponent and others.

Whether in the guardhouse, after the watch was set, he used much useless and abusive language to one person and another?

Answers, Yes, but especially to Mr Adriaen, calling him a burgher's dog and boy, yes, the dog of all the burghers.

Whether, he, the deponent, has any further statements to make in the matter?

Answers, No.

The deponent has with uplifted fingers confirmed these answers by oath.

Goosen Gerritsz, being heard, declares that last summer, the precise time he does not know, Jacob Jansz Stoll, after the mounting of the guard, made some trouble and out of mischief fired the gun which he had with him.

Resolved that the defendant shall be examined once more on the above interrogatories on the next court day.

Interrogatories for the examination of Jan Machielsz and Gerrit Jansz from Swoll.

How old they are and where born?	Answers, Jan Machielsz, aged 55 years, born at Edam, and Gerrit Jansz born at Swoll.
Whether last year they did not come to the guardhouse as burghers to do guard duty?	They say, Yes, when it was their turn.
Whether they did not see Jacob Jansz Stoll go to his house to get his sword to attack therewith the burgher watch and insult them?	They declare, Yes, and that they saw the sword, but do not know who brought it there or gave it to Jacob.
[93] Whether he did not try to attack Jochem Becker, the corporal of the burgher guard, with his sword and wanted to fight with him with his naked sword?	Answer, that he, Jacob, challenged the corporal to fight.
Whether he did not make other trouble at the guardhouse at that time?	Answer, Yes, and he struck Mr Adriaen van Ilpendam, standing by the fire, without cause.
Whether it was his watch?	They say, No.

The deponents have with uplifted fingers confirmed the above statements by oath before this court.

Interrogatories on which this court is to examine Marcelis Jansz from Bommel, former servant of Mr Johan de Hulter.

First, how old he is and where born?

Answers, at Bommel, 25 years of age.

Whether, about four months ago, he, besides Commissary Dyckman and Lourens Jansz, did not hear Christoffel Davits say that at one time alone he sold 22 *mutsgens* of brandy to the savages?

Answers, Yes, and that he, Davits, said so in the presence of still others.

Whether from this selling of brandy and drinking of the savages no trouble resulted and arose and whether the sachems of the savages there did not come to said Davits and in their way forbade him to sell any more brandy to the savages and begged him not to do so, as they got into great trouble and disputes with one another while being drunk?

Answers, Yes, that he himself understood and heard Christoffel Davits say so.

Whether he did not see Christoffel Davits now and then sell some brandy to the savages?

Answers, Yes, but that he does not know the quantity.

Whether he knows or has been informed that some trouble among the Christians and the savages has resulted therefrom, especially with the Christians?

Answers, Yes, especially because the horses of Thomas Clabbort had been in the corn.

He, Marcelis Jansz, has with uplifted fingers confirmed these answers by oath.

Herman Bastiaensz, carpenter, appearing before the court, requests payment of fl.106:5:-, due him for wages earned in building the Hon. Company's new house. It is decided that he will be paid in three months, if the treasury allows it.

On the petition of Andries de Vos, presented on the 20th of the preceding month, praying for some land behind his lot, stretching toward the woods, to be used as a pasture and meadow, it is resolved to make the following apostil: Inasmuch as the people here intend for their support, each one according to his needs, to pasture and keep some cattle there themselves, the said request is for the reason aforesaid for the present denied and not granted.

Upon the request of Annetge Bogardus, permission is given her from now on to take possession of and use the garden of, or heretofore granted to, Jacob Jansz Schermerhoren.

> JOANNES DYCKMAN
> RUTGER JACOBSZ
> ANDRIES HERBERTS
> JACOB SCHERMERHOOREN
> CORNELUS THONISEN
> JAN THOMASZ

[95] Tuesday, February 10, 1654

Present:

   Omnes

Commissary Joannes Dyckman, [plaintiff, against] Goosen Gerritsz, defendant.

Defendant's first default. Likewise Lourens Jansz, to testify concerning the shooting done by Jacob Jansz Stoll after the mounting of the guard.

Willem Fredrixsz, being summoned to appear in court, declares that Jacob Symontsz Klomp, fourteen days ago, used much abusive language toward this court, Adriaen Jansz from Leyden and himself and also that he was thereby forced to leave and go out of his house, as otherwise he would have been forced to make a stand against him, Clomp, with his knife in his hand.

Pieter Bronk, being summoned to appear, declares that Jacob, the carpenter, and Willem Jansz Prins, on Sunday, or the day before yesterday, bravely fought at his house and in order that they should not injure each other with knives, he, Bronck, had broken both their knives in their pockets before they began to fight.

Jacob, the carpenter, summoned to appear in court on account of fighting, defendant is in default.

Willem Jansz Prins declares that he does not know much about having been fighting, as he was dead drunk, but admits that on Sunday, even during the service, he was drinking at the house of Pieter Bronck.

Resolved to have them both summoned to appear again on the next court day.

Adriaen Jansz from Leyden, being summoned to give testimony of the truth in regard to what was done and said in his presence two weeks ago at the house of Willem Fredrixsz by Jacob Symontsz Clomp, the first default is entered against the witness and it is decided to have him cited again to appear on the next court day.

Upon resumption of the matter, it is resolved to adjourn the case of Jacob Luyersz, delinquent, for mischief committed on the street, until the arrival of the Hon. Director General, for reasons submitted and known to this court.

The Hon. Jacob Jansz Schermerhoren and Jan Thomasz, [96] magistrates of this court, are authorized to lay out for Hendrick Marcelis a lot on the hill, or wherever it may be most convenient and to make a report thereof to this court.

Whereas Luykas Andriesz, skipper, complains that some money is due him by Willem Albertsz from Monickendam and that for that reason he had taken possession of a boat belonging to said Willem Albertsz, it is decided by this court that he, Luykas Andriesz, may keep possession of said boat until he is paid and satisfied.

Interrogatories on which this court is to examine Jan Roelofsz, burgher of Beverwyck.

First:
How old he is and where born?

Declares and answers as follows:
20 years and born in this country.

Whether last year he did guard duty here in this fort together with other burghers?

Answer, When it was his turn.

Whether among other things he did not see Jacob Jansz Stoll, coming to the guardhouse drunk with a loaded gun, make much noise and commotion in the guardhouse?

Declares, Yes, and that he heard him fire off his gun after the mounting of the guard.

Whether he has any other statements to make concerning it?

Answers, No.

Upon the request and complaint made to this court by the purchaser of the house of Merten Herpertsz, mason, sold by this court on the 19th of the preceding month of January, now occupied by Mr Johan de Hulter, who is having a cellar dug on the lot next to the house, which the purchaser claims and considers to be detrimental to the aforesaid house, it is resolved and decided to order the court messenger, as he is ordered hereby, in the name of the court to forbid Mr de Hulter aforesaid to have said work done, with order not only to stop said work, but also to replace the dirt and to have the lot put back in the state in which it was before the work was commenced. Furthermore, as according to the custom of the fatherland [97] delivery of all houses, lots and other pieces of real estate sold by the court pursuant to a writ of execution is made promptly on payment of the first instalment and a quitclaim deed therefor is given on payment of the final payment, this serves as a warning to Mr de Hulter aforesaid that on the first of May next the court will make delivery of the aforesaid house and lot to the purchaser on payment of the first instalment, notwithstanding the fact that Mr de Hulter according to the contract might have the lease of the aforesaid house a little while longer, as this court, as stated above, governs itself according to the law and customs of the fatherland. And whereas by the terms and conditions of sale it was expressly stipulated that [the court] was selling everything as it was, without [the parties] having the right to raise any questions from any cause whatsoever, this serves to inform Mr de Hulter that on the first of May next he shall have to vacate the aforesaid sold house, in order that proper delivery thereof may be made; also that he must not make any further repairs; the court declaring further that inasmuch as the lessee had certain knowledge of the sale, he shall have to bear all expenses which were incurred by him on the aforesaid house and lot since the sale or which he may incur in the future.

JOANNES DYCKMAN
RUTGER JACOBSZ
ANDRIES HERBERTS
JAN VERBEECK
JACOB SCHERMERHOOREN
JAN THOMASZ
CORNELUS THONISEN

[98] Tuesday, February 17, 1654

Present:

Dyckman
J: Verbeeck
Schermerhoren
Jan Thomasz

Adriaen Jansz from Leyden, being summoned to testify to the truth of what was done in his presence two weeks ago today at the house of Willem Fredrixsz by Jacob Symontsz Clomp, declares that he, Clomp, spoke many abusive words to him and challenged him to come outside the door, but that he did not draw a knife.

The court having considered what is above written and also the declaration made in regard to it at the last session of the court and having further taken into consideration that on Saturday a week ago he fought with Jacob van Loosdrecht, they condemn the aforesaid Clomp to pay a fine of fl. 12 to the officer, with costs.

Jan Barentsz Poest being cited to appear before the court to show his authority for fencing off the lot next to Gysbert Cornelisz, deceased, on the south side, has exhibited his ground brief thereof granted by the Hon. Director General, of which this serves as notice.

Lourens Jansz from Hoesem, being summoned by the court, has answered the following interrogatories as indicated in the margin.

Interrogatories on which this court is to examine Lourens Jansz, burgher of Beverwyck.

How old he is and where born?	Answers, at Hoesem,[20] 48 years old.
Whether last year he did not do guard duty in the fort with other burghers?	Declares, [Yes], when it was his turn.
If, among other things, he did not see Jacob Jansz Stoll, having come to the guardhouse drunk or at least quite full, fire off his gun out of mischief after the guard had gone on duty?	Answers, Yes, that he heard it and that [Jacob] was using much abusive language.
Whether he has anything more to state about it?	Answers, No.

The honorable treasurers, Abraham Staets and Sander Leendertsen, having appeared before the meeting, declare that they have gone the rounds to collect the fifteen guilders ordered to be assessed on each house for the completion of the bridges in

---

[20] Husum, a seaport town of Sleswick.

Beverwyck, pursuant to the order of the Hon. General and this court, but that they did not succeed very well. It is resolved thereupon to have the following notice posted immediately in three suitable places. [The notice] reads as follows:

The honorable magistrates of this court order all burghers and inhabitants belonging to this jurisdiction who have any house or houses standing in and therefore belonging to this jurisdiction to pay within fifteen days from this date fifteen guilders to the appointed honorable treasurers, Abraham Staets and Sander Leendertsen, pursuant to the order of the Hon. Director General and this court, for the building of the bridges contracted for in the village of Beverwyck and to defray other expenses already incurred or still to be incurred. Furthermore, every one who has been granted a lot, on which he has not yet built and which still lies vacant, shall pay half as much; and each free person residing in this jurisdiction and exercising his trade there six guilders; on pain, in case of failure to pay within the aforesaid appointed time, of forfeiting the first day after the period when payment should have been made three guilders, the next day six guilders, and so on successively each day twice as much, and finally of peremptory execution. And in order that no one may claim ignorance hereof, the honorable court aforesaid has caused this to be posted in the usual places. Thus done, ratified and considered the second time by the aforesaid court in Fort Orange, this 17th day of the month of February 1654. Underneath was written, By order of the honorable court in this place, and was signed, Joannes Dyckman.

It is resolved to summon the surveyor, Abraham Pietersz Vosburgh, to appear on the next court day, with reference to the garden heretofore granted to Jacob Jansz Schermerhooren, which it is understood has been given to Andries de Vos without the knowledge of this court.

[100] It is resolved to order the surveyors to measure the lot behind the lot of Sander Leendertsen and inclosed by him. Whereupon the aforesaid Sander Leendertsen being summoned,

he is asked whether the aforesaid small lot was also granted to him? He says that it was promised to him, but that it is not yet mentioned in his ground brief. It is resolved to communicate this to the magistrates of this court who at present are at the Manathans and about this and other points to send them a letter reading as follows:

To the Honorable Magistrates Rutger Jacobsz, Andries Herpertsz and Cornelis Theu. van Westbroeck, at present at the Manathans.

Honorable, Wise, Prudent and Very Discreet Friends and Fellow Members of this Court:

Inclosed herewith are authentic copies of the terms of sale of the house of Merten Herpertsz, mason, and the subsequent resolution passed at the request of the purchaser, on account of the digging of a hole for a well or a cellar in the purchased lot, together with a memorandum for your honors in case Monsieur de Hulter should make any further request there to remain in the house that was sold as lessee during the term of the lease, in which [copies] we hope you will find sufficient arguments and reasons against the frivolous contentions of Monsieur de Hulter aforesaid, trusting further to what your honors in such case may be pleased and able to advance in support thereof.

Herewith go also the measurements of the lot of Sander Leendertsen, showing how much was granted to him and how much he has inclosed with posts contrary to orders, which person, being on that account by order of the officer legally summoned to appear before the court, declared yesterday that the addition to his lot is not mentioned in his ground brief, but was promised to him, so that your honors will be pleased to make further inquiry about it. As far as we can judge, Sander Leendertsen has done this on his own authority; if so, the officer here will have to institute proceedings against him to prove his title. On the other hand, we should like to see this place [101] [disposed of] as we with the consent of the Hon. General decided, namely, to have Rutger Jacobsz and Willem Fredrixsz build a good horse mill on it, for the use and convenience of the burghers here, the said place being all the more suitable therefor because it is close to the kill and the river, so that it is convenient to convey the grain to and from it by water. We have thus far not been able to find a more suitable location for this necessary structure. Furthermore, as Herman Bastiaensen has sold his house and should like to build another dwelling house on his lot on the first kill, also toward the river side, so far from the fort that it will obstruct this fort very little, [we hope] that he will be permitted to build, as he must have a place to live in.

Having nothing further [to communicate] for the present, we commend your honors, with our greetings, to the grace of God and remain,

> Your honors' willing servants and friends and fellow members of this court, the president and magistrates of the court of Fort Orange and Beverwyck.

Fort Orange, February 18, 1654

> Was signed: JOANNES DYCKMAN
> JACOB SCHERMERHOREN
> JAN VERBEECK

The memorandum follows:

> Memorandum for the magistrates Rutger Jacobsz, Andries Herbertsz and Cornelis Theunisz van Westbroeck, who have gone to the Manathans.

That herewith go authentic copies of the conditions of sale of the house of Merten Herpertsz, mason, and the resolution passed at the request of the purchaser concerning the digging of a hole for a cellar or a well in the lot sold next to the aforesaid house.

Which memorandum is intended to serve their honors at the Manathans if necessary in case Monsieur de Hulter should make there any further request to remain in the aforesaid house according to the lease drawn up between the aforesaid mason and de Hulter.

First, that he, the mason, had no right to lease the said house in this manner, because various judgments against him, upon evidence of debt, had been given by this court before he leased the aforesaid house, to wit, that [102] he must make payment to his creditors within six weeks, according to the aforesaid judgments, on pain of execution.

That he being unable to satisfy his creditors within the aforesaid time, [the court] was forced to proceed to execution.

That the sale, having been made by the court, necessarily breaks the lease, as he had no right to grant it.

It being the accepted rule in such cases that sale breaks the lease, according to the custom of the fatherland and that although this is not stipulated in the terms of the lease, the lease becomes void of itself, notwithstanding ordinarily the amount of the rent and the period of the lease are specified, which is done only to make the houses and real estate bring higher prices and which has also been the sole aim of this court in stipulating that the first payment must be made on the first of May next.

In the fatherland delivery takes place on payment of the first term, being the day on which the leases of houses usually begin.

No one may lease his real estate for a year and a day whose affairs are in a shaky condition and whose creditors have already secured several judgments against him;

For in the fatherland all leases in such case are void when the first payment is made.

Even the insolvent person, if he lives in one of his houses, must vacate the same when the first payment is made;

For otherwise the insolvent person would allow himself as much time to live therein as he pleased, which is not permitted by the courts in Holland, as may be seen by thousands of cases, but must vacate at the time stated.

Furthermore, a mortgage on the aforesaid house for a year and a day has been granted and executed with the knowledge and at the request of the lessor, which contains that the aforesaid house is specially mortgaged to Jan Jansz from Gottenburgh, to be sold by him when he pleases [103] and whereas the purchaser has furthermore offered instead of the first payment only to pay the full amount upon delivery, it would be a great loss and detriment to the general creditors to whom larger or smaller amounts are due if, on account of this lease, they would have to wait a year and a day before being paid and thereby be deprived of considerable interest;

For the net interest per year, as calculated in this country, on the purchase price of the aforesaid house, plus the cost of necessary repairs to be made, will far exceed the stipulated rent paid by the lessee.

Furthermore, it is expressly stipulated in the terms of sale that the honorable court sells everything as it is, without either the purchaser or the lessee having the right to raise any questions, from whatever cause it may be.

And whereas Monsieur de Hulter at present dwells in this jurisdiction and therefore can not be regarded otherwise than as a subject and burgher thereof, it is surprising that without notifying this court he brings further suit in the matter there.

If he denies that he is a burgher and subject of this jurisdiction, he must without any gainsay depart therefrom according to the opinion of all reasonable minds;

For no one may reside therein, not only in this but in all other jurisdictions, without duly respecting and obeying the government and courts thereof.

In case he acknowledges it, it is surprising that he ignores his own competent judges and there seeks judicial relief.

Commissary Dyckman, plaintiff, against Jacob from Loosdrecht, defendant.

Defendant's second default.

JOANNES DYCKMAN
JAN VERBEECK
JACOB SCHERMERHOOREN
JAN THOMASZ

[104] Tuesday, March 3, 1654

Present:

J: Dyckman   J: J: Schermerhoren
J: Verbeeck   Jan Thomasz

Commissary Joannes Dyckman, plaintiff, against the following persons:

Jan Hendrixsz. Defendant's first default.

Hendrick Gerritsz, for having been drinking at Hendrick Jochemsz, after the ringing of the bell. Also first default.

The commissary, plaintiff, against Jurriaen Theunisz, glazier and innkeeper, and Claes vande Hooge bergh, on account of fighting on Shrove Tuesday at the house of Jurriaen Theunisz.

Jurriaen Theunisz, appearing, declares that his opponent came into his house drunk and beat him, thereby committing violence in his house.

It is decided to have the parties summoned again at the first opportunity.

Abraham Pietersz Vosburgh declares that having some time or some days ago been called upon to survey the lot of Dirck Bensingh and being busy therewith and things not going as he, Bensingh, liked, he said to the aforesaid surveyor: "The stake which stands there is more trustworthy than you are and if you do not survey according to the stakes which stand there, you survey falsely," and other similar remarks. The aforesaid surveyor maintaining that the above written statements were made, it is resolved and decided to have the said Dirrick Bensingh and both the surveyors summoned again to appear on the next court day.

The commissary aforesaid, plaintiff, against Jochem Becker and Jacob Willemsz de Wolff, defendants, on account of fighting which took place last Saturday evening at the house of Jacob Willemsz.

Jacob Willemsz declares that the old captain's hens sitting on the nest to lay, they were chased off the nest by Jochem Becker, who said that they were his hens, and when Jacob said,

"What do you mean? they are the old captain's hens," Jochem Becker challenged Jacob Willemsz to come outside the door. The latter not coming, he ran into the house after Jacob, grabbed him by the throat or neck and gave him a sound beating besides, calling him an old dog, without the deponent having hit him in return.

The old captain, Willem Juriaensz, being summoned by the court, declares that what Jacob testified to above, happened as he said.

[105] Willem Hoffmeyer being also summoned to testify to the truth in regard to the matter aforesaid, the first default is entered against him, but it is decided to have him summoned again to appear on the next court day.

Jochem Becker declares that Jacob returned the blows and pulled him by the hair and called him a dog and a son of a bitch. Resolved to summon him to reappear also.

Jacob from Loosdrecht, carpenter, having been fighting twice, once at the house of Hendrick Jochemsz and once at Pieter Bronck's, is ordered to pay to the officer here the sum of ten guilders, with costs, to be paid immediately.

Abraham Crabaat, for having last Shrove Tuesday walked along the street in woman's clothes, is, although it is the first time and he offers the excuse that he did not know that he was doing wrong, condemned to pay a fine of six guilders for the benefit of the poor, with costs, to be paid immediately, provided that if he, Crabaat, or any one else should hereafter undertake to do this again, he shall be arbitrarily punished as an example to others.

Albert Gerritsz, plaintiff, against Rut Arentsz, tailor, defendant, for fl.76:— in seawan and fl.32 in beavers, which defendant owes plaintiff for wages earned and other things.

The court having heard the arguments on both sides, condemn the defendant to satisfy and pay the plaintiff what is hereinbefore written within the space of twenty-four hours, on pain of peremptory execution.

Jan Labatie, plaintiff, against Jochem Becker, defendant, about some dispute concerning their respective lots. Resolved that this court itself will this afternoon make an inspection in order to be able to render a proper decision and to settle their dispute in accordance with the merits of the case.

[106] Thomas Sandertsen, smith, appearing before the court, declares his inability to pay the assessment of fifteen guilders on each house, nevertheless expressing his willingness in the matter.

The court having heard his reasons for being excused, accepts them in so far that instead of fifteen guilders, he will have to pay only five guilders, once, to the treasurer, being thereby for this time excused from making further payments, without any precedent being established thereby.

The court having seen and examined what the commissary ex officio as plaintiff has exhibited in writing against the delinquent, Jacob Jansz Stoll, order the defendant aforesaid to present his written answer thereto promptly on the next court day, on pain, etc.

The schout of the colony of Rensselaerswyck having come into court has delivered the following writing:

> To the Honorable Judges of the Court of Fort Orange and Beverwyck

As officer of the colony of Rensselaerswyck, I respectfully petition your honors aforesaid as follows: Whereas it has pleased the Hon. Joannes Dyckman some time ago, at the house of the lord patroon, at the close of divine service in the afternoon, to read publicly to the congregation a protest concerning the announcement of the departure of Brant van Slichtenhorst, formerly director of the aforesaid colony, and it is [but] just that one should have positive knowledge, which one can not gather from hearsay alone, according to all [legal] customs, therefore, in my official capacity aforesaid, I request that an authentic copy of the aforesaid protest which was read may be exhibited and delivered to me, in order that I may know the matter itself and the foundation thereof, whereupon I expect your honors' apostil and consent to be written in the margin hereof. Underneath was written, Your honors' willing servant, and was signed, Gerrit Swart, officer. Done this 3d of March A° 1654, at the house of the lord patroon of the aforesaid colony.

Whereupon it is resolved to make the following apostil:

The Honorable Schout and officer of the colony of Rensselaerswyck having come into court, [107] has delivered a certain writing whereby a copy is requested of the protest against the reading or announcement made from the pulpit in regard to the affairs of Brant van Slichtenhorst, the former director of the aforesaid colony, served by Commissary Dyckman by order of this court on the 25th of January last in the church in the hearing of the congregation who were present. It states among other things that it is just that one should have positive knowledge which one can not gather from hearsay, according to all [legal] customs, and requests that an authentic copy of the aforesaid protest may be exhibited and delivered to him, in order that he may know the matter itself and the foundation thereof and that an apostil may be entered on his petition. This serves therefore to state that the court in so far does not judge his request unjust and therefore shall furnish him with an authentic copy, subject only to this condition that his honor shall first or at the same time deliver to this court in exchange a copy of what that forenoon was proclaimed in the matter by the Reverend Domine Gidiony Schaets, such being in accordance with all legal custom. This court is unable to see that it is otherwise bound to do so and therefore also intends not to send the protest to his honor or whoever else may demand the same in such a manner, which is deemed impudent, unless it receives beforehand what was read from [the pulpit]. Otherwise, it intends to delay the same until the arrival of the Honorable Director General, who according to his honor's letter meanwhile received we expect at the first opportunity and to whose wise judgment we shall gladly defer the matter, considering it without reason that in case the proclamation is refused us, this court should be bound to send and furnish the protest to their honors of the colony, but being ready and willing, if the proclamation is delivered to this court, immediately to remit a copy as aforesaid of the protest to the officer aforesaid, or whoever may ask for the same in the name of the colony.

JOANNES DYCKMAN
JAN VERBEECK
JACOB SCHERMERHOOREN
JAN THOMASZ

[108] Extraordinary Session, Friday, March 13

Present:

J: Dyckman   J: Verbeeck   C: Thuenisz
A: Herpertsz   J: J: Schermerhoren   J: Thomasz
R: Jacopsz

Pieter Adriaensen Soo Gemackelyck, plaintiff, against Cornelis Vos, defendant.

Defendant's first default. About a tub of butter shipped by plaintiff's mother at the Manathans in defendant's yacht and not delivered to the plaintiff, according to the exhibited letter written by plaintiff's mother to plaintiff for that purpose, in which it is stated, as shown to this court, that there were 33 pounds of butter in it.

Furthermore, that the defendant the day before yesterday, at the house of Willem Bout, twice drew his knife and several times made a stab at the plaintiff with it, close to his body or belly.

The first case is adjourned until the arrival in person of the plaintiff's mother herself, who is expected here any day from the Manathans, and the second case until later. Meanwhile, the plaintiff is ordered to advance the money to pay for the expenses of the court, further disposition in the matter to be made when it shall have been established who is right and who is wrong.

Herman Bastiaensen, plaintiff, against Pieter Adriaensen Soo Gemackelyck, defendant, for fl.750:– for wages earned by him, of which fl.150:–, or thereabouts, are alleged to have been paid. The plaintiff demands payment of the entire amount, notwithstanding the defendant says that the contract made between them, which is exhibited, is not yet fully carried out, he being willing to pay the first five hundred guilders and the balance as soon as the work is finished according to the contract.

The court, having heard the arguments and debates on both sides, orders and adjudges that the defendant shall remain in custody until the work shall have been inspected by two impartial carpenters and that after they have made their report he shall be allowed to go home on bail. Claes Jansz from Baere[21] and Claes from Rotterdam are appointed inspectors to inspect the work this day and [109] to report their findings to this court, as compared with the specifications, of which a copy or the originals will be put into the hands of the appointed carpenters. The expenses involved therein shall be paid by the guilty or delinquent party, on pain of peremptory execution.

JOANNES DYCKMAN
RUTGER JACOBSZ
ANDRIES HERBERTS
JAN VERBEECK
JACOB SCHERMERHOOREN
CORNELUS THONISEN
JAN THOMASZ

---

[21] Baarn, in the province of Utrecht.

Tuesday, March 17, 1654

Present:

The Hon. General	Rut: Jacopsen	Cor: Theunesz
Mr Sille	An: Herpertsen	Jan Thomasz
J: Dyckman	J: Schermerhoren	

Herman Bastiaensen, carpenter, plaintiff, against Pieter Adriaensen Soo Gemackelyck, defendant, about a certain dispute brought before the court on Friday last about wages earned in building the house of the aforesaid Gemackelyck.

The court having heard the debates and arguments on both sides and having also examined the written report of the two impartial carpenters appointed last Friday to inspect the work, order and adjudge that the plaintiff must still make in the aforesaid house a *Bol Cosyn*,[22] tongue and groove and make tight the ceilings, and hang the doors and windows. As to the one gable, which has not been tongued and grooved and planed according to the contract, but nailed down, the board overlapping one another, this shall remain thus as an offset against the extra work that has been done according to the written report. The court further condemn the plaintiff to pay the costs of the suit and order the defendant, as soon as the aforesaid work shall have been done, promptly to pay the stipulated wages.

Resolved to draw an order on the honorable treasurers here in favor of the carpenter, Abraham Pietersz Vosburgh, in the sum of two hundred guilders to be deducted from the amount which he has asked for making the two bridges here in Beverwyck.

The court of Fort Orange and Beverwyck on the safe arrival here of the Hon. Director General and the Hon. Nicasius Sille, have deemed it necessary and proper to submit to their honors the following request, which was this day delivered to their honors:

---

[22] A window with three lights, the lower sashes swinging in or out, and the upper one being stationary.

That this court, [110] from experience, for reasons hereinafter stated, can (subject to correction) come to no other conclusion than that they are forced to request that the bench of Justice of the colony of Rensselaerswyck, which until now has been allowed to continue in the place where it was accustomed to meet, may be removed and ordered to [hold court] outside of this jurisdiction or the established limits.

For it is evident that they have caused the minister, Gidion Schaets, to announce and serve public notice in the church standing in this jurisdiction that all the inhabitants of this as well of their jurisdiction who had any charges to bring against the person of Brant van Slichtenhorst must make them known and plead before their bench of justice, on pain of keeping for ever silent, and that without regard of persons, whoever they might be, which can not be understood otherwise as to include also (with all due respect) your honors and the respective members of this court.

How impudent this is, your honors can [readily see], it being contrary to your honors' express written orders and command given almost two years ago to those of the colony, when this bench of justice was erected and established, we on our side, according to our bounden duty, having never attempted to treat the court of the colony in any other than a friendly way, saving the privileges of each, nor sought to be with the court of the colony aforesaid on any other terms than those of love and friendship, the two jurisdictions mutually respecting each other's rights.

[Praying therefore,] that it may be ordered and decreed that all persons residing in this jurisdiction may (saving the right of appeal) be summoned only before this bench of justice, without regard of persons.

And whereas those of the colony judge [otherwise, that] all, or such as have taken the oath to the patroon, who at present reside in this jurisdiction and who intend to remain there, may be ordered, whenever the occasion may require it, to plead their causes before this bench and to stand trial here, after being legally cited or otherwise summoned to appear, if need be.

That the same, when residing in this jurisdiction, [111] may also be bound to take the common burgher oath, or in case of refusal be ordered to depart, since without it they can not be deemed or adjudged otherwise than in contempt. An example whereof was seen by this court in the person of Brant van Slichtenhorst who, having been three times legally cited to appear in court by a private person of this jurisdiction, gave for answer that this court had no jurisdiction over him, as he had taken the oath to the patroon.

And if the court of justice of the colony should remain where it is, this can only tend to the great prejudice of this court, as they daily make the inhabitants of this jurisdiction believe that there is to be a change and that, being returned under the jurisdiction of the patroon, they will be regarded as perjurers, in consequence of which the inhabitants here can not be held as well as they should to their bounden duty and obedience, but become refractory and on the contrary forget the respect which they owe this court.

The colony extends far and wide and between the farms established by the patroon there are still many lands which are not yet bought or occupied by the patroon or his subjects, but are cultivated by the natives themselves, to the great prejudice of this country; for the savages being allowed to plant them, they imagine after a time that they belong to them and thereafter use the lands as their own, to the great loss and detriment not only of the inhabitants, but also of the land itself, which otherwise might be bought, paid for and cultivated by the inhabitants, to the great convenience of themselves and consequently of the country. It is therefore requested that these lands, which have not yet been purchased of the natives, may by order of your honors be bought, paid for and occupied and cultivated by the private inhabitants, according to your honor's pleasure and with your consent.

As on the 8th of April next three of the magistrates will have been for two years in consecutive service and the term which they agreed to serve will therefore expire and the time arrive for others to take their places, we have below nominated a [112] double number of five persons, from whom three are to be chosen by your honors to fill the vacancies.

Abraham Staets
Volckert Jansz } left the service last year
Jan Labatie

Rutger Jacobsz
Andries Herpertsen } whose time expired on the 8th of April
Cornelis Theunisz

Jan Verbeeck
Jacob Schermerhoren } have served one year
Jan Thomasz

Nomination of four to complete the number of twelve, or to serve as magistrates:

Pieter Hartgers is one of the twelve
Frans Barentsz
Sander Leendertsen
Gerrit Jansz from Swoll
Adriaen Jansz from Leyden

The rest of what this court has to propose and to request, they request permission to propose orally, whereupon they expect your honors' favorable apostil.

Fort Orange,
March 16, 1654

Your honors' very obedient and faithful [servants], the commissary and magistrates of Fort Orange and Beverwyck.

Delivered this day to the honorable gentlemen and signed by all the members of this court. After some verbal questions had been asked of their honors, orders were given to put them into writing and to deliver [the petition] to their honors, which was done, the contents or tenor being as follows:

> To the Hon. Director General Peter Stuyvesant and the Hon. Nicasius Sille

Shew with due reverence to your honors, Commissary Joannes Dyckman and the magistrates [113] of the Court of Fort Orange and Beverwyck, that they, the petitioners, find by experience that notwithstanding the placards that have been issued, whereby all tapsters residing in this jurisdiction are required to pay the regular and appointed tapsters' excise on wine, beer and distilled liquors which they tap, retail or sell, in such way as the ordinance provides, the wine, beer and distilled liquors are not entered as they should be, but that much smuggling is going on and that the burghers here have to pay the tax put by the tapsters on the aforesaid liquors, whether they smuggle and thereby pay no excise, or not. The petitioners, therefore, would not be surprised if, in order to prevent the smuggling in the future, it were better to have the excise on beer, wine and distilled liquors publicly farmed out to the highest bidder, and left to the farmer first for a year and thereafter for longer, according to your honors' pleasure and decision, provided that the tapsters of the heavy beer and wines, before they are allowed to have these carried or brought into their houses or cellars, must obtain from the appointed collector, or farmer, or farmers, of the excise a proper certificate that they have paid the excise, and furthermore that every burgher must also get a similar certificate from the collector or farmer of the [excise on] beer, wine and distilled liquors, without however having to pay any excise, but only the fee for writing the certificate, under the penalty to be provided by your honors.

It is furthermore to be considered whether in the future those of the colony ought not to pay the established tapsters' excise as well as the tapsters in this jurisdiction, who complain that they sell their beer, wine and distilled liquors as cheap as those of the colony, notwithstanding the fact that they must pay the excise and in addition must do guard duty, as they [114] did last year, from which those of the colony are exempt, which they consider to be of benefit to the colony as well as to this jurisdiction. Also that they are bound, together with the other burghers of this jurisdiction, to bear the extraordinary charges for the maintenance of bridges, etc., which however are used also by the residents of the colony, yes, even had to help build up and fortify this fort, although in times of need it would serve as a place of refuge for those of the colony, as well as for themselves and other burghers, and other such like reasons.

Upon the complaint of the burghers here, the petitioners find and have daily experienced that the bakers do not act in good faith in the matter of baking bread for the burghers, but bolt the flour from the meal and sell it greatly to their profit to the savages for the baking of sweet cake, white bread, cookies and pretzels, so that the burghers must buy and get largely bran for their money, and even then the bread is frequently found to be short of weight, and they ask one guilders, yes, as much as 24 stivers for such poor and short-weight baked bread. Which the petitioners in the interest of this community have thought it necessary to bring to your honors' attention, in order that in the future your honors may provide herein as you shall see fit, in the interest of the community here and especially of the plain and common people, who can not bake themselves, so that if this continues the Christians must eat the bran while the savages eat the flour; [praying therefore] that a proper weight and a price for the sale of proper bread may be set.

Whereas the people here, at Katskill, Esopus and elsewhere are very short of schepel measures, whether whole, half, or quarter schepels, to measure grain and other commodities, your honors are requested to be pleased to order a reasonable quantity from *patria* to supply the people therewith [115], provided that every one who receives one is to pay for it. Otherwise, one person and another measuring with a little tub or keg, great disputes are likely to be caused and to arise among the people.

Furthermore, as the petitioners are often compelled to take off time to attend to the duties of this, their accepted office, to the great loss and detriment of themselves and the public service, they request your honors to be pleased to authorize that each of the magistrates during the term of his service or office be given a yearly salary at the discretion and pleasure of your honors, the same to be paid out of the excise, the general or other funds.

Expecting hereupon your honors' favorable apostil, they are and will remain,

> Your honors obedient and faithful servants, the magistrates of the court of Fort Orange and Beverwyck.

Fort Orange, this 17th
of March 1654.

Delivered this day to their honors, signed by all the members of this court. Received for answer that the written order and answer to this and the preceding petition would be sent at the first opportunity from the Manathans.

> JOANNES DYCKMAN
> RUTGER JACOBSZ
> ANDRIES HERPERTS
> JAN VERBEECK
> JACOB SCHERMERHOOREN
> CORNELUS THONISEN
> JAN THOMASZ

[116] Tuesday, March 31, 1654

Present:
    Omnes

Jacob Luyersen, being summoned by the court to pay to the treasurers the fifty guilders levied on every house pursuant to the resolution, has requested eight days' grace, which are granted him, when he must promptly pay the aforesaid sum to the treasurers.

Roeloff Jansz and Jacob Gerritsz, who have leased the house of Cornelis Theunisz for the unpaid half [of the tax], are ordered to pay each one half as required.

Commissary Dyckman, plaintiff, against Jochem Becker and Jacob Willemsen de Wolff, defendants, on account of assault and battery by Jochem Becker upon Jacob Willemsz de Wolff at his house on the last of February preceding.

The court having heard the statements of both sides and also examined the evidence, it is resolved to condemn Jochem Becker to pay a fine of thirty guilders to the officer here within the space of forty-eight hours, on pain of execution and to order the aforesaid Becker, as is done hereby, to leave his neighbor, the aforesaid Jacob Willemsz, and all others henceforth unmolested and in peace, on pain of arbitrary correction.

Commissary Dyckman, plaintiff, against Dirrick Bensingh, defendant, on account of abusive words spoken to the surveyors, which being further investigated by the court, it is decided to condemn him to pay a fine of twelve guilders to the officer before sundown.

Jan Thomasz, as attorney for Claes Thysz Cnyver, plaintiff, against Willem Albertsen from Monickendan, defendant, about the delivery of some casks to the value of fl.144:–, to be paid in grain or beavers.

The court having heard the statements and arguments on both sides, [117] it is resolved to condemn the defendant to pay the sum of fl.144:– demanded by plaintiff, within the space of six weeks, on pain of execution. Also, that meanwhile the defendant is not to depart from here without giving proper security for the payment aforesaid, provided that whatever the defendant has paid on account shall be deducted from the aforesaid sum.

Dirck Bensingh, having appeared before the court, requests a strip of ground in the rear of his lot. The magistrates, or some of them, are requested to make an inspection of the same.

Jacob Luyersen is notified that he must file his answer to the written complaint of the officer, sent to his house by order of the court, on or before the next court day, subject to the penalty provided.

It is resolved to have Lambert van Valckenburgh summoned to appear in court on account of the things done or committed by him last Wednesday two weeks ago at the house of Gerrit Jansz from Swoll, together with the witnesses who were present.

The request of Philip Pietersz Scheuler to enlarge his lot on the hill somewhat is granted, the president and Andries Herpertsz and Jacob Schermerhoren being appointed a committee to show him how far [he may go].

Albert Andriesz appearing in court complains that besides the boards received by him from Merten Herpertsz from de Hulter's lot, there is due to him fl.70:3:12. Resolved to summon Merten Herpertsz to appear on the next court day to see if Mr de Hulter can not spare some more boards.

Resolved to draw the following orders on the treasurers for materials delivered to this fort and for wages:

To the carpenters, in the sum of fl.128:10, in settlement of an account of fl.242:-

Albert Andriesz, for 116 boards @ 24 stivers, fl.139:4:-

Also to Rut Jacopsz for boards delivered, per account to be shown.

     JOANNES DYCKMAN
     RUTGER JACOBSZ
     ANDRIES HERPERTS
     JAN VERBEECK
     JACOB SCHERMERHO[OREN]
     CORNELUS THONISE[N]
     JAN THOMASZ

[118] Extraordinary Session, Thursday, April 2, 1654

Present:

Omnes dempto Cornelis Theunisz

Commissary Dyckman, plaintiff, against Claes van den Hoogen Bergh, defendant, about fighting of the defendant and Juriaen Theunisz on Shrove Tuesday at the house of Juriaen Theunisz. According to the declaration made by Juriaen Theunisz before this court on the third of March, the defendant came into his house drunk and assaulted and beat him.

The court having heard the declarations and arguments of both parties, order the defendant to pay a fine of sixty guilders, once, within the space of twenty-four hours, and not to go outside the limits [of this jurisdiction] until he has paid, on pain of further punishment. This covers also the abusive and threatening language addressed by the defendant to one of the members of this court while still in session, to wit, that if he, the defendant, had him in another place, he would teach him differently, etc.

Theunis Dirrixsz, appearing in court, requests that, Rut Arentsz, tailor, having died, he may undertake the settlement of the estate of the deceased, provided that this court nominate and appoint two curators besides him.

The matter being taken into consideration, the appearer's request is granted, he being accepted and appointed as curator and the Hon. Rutger Jacopsz and Goosen Gerritsz being associated with him, the three of them as curators to settle the estate of the aforesaid deceased as best they can and in due time to render a proper accounting thereof to this court.

JOANNES DYCKMAN
RUTGER JACOBSZ
ANDRIES HERPERTS
JAN VERBEECK
JACOB SCHERMERHOOREN
CORNELUS THONISEN
JAN THOMASZ

[119] Tuesday, April 21, 1654

Present:

Omnes dempto Rutger Jacopsz

Marritgen Claes' daughter, plaintiff, against Roeloff Jacopsz, defendant, about an anker of brandy furnished by plaintiff to the defendant and money advanced to him.

The defendant's wife, appearing, says that the plaintiff sold two ankers of brandy to the defendant, of which to her knowledge she had one taken out of the cellar again, notwithstanding it had already been entered.

The court having heard the statements and arguments of both parties, condemn the defendant to pay the plaintiff within the space of three days nine whole, good, merchantable beavers, leaving it to the choice of the plaintiff to deliver the other or second anker of brandy to the defendant and to receive ten beavers for the said anker and the money advanced, or, in case of failure to deliver said anker, to receive nine beavers. And in case the payment does not take place within the aforesaid time, it is ordered to proceed to peremptory execution.

Jacob Hendrixsz Sibbinck, plaintiff, against Jacob Adriaensen, wheelwright, defendant, for ten beavers for wages earned on the house in which the defendant dwells.

Defendant's first default.

The Hon. Andries Herpertsz and Jacob Jansz Schermerhoren are appointed to lay out for Jacob Hendrixsz Sibbinck a garden next to the garden of Gillis Pietersz.

Commissary Dyckman, plaintiff, against Hendrick Biermans, defendant, for assault and battery.

Defendant's first default.

Pieter Bronck, for himself as well as for Anker Brynsen and Lourens Lourensen, asks for six months' extension of time without having to pay any fines [for not building] on the lots granted to them in Beverwyck, because they can not get nails and for other reasons. Their request is granted.

[120] Jacob Luyersz being summoned by the court on account of previous misdemeanors, the court for various reasons them thereunto moving have resolved to pardon the aforesaid person with reference to the misdemeanor committed by him and the hereinbefore mentioned abusive words spoken to the officer.

The defendant appearing in court has begged forgiveness and stated that he knows nothing of the commissary and Officer Dyckman and his wife but what is honorable and virtuous. He is condemned however for assault committed on the public street to pay the officer at once a fine of 25 guilders, for the benefit of Officer Dyckman.

Joannes Withart, plaintiff, against Volckert Jansz and Pieter Hartgers, defendants, about payment for goods left in the year 1652 by Evert Tesselaer in the hands of the defendants.

Parties are referred to referees, Commissary Dyckman, Arent van Curler, Jan Baptista van Rensselaer and Anthonis de Hooges, to agree on such terms as they can, the referees to report their findings to this court.

JOANNES DYCKMAN
ANDRIES HERPERTS
JAN VERBEECK
JACOB SCHERMERHOOREN
CORNELUS THONISEN
JAN THOMASZ

[121] Tuesday, April 28, 1654

Present:

Omnes

Jacob Hendrixsz Sibbinck, plaintiff, against Jacob Adriaensen, wheelwright, defendant, about ten beavers which are due to the plaintiff from the defendant for wages earned on the defendant's house sold to Cornelis Segertsen.

The defendant admits the aforesaid debt.

The court orders the defendant to pay the aforesaid ten beavers to the plaintiff promptly on the first of May, which payment is to be made out of the first term of payment of the purchase money of the house, without any gainsay.

Jacob Jansz Schermerhooren, plaintiff, against Jacob Adriaense, wheelwright, defendant, for fl.118:13:—, which the defendant owes to Elysbet Cornelis, of whom he has a power of attorney to collect the aforesaid money.

The defendant admits the aforesaid debt.

The court orders the defendant to pay the plaintiff the aforesaid fl.118:13:— in the following instalments, to wit, fl.50:— out of the first payment of the purchase money of the house sold by him to Cornelis Segertsen and the balance until the payment in full of the aforesaid sum out of the second payment, promptly, without any exceptions.

Claes Gerritsz, plaintiff, against Brant van Slichtenhorst, defendant, for 20 beavers of the defendant in the hands of the Hon. Rutger Jacopsz, attached by the plaintiff.

Defendant's first default.

Goosen Gerritsen, plaintiff, against Merten, the mason, for fl.75:8:8–, entered here for the sake of notification.

[122] Jan Witthardt, plaintiff, against Pieter Hartgers and Volckert Hansz, defendant, about a claim for goods left by Evert Tesselaer in the hands of the defendants.

The court having heard the statements and arguments on both sides, order that the defendants may retain the sum of fifty guilders out of the plaintiff's moneys in their hands, which has regard to the money advanced and expenses incurred on the side of the defendants during the litigation carried on by the contracting parties in Holland, upon condition that in case the plaintiff, or his principals there, are condemned to pay the costs of the suit, they shall have and receive therefor the aforesaid sum. But in case it hereafter turns out to be otherwise and the defendants have definite advice and proof that the plaintiff is not condemned there in the costs aforesaid, the defendants shall be bound, instead of the fifty guilders which they retained, to pay promptly to the plaintiff or the authorized agents of Evert Tesselaer one hundred guilders, upon proof and evidence as aforesaid. Furthermore, the defendants are ordered to satisfy and pay immediately and promptly to the plaintiff the balance of the money for the goods which were left by Tesselaer in the custody of the defendants.

Gerrit Jansz from Swoll being summoned by the court to give testimony to the truth in regard to the dispute which took place at his house between Andries Herpertsen and Lambert van Valckenborgh at the time of the departure of the Hon. General, the defendant's second default [is entered against him].

Commissary Dyckman, plaintiff, against Hendrick Bierman, defendant, for assault and battery.

Defendant's second default.

Commissary Dyckman is ordered by the court to pay to Willem Albertsen from Monickendam, instead of fl.108: which he owes him, eighty-eight guilders precisely within the space of fourteen days, and this on account of some abusive language addressed to the commissary according to the affidavits exhibited; he, Willem Albertsz, declaring before this court that he knows nothing further about the said commissary but what is honorable and virtuous.

[123] A petition was read of Anthonio de Hooges, demanding payment by Jacob Adriaensen, wheelwright, first, of fl.228:— for boards delivered by his father-in-law, Albert Andriesz; secondly, also by Jacob Adriaensen, of the sum of 35 beavers due to Jan Tjebkens Schellinger for merchandise delivered by said Schellinger to Jacob Adriaensen, according to the note, the petitioner being authorized to receive both sums aforesaid.

Jacob Adriaensen admits before this court that he owes both of said sums and whereas said de Hooges requests that payment be made out of the first payment on the house sold by Jacob

Adriaensen to Cornelis Segertsen,[23] it is decided and ordered that the said payment shall be made in two terms, to wit, the half of both amounts out of the first payment and the remaining half out of the second payment which Jacob Adriaensen is to receive for the aforesaid house.

And as regards the said de Hooges's third request contained in this petition, to have added to his lot one and a half rods, extending south and north, which according to his ground brief it was heretofore measured short, the same is granted him.

It is decided to have Merten Herpertsen, mason, summoned to appear on the next court day to answer various complaints on the part of his creditors.

Robbert Vastrick, in the name of his brother, Gerrit Vastrick, demands of Jacob Adriaensen, wheelwright, for merchandise delivered, according to his note of hand, the sum of fl.379:-, of which he, Jacob Adriaensen, has paid four beavers on account.

Jacob Adriaensen acknowledges the aforesaid debt.

Robbert Vastrick demands payment out of the first payment for the house sold by Jacob Adriaensen to Cornelis Segertsen.

The court condemns and orders Jacob Adriaensen, wheelwright, to pay the aforesaid fl.379:-, less four beavers, as follows, to wit: one hundred guilders before the departure of the returning ships sailing from here for *patria* and the balance out of the second payment to be received for the house sold by him, according to the contract made.

[124] An order drawn on the treasurers in favor of Goosen Gerritsz, in the sum of fl.6:10:-, for 13 lbs. of nails delivered for the fort.

Cornelis Segertsen having a claim of fl.41:10 against Jacob Adriaensen, wheelwright, asks permission to deduct this from the first payment for the house purchased by him, which is granted. And in order that the receipt and distribution or payment to the creditors of Jacob Adriaensen, wheelwright, may

---

[23] In the margin is written: " The attachment of the money is declared valid."

proceed more orderly, the honorable magistrates, Andries Herpertsen and Jan Thomasz, are appointed and charged therewith.

Carsten, living with the Hon. Jan Thomasz, is for the present excused from paying the fine for his lot in Beverwyck due on the first of May.

JOANNES DYCKMAN
RUTGER JACOBSZ
ANDRIES HERPERTS
JAN VERBEECK
JACOB SCHERMERHOOREN
CORNELUS THONISEN
JAN THOMASZ

Friday, May 30, 1654 [April 30, 1654]

Present:

J: Dyckman	J: Schermerhoren	A: Herpertsen
J: Verbeeck	J: Thomasz	C: Thonisz
R: Jacopsz		

Willem Fredrixsz Bout is hereby ordered to take his choice, either, as soon as this is shown to him, to stop furnishing imported beer to retailers, or to stop tapping; also not to lay in large quantities of small beer in his house; he, Willem Fredrixsz, being ordered to give his answer to the court messenger upon the exhibition hereof and to state which of the two things according to the custom of Holland he intends to and will do, the court messenger to note the statement or answer hereon and to make his return thereof on the next court day.

Abraham Pietersz Vosburgh is ordered to begin the bridge across the third kill within eight days and to proceed with the work until completed; and in case he does not comply herewith, the contract shall again be let by the court at the said Vosburgh's own expense and charge.

[125] According to the communication from the Hon. General and the Supreme Council in regard to the nomination of officers made by this court, there have been chosen this day, in the place of the retiring magistrates, Rutger Jacopsz, Andries Herpertsz and Cornelis Theunisz van Westbroeck, whose term of office has expired, the Hon. Sander Leendertsen, Pieter Hertgers and Frans Barentsz Pastoors, who being summoned to come into court have taken the following oath of fidelity before the commissary:

We, the undersigned, Sander Leendertsen, Pieter Hartgers and Frans Barentsen, in the capacity of magistrates and judges of the bench of justice of Fort Orange and Beverwyck, promise and swear in the presence of Almighty God and our fellow brethren that we shall help to do true equity and justice between man and man and further in all matters to promote and assist the administration of justice and the government according to the best of our knowledge and ability; also, that we shall in every way conduct ourselves loyally and faithfully toward the Hon. States General of the United Netherlands, the Hon. Directors and Masters of this New Netherland province and the Hon. Director General and Council residing at New Amsterdam; with the further promise that we shall help to maintain here the Reformed Religion according to the Word of God and the regulations of the Synod of Dordrecht and not to tolerate publicly any sect, all in the best interest of this jurisdiction and community. So truly help us God Almighty.

The honorable retiring or former magistrates, Rutger Jacopsz, Andries Herpertsz and Cornelis Theunisz, are duly discharged from their oath and most highly thanked for their honors' former good fellowship and the good service rendered to the company and to the public.

[126] Tuesday, May 5, 1654

Present:

J: Dyckman   San: Leendertsen   J: Schermerhoren
J: Thomasz   F: Barentsen   P: Hergers
J: Verbeeck

Rutger Jacobsz, plaintiff, against Willem Albertsen from Monickendam, defendant, about fl.35:— for beer delivered.

The defendant admits the aforesaid debt.

The court orders the defendant to pay the aforesaid fl.35:—, or the sum demanded, to the plaintiff within the time of six weeks, on pain of execution.

Rutger Jacopsz requests to have a garden to go with the house which he intends to build within a short time on his lot next to his dwelling house, which request is granted. And as to the request of Leendert Philipsz, the Hon. Magistrates Jacob Schermerhoren and Sander Leendertsen are appointed a committee [to consider the matter].

Willem Albertsen appearing before the court acknowledges that he is satisfied by Rutger Jacopsz for two months' hire of his yacht, leased for the service of the Hon. General.

Hendrick Driesz,[24] plaintiff, against Jochem Becker, defendant, for shooting plaintiff's dog three days ago on the public street.

Parties have compromised before this court, the defendant offering to have a young dog trained with others and when trained to deliver it to the plaintiff in the place of the dog that was killed; but as the deed was done in the public street and the plaintiff's dog was killed, the officer is allowed one beaver, which the defendant is to pay within twenty-four hours.

Hendrick Driess, plaintiff, against Merten Herpertsen, mason, defendant, for fl.200:—, which defendant is alleged to owe plaintiff according to the note exhibited.

---

[24] Hendrick Andriessen, from Doesburg.

The defendant admits the aforesaid debt, which is entered here only for the purpose of notification.

Jan van Twiller, appearing for Gerrit Vastrick, has exhibited a note of Merten Herpertsen in the sum of fl.449:–, which the said Herpertsen admits he owes.

[127] Willem Albertsen from Monickendam, plaintiff, against Pieter Bronck, or Eldert de Goyer, defendants.

Defendant's first default.

The commissary, plaintiff, against Hendrick Biermans, defendant, for assault and battery.

The defendant declares that he knows nothing about it. Case adjourned until some other time. Meanwhile, the commissary is to make further inquiry.

Jochem Becker is ordered to sheet the [bank of the] kill on the side of Jan Labatie, as far as he, Becker, has dug it up, provided that the small corner of land provisionally added to his lot, to wit, Labatie's, shall be left until further order of this court, an extract from this record to be sent to the homes of both of them to regulate themselves accordingly.

Merten Herpertsen acknowledges that he owes the following amounts:

Gabriel Leendertsen	fl.18:–
Hendrick Jochemsz	fl.80:–
Dirrick Jansz Kroon, acording to obligation	fl.27: (beavers)
Volckert Jansz	fl.31:–
Pieter Hartgers, for beer delivered, that is to say, a beaver coat delivered	fl.32:–
Sander Leendertsen, for nails	fl.17:3:–

Willem Fredrixsz coming into court requests permission to continue the wholesale trade in beer, on condition that he will not lay in any beer in his house, other than that which is used for tapping and will enter this each time. It is decided that he may provisionally do so on that basis, provided that the beer which he does not tap, he must have the people themselves fetch from the brewery and that he may in no way take in or lay in any small beer in his house.

Claes Gerritsz, plaintiff, against Mr Brant van Slichtenhorst, defendant, about 20 beavers due by defendant, attached by plaintiff in the hands of Rutger Jacopsz.

The plaintiff, appearing, submits a copy of a certain judgment given or pronounced by the Hon. Director General and the Supreme Council of New Netherland under date of July 19, 1652, whereby it appears that the defendant [128] on his third default of appearance was condemned at the Manathans by the Hon. General and the Supreme Council aforesaid to return the peltries and goods which he had taken out of the plaintiff's chest, or the value thereof.

It is decided by this court that if the defendant has any objection to make against this, he may appear in person on the next court day, the plaintiff declaring that he intends to have the defendant for the third time legally summoned to appear at that time.

The commissary and president of this court is this day appointed to examine and look over the account of the collector, Pieter Ryverdingh, and to make a report of his findings.

> Interrogatories upon which this court is to examine Volckgen Jan's daughter, the wife of Jan Fransz van Hoesem, and Jan Bembo, a soldier.

How old they are?	Of competent age.
Whether the evening before the Hon. General came up here, the commissary did not come to the house of Jan van Hoesem?	Answer, Yes.
Whether the commissary, coming there, did not find a party of drunken savages?	Answer, Yes.
Whether among them there was not a savage who sat and drank good beer?	Answer, Yes.
Whether they know where it was obtained, that is to say, the good beer?	Answer, From the house of Willem Bout.
How large was the can?	Answer, a *mengel* can.
Whether the commissary did not give the savage twelve stivers to have the can filled again?	Answer, Yes.
Whether they did not taste whether it was black beer?	Answer, Yes.

[129] Resolved that Sander Leendertsen, Willem Bout, Jan Machielsz, Jan Hendrixsz and Herman Bastiaensen shall build a convenient bridge in the road across the sewer which they have dug together. Also, that they must do so at the first opportunity, under the penalty to be provided, as otherwise it tends to obstruct the public road.

JOANNES DYCKMAN
JAN VERBEECK
JACOB SCHERMERHOOREN
JAN THOMASZ
SANDER LENRSEN
PIETER HERTGERTSZ
FRANS BARENTSEN PASTOORS

Tuesday, May 12, 1654

Present:

Omnes

Willem Fredrixsz, plaintiff, against Rutger Jacobsz, defendant.

The plaintiff appearing much intoxicated before the court is ordered to depart.

Jan van Hoesem, plaintiff, against Merten Herpertsen, mason, defendant, for fl.52:8:–, which the defendant owes plaintiff.

The defendant admits the aforesaid debt, which serves here by way of notification.

Jan Labatie is ordered to return at the first opportunity the ten barrels of lime and the 1600 bricks which he borrowed from the commissary, which he agrees to do accordingly.

Jan Labatie, plaintiff, against Gillis Pietersz, defendant, about the purchase of plaintiff's house at the Manathans, sold by the defendant for the plaintiff, and some nails left by the plaintiff in the defendant's hands, requesting a proper accounting of both.

The defendant says that he rendered an accounting at the Manathans in the presence of the purchaser of the house. [130] The defendant undertakes further at the first opportunity to write about the account to the Manathans, so as to be able to make an accounting of one thing and another in proper form.

It is decided to give the defendant four weeks' time from this date and if within that time no accounting is made by the defendant, the plaintiff may apply to this court, when further action will be taken in the matter complained of.

Claes Gerritsen, plaintiff, against Mr Brant van Slichtenhorst, defendant, about 20 beavers due by the defendant attached by the plaintiff in the hands of Rutger Jacobsz.

Defendant's third default.

The court orders Rutger Jacopsz to let the plaintiff have the 20 beavers and to satisfy him, upon sufficient security, in accordance with the judgment rendered by the Hon. General and the Supreme Council.

Symon Groot is ordered to build within two months upon the lot that has been granted to him, on pain of having to pay the full fine.

Symon Groot, on account of Jan Peeck, demands of Merten, the mason, fl.61 :— according to the account.

Merten, the mason, admits the aforesaid debt. Entered here [by way of memorandum].

Pieter Lot is given until [Amsterdam] fair [25] to build upon the lot granted to him. In case he does not build by that time, he shall pay the full fine and because he has not yet begun, he must pay one beaver to the officer.

Hendrick Gerritsen is to pay two beavers for not having built upon his lot.

Jacob Hendrixsz Sibbinck likewise two beavers.

Jacob Hendrixsz Sibbinck is granted a garden, adjoining on the west Gillis Pietersen, on the north Pieter Hartgers, on the east the wagon road and on the south the cripple bush, in length 7 ½ rods and in breadth on the north side 4 rods and 10 feet and on the south side 4 rods.

Wynant Gerritsen is ordered to pay a fine of fl.25 :— to the officer for not having built upon his lot and fl.6 :— for having fought; to be paid within 48 hours.

Luykas Pietersz fl.25 :— for not having built upon his lot, to be paid within 48 hours.

[131] Machiel Ryckertsen is condemned to pay four guilders to the officer for having last day of prayer sat drinking at the house of Jacob Luyersen during divine service.

Gabriel Leendertsen is ordered to hold back fl.25 out of the money which he must pay Lourens Jansz on account of the purchase of the house and to pay this to the officer because Lourens Jansz has not fenced in his garden.

Resolved that the gardens which have been laid out shall this afternoon be distributed by lot or otherwise to those who have made request therefor.

---

[25] September 23d.

Abraham Pietersz Vosburgh being summoned by the commissary and officer to appear in court to settle as far as possible the disputes which have arisen among the burghers on account of the faulty surveying and also on account of some gardens which without the knowledge of this court are being fenced in or have been granted away, the said Vosburgh is ordered to deliver in to this court his surveyor's book, which he, Vosburgh, said he would consider doing. However, it is decided that the court messenger shall immediately go with the said Vosburgh to his house, he, Vosburgh being ordered to give the aforesaid book to the court messenger; but as the court messenger reports to this court the said Vosburgh's unwillingness in this matter, it is decided for the second time and per superabundance to send the court messenger to him, Vosburgh, with the same order as aforesaid. The said messenger reporting for the second time [Vosburgh's] unwillingness, it is resolved that tomorrow, upon his refusal to deliver the aforesaid surveyor's book kept by him, the officer shall take him into custody until further order of this court.

Upon the request of Elysabet Cornelis' daughter, the Hon. Pieter Hertgerts, together with the Hon. Jacob Schermerhoren and the Hon. Cornelis Segertsen are appointed guardians of the two children left by Gysbert Cornelisz, deceased.

JOANNES DYCKMAN
JAN VERBEECK
JACOB SCHERMERHOOREN
JAN THOMASZ
SANDER LENRSEN
PIETER HERTGERTS
FRANS BARENTSEN PASTOORS

[132] Tuesday, May 19, 1654.

Present:

J: Dyckman   Sander Leendertsen   J: Schermerhoren
J: Thomasz   Frans Barentsz Pastoors   Pieter Hertgerts
J: Verbeeck

Willem Fredrixsz, plaintiff, against Rutger Jacopsz, defendant, about a barrel of beer or twenty guilders which defendant claims to have delivered to plaintiff upon mutual settlement of accounts and execution of a general receipt for beer delivered by defendant to the plaintiff.

Plaintiff denies this and refers to the receipt executed and signed jointly by the defendant and Goosen Gerritsen.

Plaintiff is ordered to produce the aforesaid receipt in court together with the delivery book of the defendant, in order that the date, etc., may serve as evidence and the judgment of this court in the case may thereupon follow.

Leendert Philipsz being summoned to appear in court in regard to the lot granted to him and the officer's claim that it has not been built upon within the appointed time, the defendant, appearing, claims that the person of Herman Bastiaensen gave him permission to delay. Decided that Herman Bastiaensen shall be summoned to appear on the next court day together with his opponent.

Isaac Allerton, plaintiff, against Thomas Sandertsen, smith, defendant.

Plaintiff demands of defendant fl.195:— according to the note signed by him.

The defendant admits the aforesaid debt and promises to pay the plaintiff through Jan van Aecken out of the first payment for the house sold by him, [paying] to him or the aforesaid van Aecken, first the sum of one hundred guilders and a year later the balance, being fl.95:—, to the plaintiff or his agent and substitute here.

The court having heard the statements on both sides and found that the parties are satisfied therewith, order that the said agreement shall be strictly carried out by the defendant, on pain, etc.

[133] Whereas it is found by experience and brought to the attention of this court that some of the inhabitants of this jurisdiction venture to sail in canoes, rowboats, or other vessels from here to the Esopus and Kats[k]il plain to sell brandy or liquor to the savages along the way, or at the aforesaid places, to the considerable detriment of the good inhabitants there, it is decided to have notices posted that no one residing within this jurisdiction and consequently belonging thereto shall be allowed to sail thither from here in any rowboats, canoes or other vessels without having the same inspected here by the officer and without having obtained proper consent to go thither from and in the name of this court, on pain of forfeiture by those who shall be found to have acted contrary hereto of the sum of fifty guilders for each offense for the benefit of the officer here.

Willem Fredrixsz Bout being summoned to appear in court on account of the sale of strong beer to the savages, the court, having also examined the affidavits and informations secured by the officer for that purpose, condemn the defendant to pay a fine of twenty-five guilders for the benefit of the officer, with costs, to be paid within 48 hours.

Merten Herpertsz, mason, being summoned to appear in court by the following persons, acknowledges that he is well and truly indebted to them as follows:

Willem Fredrixsz . . . . fl. 211:-
Jacob Jansz Stoll. 180:-

To Lourens Lourensen, twenty-six good, merchantable beavers, which is entered here by way of memorandum.

Jacob Jansz Flodder, having failed to build upon his lot granted to him in Beverwyck within the proper and specified time, is condemned to pay a fine of sixteen guilders for the benefit of the officer.

[134] Eldert Gerbertsen, because he has failed to inclose the lot that was granted to him within the proper and specified time, is condemned to pay within 48 hours a fine of ten guilders for the benefit of the officer.

Geertruyt Jeronimus, being summoned to appear in court on account of some abusive and slanderous words spoken and addressed to the members of this court that were present, the first default is entered against her.

Abraham Pietersz Vosburgh being summoned to appear in court to show why he does not begin and complete the bridge across the second kill, according to the contract made by him, has brought forward some reasons for excuse. However, the appearer is ordered to begin the aforesaid work during the coming Whitsuntide and then to complete it; otherwise, in case of further delay, the contract for the work shall at his own cost and charge be let by public bidding, as the failure to make or complete the bridge tends to the great inconvenience of the burghers here.

Jan Verbeeck, plaintiff, against Thomas Koninck, defendant, for the balance of payment due to plaintiff by defendant for the delivery and sale of a house to the defendant, in payment for which the plaintiff received some boards from the defendant, who sent them to the Manathans to Mr Jacob, the surgeon, but which are said to have been found not merchantable there.

The defendant says that he received the boards from Evert Pels, who owed him good boards.

The plaintiff says that he has not seen the boards that were delivered.

The court, having heard the statements and arguments on both sides, is of opinion that the parties must recover their loss in connection with the boards delivered from Evert Pels, who delivered them, and if they have been shipped to the Manathans, there and in such way as they shall see fit.

It is decided that Goosen Gerritsen must without delay move back the palisades inclosing his lot on the hill [135] as far as the stakes that have been set by this court on the street line, beside the palisades, on pain of incurring the penalty to be provided, without prejudice to the demands of the officer.

Upon the request of Claes from Rotterdam and Oom Dirrick that they may each obtain a lot in connection with the gardens that were granted to them, it is decided to adjourn the matter until further advice from the Hon. General and the Supreme Council.

Stoffel, the carpenter, having set a post near his lot, far outside of the line, in the common road, to begin inclosing his lot from that point, it is ordered that the aforesaid Stoffel must remove said post and the Hon. Magistrates Jacob Schermerhoren and Pieter Hertgerts are appointed to stake out the proper line and to do or cause to be done whatever is required.

Upon the request of Cornelis Segertsen to have a piece of woodland and to be allowed to fence it in as a pasture for his cattle, lying behind the inclosed land of Jan Barentsz Poest, it is decided to give for answer that this court will this day make an inspection thereof in order afterwards to pass a resolution thereon.

JOANNES DYCKMAN
JAN VERBEECK
JACOB SCHERMERHOOREN
PIETER HERTGERTS
FRANS BARENTSEN PASTOORS

[136] Friday, May 22, 1654

Present:
   J: Dyckman   J: Schermerhoren   J: Thomasz
   P: Hertgertsz   J: Barentsz Pastoors

Jacob Jansz Stoll, plaintiff, against Jacob Flodder, Eldert Gerbertsz, Willem Bout and Sander Leendertsen, defendants.

The plaintiff exhibits a written contract made the day before yesterday between him and Jacob Flodder, whereby Jacob Flodder sold to the plaintiff certain two horses belonging to the sawmills, or being his, Flodder's, which in accordance with the aforesaid sale were yesterday also delivered to the plaintiff by him, Flodder. [This,] however, [is objected to by] the sureties of the said Flodder, to wit, Sander Leendertsen and Willem Fredrixsz Bout, in view of a special contract signed by the said Flodder in regard to [the lease of] the two mills on the fifth kill, whereby his goods such as belong to mills and further all his other goods, none excepted, which he then had or might acquire or gain in the future, were specially mortgaged and pledged as security to the aforesaid sureties, as may appear more at large from the contract signed by Jacob Jansz Flodder, it being the intention of the aforesaid sureties, as they have openly declared before this court, that the horses that were sold may not be removed from there until and before Jacob Jansz Flodder shall have delivered to the lessee with the mills two similar, good horses, in the stead of those that were sold.

One thing and another being duly considered by this court, they are unable to conclude that at the request of the sureties the horses may not be removed until the aforesaid Flodder shall have brought to the aforesaid mills two hores as aforesaid in the stead of the two that were sold; on the other hand, in order to satisfy the claims which the sureties make in virtue of the aforesaid written contract signed by Jacob Flodder, he can first of all duly discharge the aforesaid sureties from the obligations of the bonds signed by them in regard to the aforesaid mills on the fifth kill, [137] since the claims of the sureties aforesaid in this matter, as soon as they are discharged, of themselves cease or become void.

Meanwhile, since the plaintiff claims that he suffers much loss, expense and damage by reason of the fact that the aforesaid horses are not delivered to him according to the bill of sale, the plaintiff can recover these from the person of Jacob Flodder, whether by further contract, arbitration, or otherwise, in all where and in such way as he shall see fit. Meanwhile the aforesaid Jacob Flodder is condemned in the costs of this extraordinary session of the court, advanced by the plaintiff.

JOANNES DYCKMAN
JACOB SCHERMERHOOREN
PIETER HERTGERTS
FRANS BARENTSEN PASTOORS

Thursday, June 4, 1654

Present:

Omnes

A letter having been received yesterday from the Hon. Director General Peter Stuyvesant of the 31st of the preceding month, regarding the rumors about the English, ordering that the soldiers be sent down, both those who are in the service and those who were discharged some time ago, and also to enlist people in the country's service and to send them down at the first opportunity, it is decided to have the drum beat and to enlist all those one can get and who present themselves, on condition that they be given a little money in hand, and further upon wages of the Hon. Company without prejudice to this court. Furthermore it is decided to reply to the aforesaid writing as may appear at length from the letter book.[26]

JOANNES DYCKMAN
JAN VERBEECK
JACOB SCHERMERHOOREN
PIETER HERTGERTS
FRANS BARENTSEN PASTOORS

---

[26] *Minuytboeck;* apparently referring to a book in which letters and possibly drafts of other documents were entered and kept for purposes of reference. No such book is now in existence.

[138] Tuesday, June 9, 1654

Present:
    Omnes

Cornelis Theunisz, plaintiff, against Roeloff Jacopsz, defendant, about ten beavers and two guilders for house rent claimed by plaintiff from defendant.

The defendant admits the aforesaid debt.

The court having heard the statements and arguments on both sides, condemn the defendant to pay the plaintiff the aforesaid ten beavers and two guilders in seawan within the time of six months, the attached property of the defendant to remain attached until he has paid or given sufficient security for the payment.

Roeloff Jacopsz, plaintiff, against Jan Gouw, defendant, about 7 ½ beavers which plaintiff owes the defendant and for which [the latter] has attached goods belonging to the plaintiff. The plaintiff says that money is due him from Jacob Adriaensen, wheelwright, and that he assigned this to the defendant in payment [of his debt]. It is decided that the plaintiff may have Jacob Adriaensen, wheelwright, summoned to appear before the court on the next court day.

The court having heard the complaint of Roeloff Jacopsz against Jan Gouw, that the latter daily goes off with his wife, etc., the case is adjourned until the next court day, or some other time when further evidence about it may be presented.

Jacob Adriaensen, wheelwright, plaintiff, against Jacob from Loosdrecht, carpenter, defendant, about some work which the defendant agreed to do for the plaintiff, and which he did not finish according to his promise, etc.

Defendant's first default.

Jan Roelofsen, for not having built upon his lot within the appointed and proper time, is ordered to pay one beaver within 24 hours.

[139] Pieter Bronck, plaintiff, against Huybert Jansz de guyt,[27] defendant, about fl. 74:– which the defendant is alleged to owe plaintiff.

The defendant admits the aforesaid debt.

The defendant is ordered to remain under arrest until he pays the seventy-four guilders demanded, or otherwise gives sufficient security that payment will be made within the space of three months.

Arent van den Bergh, plaintiff, against Arent Andriesz, defendant, on account of a dispute about a gun for which the plaintiff paid a certain sum in hand and which the defendant claims to be his gun.

The court is of opinion that the gun must be restored, provided the defendant bears part of the expense, as is proper.

Steven Jansz, plaintiff, against Merten, the brewer, defendant, about fl.45 or fl.46 for wages earned by the plaintiff [for work] on defendant's house.

The defendant says that to his inconvenience the plaintiff quit the work which he had agreed to do. Furthermore that the defendant had the timber for two window frames hewn for the plaintiff, which the plaintiff himself should have hewn.

The court having heard the arguments on both sides, refers the parties to referees, Herman Bastiaensen, surveyor, and Claes Jansz from Baere[n],[28] carpenter, who are to inspect the work this day, according to the verbal agreement, and to make a report thereof to this court on the next court day.

Evert Pels, plaintiff, against Jan Fransen van Hoesem, defendant, on account of fl. 62:–, which the defendant owes the plaintiff for the delivery of boards.

The court orders the defendant to pay the plaintiff the aforesaid sum of sixty-two guilders, according to the note, within the space of twice twenty-four hours, on pain of execution.

[140] Rutger Jacopsz and Goosen Gerritsen, in the name of those in the community here who keep cattle, have requested

---

[27] The rascal.
[28] Baarn, a village in the province of Utrecht.

permission to close the common road with gates so as to form a corral for the cattle, on condition of building a footstep on each side. Is provisionally granted until further inspection.

Andries de Vos, having a power of attorney from Abraham Pietersen Vosburgh, has delivered to the court a written answer to the written complaint heretofore presented to this court by the commissary in regard to the offenses committed by the aforesaid Vosburgh. The same being read, the commissary and officer here has agreed to make a replication thereto at the first opportunity as required by law.

There having been presented to this court the written report of the referees, Herman Bastiaensen, surveyor, and Claes Jansz from Baren, carpenter, heretofore appointed to inspect the work in dispute between Steven Jansz and Merten, the brewer, and to report thereon, it appears that Merten aforesaid, according to the best of their knowledge, is entitled to deduct the sum of eleven guilders from Steven Jansz's account. The said report is approved and Steven Jansz is condemned, as he is found to have been at fault, to make proper compensation to the referees in addition to having the eleven guilders deducted from his account.

JOANNES DYCKMAN
JAN VERBEECK
JACOB SCHERMERHOOREN
PIETER HERTGERTS
FRANS BARENTSEN PASTOORS

[141] Tuesday, June 16, 1654

Present:

Omnes dempto Sander Leendertsen

Jan Adriaensen, plaintiff, against Evert Pels, defendant, for the sum of forty-four beavers and six otters, amounting together to the sum of four hundred guilders, in part payment of which the plaintiff, or his agent, has accepted an account against the

Hon. Company for wages earned by the defendant, according to a power of attorney given to Jan Jansz from Gottenborg in favor of Willem Houttum. The aforesaid account amounts to two hundred and eighty-five guilders and four stivers, so that there is still due to the plaintiff on account of his master, Willem Houttum, or whoever it may concern, the sum of one hundred and fourteen guilders, sixteen stivers.

The court having heard the statements and arguments on both sides, are of opinion that the defendant must pay to the plaintiff the sum of one hundred and fourteen guilders and sixteen stivers before the departure of the first ship from this country for *patria*, the above mentioned account of fl. 285:4–, shown to the court and accepted in payment by the plaintiff or his attorney according to the signature, serving to make up the payment in full.

The Hon. Andries Herperts has delivered in court an account of disbursements made last year to Keese Waeye, despatched expressly with letters to the Manathans, amounting in seawan, etc., to fl.35: 8 stivers; and for cutting quarry stones for the new Company's house next to Jochem Keteluyn, twenty guilders, amounting together to the sum of fl. 55: 8 stivers, which sum the collector is ordered to pay him. But as to his honor's further claims on account of his having been sent last year to the Manathans as a delegate from this court to the general Lantdagh, the expenses whereof amounted according to the account to fl. 150:–, the payment thereof is deferred until the Hon. General shall have been written to about it.

[142] Leendert Philipsz, plaintiff, against Herman Bastiaensen, defendant, about the lot in dispute at the last session of the court.

Defendant's first default.

Jan Gouw, plaintiff, against Roeloff Jacopsz, defendant.

The defendant appeals to [the testimony of] Jacob Adriaensen, wheelwright, whom he may cause to be summoned to appear on the next court day.

Dirrick Bensinck, being summoned by the commissary and officer to appear before the court to testify in regard to the situation of his garden, drawn by lot by the Hon. Jacob Schermerhoren and with the leave and consent of this court transferred by him to the aforesaid Dirrick Bensingh, has declared as follows, to wit:

That last Whitsunday morning, while he, Bensinck, was standing in front of his door, Andries de Vos and Abraham Pietersz Vosburgh came to him and asked him, Bensinck, first, whether he had complained about his garden to this court, whereupon he, Bensingh, said: " It is still my garden, although you people have inclosed it without my consent," and that he had enough reason to complain because they had taken his garden away from him without his knowledge and that they knew that it was his garden was certain, for they had previously asked him to contribute his share in erecting the fences between them. Whereupon they replied that rather than have him, Bensinck, make much fuss about it, they would given him back his garden, provided that he would pay and reimburse them for the expenses incurred by them on the garden. Whereupon he, Bensinck, answered them that they had no power to give away the garden, but that the authority in the matter rested with this court, which had once granted it to him. He therefore requests that he may be continued by this court in the possession of this garden and be allowed to keep what was once given to him, he, Bensinck, declaring [143] further that Abraham Pietersz Vosburgh, upon resurveying [the lots], found that on the side of his house, between him and Willem Hap, there was more ground [than originally stated] and that he had allotted them each a few feet of ground.

Commissary Dyckman, plaintiff, against Luykas Pietersen, defendant.

Defendant's first default.

Interrogatories upon which the Hon. Andries Herpertsen and Cornelis Theunisz van Westbroeck, recently retired magistrates, have been examined.

Whether they gave their consent to the giving away of the garden of Dirrick Bensinck, formerly owned by Jacob Schermerhoren?	Answer, No.
Likewise of the garden which Luykas Pietersen has inclosed and for which he received a ground brief without the knowledge of this court?	Answer, No.
Likewise of the garden of Cornelis Vos, next to Mr Rensselaer's?	They declare that they know nothing about it.
Likewise in regard to the extension of the lot of Abraham Pietersz Vosburgh, where he lives?	They declare that they know nothing about the new extension and the Hon. Andries Herpertsen declares that Abraham Pietersen Vosburgh has without their knowledge, on his own authority, added a piece to Mr de Hooges's garden, given and allotted to him by this court. They offer, if need be and required, to confirm the preceding declarations by oath.

The petition of Pieter Lot for a garden to go with his lot is laid aside until the next court day.

Post Meridiem

The Hon. Volckert Jansz, formerly a magistrate, being legally summoned by this court to testify in regard to the lot of Abraham Pietersen Vosburgh, has testified as follows, namely: That he and other magistrates of this court had shown to the aforesaid Vosburgh [144] the length and breadth of the lot, [extending] to certain stakes that were driven into the ground, and that the said Vosburgh in first inclosing his lot had governed himself accordingly and that he is not aware that any additional land was afterwards granted to the said Vosburgh. Also, as sworn surveyors ought to be trusted to make the survey, that he has not verified the number of rods of the survey.

Secondly, that the lot of Cornelis Vos, near the bridge, was ordered by the Hon. de Hooges to be laid out with an angle for the greater convenience in using the road across the bridge.

Wednesday, June 17, 1654

Present:

Omnes dempto Sander Leendertsen

A petition was read from Adriaen Jansz from Leyden praying for permission to have a lot next to the palisades of Thomas Jansz for a public house instead of a city tavern, in accordance with the consent obtained from the Hon. General and the Hon. Supreme Council of New Netherland, written in the margin of his petition, dated the 30th of April last past; whereupon it is decided that the respective members of this court shall first inspect the place. Commissary Dyckman and Jacob Schermerhoren being appointed to lay out and measure off the lot, they report to this court that in virtue hereof they have for this purpose laid out a lot for the aforesaid Adriaen Jansz from Leyden, next to the road along the palisades of Thomas Jansz, in width, front and rear, five rods and eight feet, in length fourteen rods, which is entered here by way of memorandum.

> JOANNES DYCKMAN
> JAN VERBEECK
> JACOB SCHERMERHOOREN
> PIETER HERTGERTS
> FRANS BARENTSEN PASTOORS

[145] Extraordinary Session, Thursday, June 18, 1654

Present:
    As before.

A petition having been read of Andries de Vos and Abraham Pietersen Vosburgh, demanding proof of the term "delinquent" in the order issued on the statement of the offenses committed by Abraham Pietersen Vosburgh, filed in writing by the commissary and officer, it is decided to make an apostil thereon, as follows:

Whereas the Honorable Court ordered the defendant by Tuesday, being the next court day, to present his written rejoinder to a certain replication filed by the commissary and officer regarding the offenses committed by the defendant, which replication was sent to him by the court messenger and in the absence of the defendant and his wife presented by the court messenger to the defendant's attorney, the aforesaid court messenger has in a written return made to this court set forth that he received from the defendant's attorney the statement that the defendant's attorney, Andryes de Vos, was not inclined to receive any writs of the court until the charge of being a delinquent had been proved to the defendant by the officer and that the aforesaid attorney had received instructions to that effect from the defendant before his departure. Whereupon the court has concluded to order the aforesaid replication to be sent once more to the defendant's house, with the express command that he must strictly observe and comply with the order thereon issued by this court, the defendant, or his attorney, being further ordered once more [146], as they are hereby, that they, or either of them, must next Tuesday, without delay, appear before this court and at the same time deliver the documents or proofs which the defendant may have to submit in his defense, when the officer shall likewise produce his evidence to the contrary, to show that the defendant on all counts is a delinquent, as the officer fully undertakes to do.

And whereas the officer has requested that as he, in his capacity as aforesaid, is to prove the defendant to be a delinquent, the latter [may be ordered to] submit his counter proofs, if he has any, at the same time as the officer — which request the court judge to be not unreasonable — they finally order the defendant to appear on Tuesday next and to argue his case against the officer orally and in writing.

JOANNES DYCKMAN
JAN VERBEECK
JACOB SCHERMERHOOREN
PIETER HERTGERTS
FRANS BARENTSEN PASTOORS

[147] Tuesday, June 23, 1654

Present:

Omnes dempto Sander Leendertsen

Last Sunday a letter was received by this court from the Honorable General, of the 17th of this month, wherein he advises the court of the bad news received from the north and that on that account, for the better defense of the Manathans, they were not only busy repairing the old works, but also obliged to begin some new ones. Complaining of the scarcity of money in the treasury, he requests that the most prosperous of the burghers here lend a helping hand and that this court would be pleased to negotiate a loan of money, on condition that it be returned within a year, either in duties, or otherwise, for which his honor and the honorable councilors offer their persons and property as security.

After careful consideration of the matter, this court has decided to summon the most prosperous and loyal citizens and to communicate the matter to them, with the recommendation that they assist the Honorable General in this great emergency, who, having been summoned one by one and appeared in court, have signed for the following amounts, which they have agreed to furnish promptly for the purpose and on the conditions hereinbefore written, and which it is decided to send at once by the sloop of Jacob Symontsz Klomp, in company of two other sloops, which are lying ready to sail for the Manathans. They have contributed and signed as follows:

Arent Andriesz, two beavers............fl.	16:–
Cornelis Theunisz, 25 beavers................	200:–
Andries Herpertsz, in seawan................	70:–
Abraham Staets, in seawan.................	200:–
Gerrit Jansz, cooper, 50 beavers..............	400:–
[148] Brought forward from preceding page......fl.	886:–
Jan van Hoesem, four beavers...............	32:–
Herman Bastiaensen, four beavers............	32:–
Hendrick Jochemsz, in seawan...............	100:–
Jan Hendrixsz, four beavers..................	32:–
Joannes Dyckman, in seawan................	28:–
Jochem Becker, five beavers...............fl.	40:–
Jacob Schermerhoren, 12½ beavers............	100:–
Karsten Jansz, smith, 6 beavers and 2 fl. in seawan..	50:–
Pieter Looxkermans, 1½ beavers..............	12:–

Court Minutes, 1652–1656

Jacob Thysz vander Heyden, 1½ beavers........ 12:–
Adriaen Jansz from Leyden, 6 beavers and 2 fl. in
 seawan 50:–
Volckert Jansz, 20 beavers................... 160:–
Evert Jansz Wendel, four beavers............. 32:–
Pieter Bronck, 2 beavers..................... 16:–
Frans Barentsen, in seawan................... 16:–
Cornelis Vos, 2 beavers...................... 16:–
Pieter Hertgers, 12½ beavers and fl. 70 in seawan.. 170:–
Rem Jansen, 5 beavers........................ 40:–
Jan Labatie, 12½ beavers..................... 100:–
Jan Thomasz, in seawan....................... 100:–
Thomas Jansz, one beaver and fl. 2 in seawan..... 10:–
Claes Hendrixsz, carpenter, a note payable by
 Willem Beeckman, to be collected by the Hon.
 General 50:–
Willem Bout, 10 beavers...................... 80:–
Goosen Gerritsen, 15 schepels of wheat and 2
 beavers ....fl. 61:–
 ─────
Total 192 ½ beavers and fl.590 in seawan........fl. 2225:–

But in recounting the number it was found that there was one beaver too much, which was sent also, as follows:
144 whole beavers
18 *drielingen* [2/3 skins]
75 half beavers

On the 26th of June the above amount was sent off by Jacob Symontsen Clomp and by the accompanying sloop, Claes Thysz, master, the wheat, in the presence of the honorable magistrates, Jan Verbeeck and Jacob Jansen Schermerhoren.

> JOANNES DYCKMAN
> JAN VERBEECK
> JACOB SCHERMERHOOREN
> PIETER HERTGERTS
> FRANS BARENTSEN PASTOORS

[149] Tuesday, June 30, 1654

Present:

    J: Dyckman   J: Schermerhoren   Frans Barentsz
    J: Verbeeck   Pieter Hertgerts

Andries des Vos, as attorney for Abraham Pietersz Vosburgh, being summoned to appear in court, is notified and ordered once more and as an extra warning to himself and his principal that he must two weeks from this date produce in court all the evidence which he may have in defense of Abraham Pietersz Vosburgh, on pain, etc. Meanwhile the officer, Dyckman, has not been neglectful but offered to deliver to this court the documents and papers which he can produce in support of his charges against Abraham Pietersz Vosburgh and [requests] that the replication to which he must make answer be again sent to him by the court messenger.

Jochem Becker, being summoned by the commissary and officer to appear in court to testify whether Elmerhuysen Kleyn and Gerrit Slichtenhorst did not sell brandy to the savages and whether he did not have certain knowledge thereof, more than the common rumor and complaint thereof among the burghers, has declared as follows:

That about two months ago, the exact day he has forgotten,

he saw a certain savage get brandy and drink it at the house,[29] who, coming out of their house drunk, picked up a maul lying near the house of Jan van Hoesem's farm and therewith forcibly banged open the door of his house and thereupon greatly molested him and his family. Also, that when he banged with the maul on the door, the dowels came out of the casing and that he committed many other outrages. Furthermore, that afterwards a Mahican, commonly called "Whoremaster," being there in the house drunk and wishing to pay for the brandy drunk in the house, with enough money, so it seemed, was given a sound thrashing by Elmerhuysen and Slichtenhorst, and on coming out of the house made a good deal of trouble here and there.

Jacob Adriaensen, wheelwright, has requested that the attachment of the goods of Jacob from Loosdrecht at the house of Andries Herperts, might be declared valid.

The same is declared valid.

[150] Willem Jansz Stoll being summoned to appear in court on account of his having stabbed Dirrick Lammertsz, this day two weeks ago, at the house of Hendrick Jochemsz, with a knife, has sent in his stead Willem Fredrixsz, who, appearing, has requested in the name of the aforesaid Stol that the matter might be compromised, which the officer is ordered by this court to do, with this reservation, however, that in case he can not compound with the parties to his satisfaction and as is proper, in the presence of two arbitrators, he can let the action stand, to be hereafter disposed of by this court.

Meanwhile, the witnesses who were present, having been summoned by the commissary and officer to appear in court, have declared as follows:

---

[29] At this point, there is written in the margin: "He further declares that he saw them hold the glass in the hand and fill it with brandy and that he drank it in the house, tapped in their own glass."

Interrogatories upon which the honorable court are to examine Hendrick Jochemsz, Jan Gouw, Thomas Sandertsen and Wynant Gerritsen.

Whether yesterday, two weeks ago, in the afternoon, they were not at the house of Hendrick Jochemsz?

Answer, Yes.

Whether they did not see there some persons who were bowling and who they were?

They declare they themselves, with the exception of Hendrick Jochemsz, and some others were bowling there.

Whether, in the course of the game, some trouble did not arise and through whom? Who the first person was to make trouble?

They declare that they saw no trouble, except during the last game. That Dirrick said to Willem Jansz Stoll, shaking him by the sleeve, without striking him, that he should keep his mouth shut, or he would sew it up with a waxed thread. Willem said that Dirrick was a beggar. Willem said: " Go and get a sword or a rapier and strike, if you are an honest fellow!"

Whether Willem Jansz Stoll did not come with a bare knife in his hand and suddenly stabbed Dirrick?

They declare, Yes, and that he said among other things to Thomas Sandertsen: " Will you take it up for him?" stabbing and cutting in every direction.

Whether they know how Dirrick received the stab?

They declare that they paid no attention to it and do not know exactly how.

Whether Dirrick did not seek to retreat from one place to the other?

They declare, Yes, and that others meanwhile did their best to separate them.

[151] Stoffel, the carpenter, having come into court, requests payment for four bolt locks and one door lock for the guard house, the first being delivered for the bastions of the fort, amounting together to fl. 9:–. Decided to grant him and draw an order on the honorable treasurers for the amount.

JOANNES DYCKMAN
JAN VERBEECK
JAN THOMASZ
PIETER HERTGERTS
FRANS BARENTSEN PASTOORS

Tuesday, July 7, 1654

Present:
J: Dyckman   Jan Thomasz   Pieter Hertgerts
J: Schermerhoren   Sander Leendertsen Frans Barentsz

Jochem Becker, baker, being legally summoned by the commissary and officer to appear here on account of the declaration made before this court on the 30th of the preceding month, which was again read to him, Becker, he has at the request of the president and officer with uplifted fingers, by solemn oath, confirmed the said declaration regarding the sale of brandy to the savages by Elmerhuysen Kleyn and Gerrit Slichtenhorst, for so far as it appears thereby.

A petition was read of Dirrick Lammertsen from Otmarssen,[30] setting forth that yesterday three weeks ago, without any resistance on his part, he was stabbed and wounded by Willem Jansz Stoll, which said Stoll, as he understands, has compounded with the commissary and officer as to his due and the surgeon's fee, and praying therefore that for his pain and suffering and loss of time he may also be granted some compensation by this court. Whereupon it is decided to note in the margin that the lieutenant

---

[30] Ootmarssum, in the province of Overyssel, Netherlands.

may before the next court day file a statement about it with this court, when this court will take his claims into further consideration and pass a resolution thereon.

Marcelus Jansz, plaintiff, against De Paus, defendant, about a half barrel of beer.

The defendant as well as the plaintiff refer to the witnesses who were present.

The case is adjourned until the next court day, when the parties may have the witnesses summoned also.

[152] Roeloff Jacopsz, plaintiff, against Tryntgen Jacop's daughter, defendant, about an attachment levied by the defendant on some of the plaintiff's goods.

The court having heard the statements and arguments on both sides, decide and order that the goods which are attached by the defendant shall remain attached until the plaintiff pays the defendant the sum which she claims the plaintiff owes her, or else gives sufficient security for the payment thereof.

Willem Albertsz from Monickendam, plaintiff, against Ellert Gerbertsen, defendant, about reimbursement for the costs of the summons by this court, advanced by the plaintiff.

The defendant's first default.

Cornelis Theunisz van Westbroeck, being subpoenaed by the officer to appear before the court to testify whether any of the goods attached at the house of Andryes Herpertsen, belonging to Jacob Loosdreght, have since the attachment been removed from the aforesaid house and delivered to the aforesaid Loosdreght, declares, Yes, and that he had certain knowledge thereof, offering to confirm, etc.

Luykas Pietersz is ordered to pay two beavers to the officer, because he has not built upon his lot within the appointed time, the same to be paid now, promptly within 24 hours, instead of the fl. 25:— which he was heretofore ordered to pay.

Merten, the brewer, and his wife have declared at the request of the officer that last Tuesday, in the evening, Seeger

Cornelisz came and knocked at their door, wanting to drink there, and when at first he received no answer and was not let in, kicked in the door in such a way that the dowels came out of the posts and casing. Coming in with Jacob from Loosdreght, he wanted to have beer tapped, which they did not have and was not in the house. Not being able to get it, he used many vile and abusive words, calling him, Merten, a whoremaster and his wife a whore and [saying] that she was found with Frans Thomasz in the thicket. [They furthermore declare] that the lamp was put out and that Jacob from Loosdreght wanted per force to get into the woman's bed and that coming near [153] the bed, he did not hesitate to grab and touch here, but did so.

Adriaen Claesz Brant being subpoenaed to appear in court to give further evidence in the matter aforesaid, as far as it is in his power, has testified as follows:

That Seeger Cornelisz at the time mentioned first came and knocked at the door, wanting to come in, and when he received no answer, kicked it in with his feet or opened it by force in such a way that the dowels came out of the casing; that thereupon he came into the house by force, using many abusive words, but [that the witness], as he went to bed, knows nothing further about it.

Merten, the brewer, on account of various excuses offered by him, is, instead of the fl.15:– to be contributed toward the building of the bridges and other expenses, ordered to contribute promptly fl.10:–

Neis, or Jacob Adriaensz, wheelwright, plaintiff, against Jacob from Loosdreght, defendant, about claims which the plaintiff alleges he has against the defendant on account of his not carrying forward and finishing the work undertaken by him.

The defendant being absent, the court decides that the plaintiff may have the defendant summoned to appear on the next court day. Defendant's first default.

Merten, the mason, declares that he owes Hermanus Hertogh no more than ten beavers, or fl. 80:—, for goods bought and received.

JOANNES DYCKMAN
JAN VERBEECK
JAN THOMASZ
PIETER HARTGERTS
FRANS BARENTSEN PASTOORS

[154] Extraordinary Session, Friday, July 15, 1654

Present:
Omnes

After mature consideration of the present juncture of time, this court has for various reasons thought it necessary to call some of the most favorably disposed of the citizens here before the court, to propose to them the necessity and the reasons which this court thinks it has to send a present to the Maquas: first because the savages, on account of the scarcity of merchandise, have been obliged to give much more than ordinarily for the goods which they bought by the measure. It is to be noted, however, that the good inhabitants themselves had to forego what was bought out of their own much needed supply, which was the cause and origin of the high cost of the same. However, when the ships come here, [it is proposed] to promise them, according to the circumstances, to let them have the goods cheaper, on the old basis.

Secondly, to renew the old alliance and friendship between both sides.

Thirdly, in order that they shall in the future not kill our cattle, as has happened heretofore.

Fourthly, that in case the savages should again make some presents, as they are accustomed to do, these shall be divided among the [present] givers, or their order, in proportion to the amount contributed by them.

Rutger Jacobsz has presented five fathoms of seawan, a kettle and four hatchets

Sander Leendertsen, six fathoms of seawan, three kettles, three hatchets and two pounds of powder

Jacob Schermerhoren, three pounds of powder

Commissary Dyckman, four fathoms of seawan

Pieter Hertgerts, two pounds of powder, six fathoms ditto and four hatchets

[155] Jan Thomasz, five fathoms of seawan

Volckert Jansz, two pounds of powder, four fathoms of seawan

Andryes Herpertsen, four fathoms of seawan

Goosen Gerritsen, four fathoms of seawan

Frans Barentsz, three fathoms ditto

Jan Verbeeck, three fathoms of seawan

JOANNES DYCKMAN
JAN VERBEECK
JAN THOMASZ
PIETER HARTGERTS
FRANS BARENTSEN PASTOORS

Tuesday, July 31, 1654

Present:

J: Dyckman   J: Schermerhoren
J: Verbeeck   Frans Barentsen

Pieter Bronck, plaintiff, against Luykas Pietersz, defendant, about a tavern debt amounting to fl. 193:2:–.

The defendant having been summoned and an attachment issued against him, the first default is entered against him.

Willem Albertsen, plaintiff, against Ellert Gerbertsen, defendant.

Defendant's second default.

Cornelis Houtewael, plaintiff, against Claes Hendrixsz, defendant, as surety for Jacob Jansz Flodder with reference to the monthly wages claimed by the plaintiff, amounting to fl.60:—

The defendant's first default.

Cornelis Gerbrantsen, plaintiff, against Jacob Symontsen Clomp, defendant, about fl.60: 11 stivers, for wages earned on the defendant's sloop.

The court having heard the statements and arguments on both sides, have ordered, as they do hereby, that the defendant shall pay the plaintiff before his departure from here the sum of fl. 60:11:—, demanded, on pain of execution.

[156] Mr Johan de Hulter, plaintiff, against Willem Albertsen from Munickendam, defendant, about a jack loaned by the plaintiff to the defendant, which was not returned in good condition, whole and in order as it was delivered by the plaintiff to the defendant.

The defendant says that he returned the same.

The parties may on the next court day appear before this court with their evidence to show whether the jack was returned in the same condition as it was delivered, when judgment in the matter shall be given.

The case of Seeger Cornelisz is adjourned until the next court day, or the first opportunity, to take the oaths of the witnesses.

This court having carefully considered the complaints made to it by Catharina Liberis, widow of Pieter Theunisz from Brunswyck, deceased, at Katskill, and also examined the provisional will made and afterwards approved by this court at the request of the petitioner, with regard to the surviving daughter of the deceased aforesaid, have concluded that in virtue of the will made [by the deceased] the aforesaid widow shall remain in full possession of the property there until such time as she may marry or die and, furthermore, that if she can not come to a legal agreement with the aforesaid surviving daughter or her husband about the complaints made as aforesaid, they must both leave the farm at once, without being allowed to come on it again for the time of six months, or to give any orders there, on pain, etc. Meanwhile, this court shall in that case settle the matter in such a way as by both sides shall be considered reasonable and just.

[157] Abraham Pietersz Vosburgh being summoned by the commissary and officer to appear in court on account of the offenses committed by him and appearing with his attorney, Andryes de Vos, they both request that the matters pending before this court growing out of [acts] committed by him and his wife, Geertruyt Pieter's daughter, may at this [critical] juncture of time be composed and settled by arbitrators to be chosen by both sides. Whereupon the court, taking into account the present dangerous times, condescend to do so, on condition that if they can not come to any satisfactory agreement, the action shall remain unabated. On the side of the commissary were chosen and appointed the present honorable magistrates, and on the defendant's side Rutger Jacopsz and Goosen Gerritsen, whose award is inserted here as follows:

Abraham Pietersen Vosburgh and his attorney, Andryes de Vos, having this morning requested in court that the matters in dispute pending before this court [as to offenses] committed by the aforesaid Vosburgh and his wife, in actions, words or deeds, may be settled by arbitrators, it is by way of compromise agreed by the arbitrators appointed by the defendant on the one side and those appointed by the honorable court on the other side that all causes of action and claims which the officer may to this date have against the aforesaid Vosburgh shall be composed, annulled, canceled and settled, on condition that the officer shall receive from the aforesaid Vosburgh as a fine the sum of two hundred and fifty guilders, one half to be paid promptly within six weeks and the other half within six weeks thereafter. However, the aforesaid Abraham Pietersz Vosburgh is to remain deposed from his office of surveyor. Andryes de Vos is retain the garden inclosed by him, but the lot on which he [158] resides and which he enlarged far beyond its proper limits, contrary to the order of this court, he shall reduce in size according to the pleasure of this court, without any objection, and the whole extent of the garden of Luykas Pietersz shall revert, as it does hereby, to this court. Provided, finally, that the wife of Abraham Pietersz Vosburgh shall come and appear before this court and declare that she has nothing to say about any of the members but what is honorable and of good repute. For the faithful performance hereof signed with their own hands, this 15th of July 1654. Was signed: Abraham Pietersz Vosburgh. As arbitrators: Rutger Jacobsz, the mark X of Goosen Gerritsen, set with his own hand.

JOANNES DYCKMAN
JAN VERBEECK
FRANS BARENSEN PASTOORS

Tuesday, August 11, 1654

Present:
  Omnes

In response to a communication from the Hon. Director General, the Hon. Commissary and Jan Verbeeck are appointed a committee [to confer with him] in accordance with the commission and instructions to be given to their honors.

[The court] having heard the report of the honorable committee, consisting of the commissary and Jan Verbeeck, [appointed to go] to the Esopus to measure the lands there, and having furthermore examined the petition of Evert Pels, stating that the lands bought by them looked to the eye larger than they were actually found to be and requesting that he, Evert Pels, may be allowed to purchase some of the land which the Hon. General intends to keep for himself, it is decided that the committee going to the Manathans are to confer about the matter there and exhibit the aforesaid petition.

[159] Whereas some savages, both Maquas and Senecas, have this day, according to ancient custom, made a present to this court, it is, in order to give them some powder in return, thought proper to present them among other things with 25 lbs of powder. The Hon. Abraham Staets is therefore requested to let them have the same from the Hon. Company's powder which is in his honor's custody, provided that he shall be discharged by this court from the obligation to account for it to the Hon. General and hereafter communicate to his honor the contents of the present. The aforesaid savages have furthermore made some propositions to which answer in proper form was made.

JOANNES DYCKMAN
JAN VERBEECK
JAN THOMASZ
PIETER HARTGERTS
FRANS BARENTSEN PASTOORS

Tuesday, August 25, 1654

Present:
   Omnes

Cornelis Houtewael, plaintiff, against Claes Hendrixsz, or Jacob Flodder, defendant, about wages earned by the plaintiff of the defendant, amounting to the sum of sixty guilders.

The defendant is ordered to pay the aforesaid sixty guilders to the plaintiff within the space of twenty-four hours, on pain of execution.

Jochem Becker, plaintiff, against Daniel Rinckhout, defendant, about some grain measures which he gave and loaned to the defendant at the house of Broer Cornelis and which have not been returned.

The court orders the defendant to return the said loaned articles to the plaintiff within two days, on pain of paying a fine of ten guilders.

Geertruyt Pieters, having been legally summoned, the second default is entered against her.

[160] On account of [goods?] advanced for the savages, it is decided to grant and draw in favor of the Hon. Jacob Jansz Schermerhoren an order in the sum of fl. 15:–

Upon the petition of the court messenger, Pieter Ryverdingh, it is decided that of the excise money received he is to retain the sum of one hundred guilders and must charge that to his account.

For important reasons it is decided to farm out this very afternoon the wine and beer tapsters' excise from now until the first of May next, in accordance with the notices posted, and to let the farming proceed. On the conditions read to him, Jacob Hendrixsz Maat became the farmer and gave security in the sum of fl.1300:– for the period aforesaid.

Gerrit Seegertsen having made a request for a building lot, the matter is postponed until the return of the honorable committee [now] going to the Manathans.

    JOANNES DYCKMAN
    JAN VERBEECK
    JAN THOMASZ
    PIETER HARTGERTS
    FRANS BARENTSEN PASTOORS

Tuesday, September 1, 1654

Present:
  J: Dyckman   Pieter Hertgertsz
  J: Thomasz   Frans Barentsz

Geertruyt Pieters, the wife of Abram Pietersz Vosburgh, being legally summoned by the commissary, the third default is entered against her.

Jacob Hendrixsz Maat having a week ago bid in the farming of the usual tapsters' excise on wine and beer, has presented a certain writing whereby he requests that in order the better to prevent frauds in the matter, the burghers as well as [161] the tapsters may be ordered to obtain a proper certificate from the farmer or the impost master, to wit, of wines and strong beer only, paying two stivers for each certificate, before they be allowed to take them into their houses or get them from the brewers, or unload them from the incoming sloops and store them, and that the former ordinances on the subject may be renewed.

Whereupon it is decided to make the following apostil: Proper action thereon will be taken and for that purpose the ordinances will be published and posted anew and the same will in every way be enforced as is proper.

As to the second point, regarding the brewers, he may at any time inquire, or have inquiry made, what beer is brewed or imported, without being necessitated thereby to make an inspection of the brewers' houses. But the brewers shall not be allowed to furnish any strong beer to the burghers or tapsters until a proper certificate from the farmer, or impost master, or his collector, is shown to them, on pain, etc.

As to the third point, regarding the time within which every one shall be obliged to get a certificate, or certificates, from the farmer, this is approved, on condition that the impost master shall have to post a notice, or notices, to that effect, stating where the collector resides, or where the certificates may be obtained.

[162] The impost master is promised, however, that [the regulations] will in all respects be properly enforced.

The Hon. Jacob Jansz Schermerhoren having this day a week ago resigned from this court in order to go to *Patria*, his honor is with a clasp of the hand thanked for his good comradeship, the pains which he has taken and the good service performed by him as a magistrate of the honorable court here, both in the interest of the people and of the Hon. Company. At his honor's request, an extract herefrom will be placed in his hands to serve him by way of testimonial in case of need.

JOANNES DYCKMAN
JAN THOMASZ
PIETER HARTGERS
FRANS BARENTSEN PASTOORS

Wednesday, September 2, 1654

Resolved to give Abraham Pietersz Vosburgh in part payment [of his bill] for the two bridges made in Beverwyck an order on the honorable treasurers for the sum of fl.75:—

JOANNES DYCKMAN

[163] Tuesday, September 9, 1654 [31]

Present:

J: Dyckman	Pieter Hertgerts
J: Verbeeck	Frans Barentsz [32]
J: Thomasz	

Pieter Bronck, plaintiff, against Jacob Jansz Flodder, defendant, about fl. 920:—, which the defendant acknowledges that he owes, less thirty guilders for some freight brought up the river for the plaintiff.

The parties are to agree about the payment if possible, otherwise they may apply again to this court.

Pieter Bronck, plaintiff, against Luykas Pietersz, defendant, about a tavern debt amounting to fl. 192:13:—.

The defendant admits the debt.

---

[31] Thus in the original. The date should be September 8, 1654.
[32] The original has Frans Brantsz.

The defendant is ordered to pay the aforesaid sum of fl.192:13:– to the plaintiff within the time of six weeks, on pain of execution.

Jan Hendrixsz, plaintiff, against Jan van Aecken, defendant.

Claes Gerritsz being subpoenaed by the court declares that Jan van Aecken let Jan Hendrixsz have a half interest in the purchase of the house of Thomas.

Defendant's first default.

JOANNES DYCKMAN
JAN VERBEECK
JAN THOMASZ
PIETER HARTGERTS
FRANS BARENTSEN PASTOORS

[164] Friday, September 12, 1654 [33]

Present:

J: Dyckman
J: Verbeeck
J: Thomasz
Pieter Hertgerts
Frans Barentsz Pastoors

Jacob Hendrixsz Maet, being subpoenaed by the court to testify whether he has not seen like the commissary that Maria Jans, the wife of Steeven Jansz, sold some brandy to the squaw or to the savages, declares that Maria Jans tapped and gave to the squaw some brandy in a small pewter bottle and received therefore some seawan in the presence of others, such as Cees Pott, Claes Hendrixsz and Ariaen Claesz, who for so far as they have seen it have confirmed this statement on oath. Ariaen Claesz declares that he saw a pewter bottle with brandy, which brandy to the best of his knowledge was tapped to the squaw by Maria Jans. The same is also sworn to by Jacob Hendrixsz Maet, who testifies that she poured the brandy which she gave

---

[33] Should be September 11, 1654.

to the squaw from a bottle in her cupboard, which he confirms on oath. Claes Hendrixsz declares that he tasted the brandy, but that he did not see from whom or how the squaw got the brandy.

      JOANNES DYCKMAN
      JAN VERBEECK
      JAN THOMASZ
      PIETER HARTGERTS
      FRANS BARENTSEN PASTOORS

    Tuesday, September 28, 1654 [34]

Present:

 J: Verbeeck   J: Thomasz   F: Barentsz

Interrogatories on which this Honorable Court is to examine Marten Ottensen, commonly called Swager [35] Merten.

How old he is and where born?	Answer: Thirty-four years, born at Amsterdam.
Whether he has not been at the house of Jacob Luyersz, where Cornelis the Swede, now sailing on the *Karreman,* was present and on what day?	Says: Yes, and that he was there about the 25th of this month.
[165] Whether he was not called outside by the said Swede?	Answer: Yes.
Whether among other things the said Swede did not ask whether he was in any service and had sailed to the Cape?	Answer: Yes.
Whether he did not ask said Marten if he was willing to serve the Queen?	Answer: Yes.

---

[34] This should be, September 29, 1654.
[35] *Swager* means brother-in-law.

Whether he did not say, "I have something secret to tell you, but you must keep quiet?"

Answer: Yes.

Whether he did not say, "I have come here by order of the Queen to spy out this place?"

Answer: Yes.

Whether he did not [ask him] again to keep still, as otherwise it would cost them both their lives?

Answer: Yes.

Whether thereupon he did not promise to [let him] be his lieutenant in this service?

Answer: Yes.

Whether he, Swager Marten, the next day, asked the aforesaid Cornelis, the Swede, if he knew what he had said to him?

Answer: He said, "Yes, but keep still about it."

Whether further he did not ask Swager Marten whether he had two or three guns?

Answer: That he did have them at the Manathans. Whereupon he, Cornelis the Swede, said, "All right, keep still; we shall see what to do further in sailing thither."

This day, the 28th of September, Swager Marten has taken the usual oath on the aforesaid questions and answers in the presence of the attending magistrates.

JAN VERBEECK
JAN THOMASZ
FRANS BARENTTSEN PASTOO[R]S

[166] Extraordinary Session, September 30, 1654

Present:

    J: Verbeeck   P: Hertgerts   J: Thomasz

Andryes Herpertsen, plaintiff, against Femmetgen Westerkamp, widow of Hendrick Jansz Westerkamp, deceased, defendant.

The plaintiff demands that the defendant's daughter serve out and fulfil her term of service according to her promise and contract.

The defendant requests [permission] to take away her daughter in accordance with the promise which she made her deceased husband on his deathbed, unless the plaintiff's contract be held valid.

The court, having heard the statements and arguments on both sides, order that the promise made by the defendant to her deceased husband on his deathbed shall be carried out, on condition that the defendant's daughter shall remain five weeks longer with the plaintiff, in order that he may in that time look out for another servant.

Uldrick Kleyn having come into court requests that he may be released from confinement and set free, which is granted him on condition that he shall hereafter at the request of this court come to justify himself.

                              JOANNES DYCKMAN
                              JAN VERBEECK
                              JAN THOMASZ
                              PIETER HARTGERS

Extraordinary Session, Thursday, October 15, 1654

Present:

| J: Dyckman | J: Thomasz | Pieter Hertgerts |
| J: Verbeeck | Sander Leendertsen | Frans Barentsen |

Maria Jans, the wife of Steeven Jansz, plaintiff, against Abraham Crowaet,[36] defendant, for payment of fl. 148 and one stiver according to a judgment of the court of the colony of Rensselaerswyck dated the 27th of August last past. At the request of the commissary and officer, the plaintiff declared that the attachment levied on the goods in the sloop of Jacob Symontsz Clomp was not vacated before his departure from here.

Eldert Gerbertsz, plaintiff, against Jacob Symontsz Clomp, defendant, about one hundred guilders which Jacob Clomp or the defendant received from the plaintiff and for which [167] he promised to deliver hogs to the plaintiff. [The plaintiff alleges] that the defendant brought some hogs up the river but sold them to others for eighty guilders.

The court, having heard the arguments and debates on both sides, enjoin the defendant from leaving here without having given sufficient security. Meanwhile the officer here is requested and ordered on account of the wounding of Ariaen Claesz to take the sails and the rudder from board the defendant's sloop.

The wife of Pieter Cornelisz having requested a lot, consent is given, but the granting of the lot is postponed until the surveying of the lots.

JOANNES DYCKMAN
JAN VERBEECK
JAN THOMASZ
PIETER HARTGERS
FRANS BARENTSEN PASTOORS

---

[36] Meaning: Abraham, the Croat.

Tuesday, October 20, 1654

Present:

J: Dyckman   J: Thomasz   Frans Barensz Pastoors
J: Verbeeck   Sander Leendertsz

Steeven Jansz, plaintiff, against Abraham Crowaet,[37] defendant, about the preceding claims.

The court decides that the chest of Abraham Crobaet on board the sloop of Jacob Symontsz Clomp shall remain attached until the claim is satisfied.

Jan Hendrixsz, plaintiff, against Jan van Aecken, defendant.

The plaintiff says that in company with Jan van Aecken he bought the house of Thomas Sanders. Parties are referred to Mr Anthonius de Hooges, Goosen Gerritsen, Gillis Pietersz and Rem Jansz, referees, to agree if they can.

Adriaen Dirrixsz de Vries, being summoned to appear in court, complains that some time ago the officer served a notice on him and used many abusive words, complaining of the violence committed.

Cors Boutsen, appearing, requests to know the reasons for his detention. Is told that they will be communicated to him at the proper time.

Marcelis Jansz declares that Cors Boutsen [168] came to his house with the knife on his hat, wanting to assault him, and complains of violence committed at his house by Cors Boutsen, Luykas Pietersen and Herman Janssen.

Gillis Pietersen declares that Cors Boutsen stood with the knife on his hat and challenged whoever was willing to a fight.

Uldrick Kleyn declares that he heard the window crash through which the aforesaid three, to wit, Cors Boutsen, Luykas Pietersen and Herman Jansz, broke in.

Eldert Gerbertsz still demands payment for the 100 boards delivered to Jacob Symontsz Clomp, for which he promised to

---

[37] The original has "Abrabraham Crowaet," and in the next line, "Arabraham Crobaet."

bring him hogs from the Manathans, but which he sold and delivered as security to others, requesting that payment be made therefor and that the goods attached under the warrant of attachment against Jacob Symonsz Clomp may remain attached until he is satisfied. The request is granted.

Lambert van Valckenburgh has requested to have a lot. Postponed until the drawing of lots.

Hendrick Gerritsz requests to have a garden in connection with the house which he built on the lot purchased by him. He is notified that the matter will be taken into consideration at the first opportunity.

Theunis Cornelisz van Slingerlant requests a lot. Postponed until the drawing of lots. Likewise [the requests of] Albert Andriesz and Barent Albertsen.

Claes Jacopsz requests a lot. Postponed until the drawing of lots.

Joannes Magapolensis having requested to have a lot, a lot will be assigned to him on the hill, when the drawing of lots takes place. Carsten Carstensen and Gerrit Segertsen have also requested lots. Postponed as above.

JOANNES DYCKMAN
JAN VERBEECK
JAN THOMASZ
FRANS BARENTSEN PASTOORS

[169] Extraordinary Session, Wednesday, October 21, 1654

Present:

J: Dyckman   J: Thomasz   Frans Barentsen Pastoors
J: Verbeeck Sander Leendertsen

Gillis Pietersen being duly subpoenaed and summoned, declares that Marcelis Jansz and Cors Boutsen both had their knives out and that Cors Boutsen came with his knife on his hat to Marcelis's house and again challenged whoever would [to a personal combat].

Uldrick Kleyn declares that when they first came to the door they wanted perforce to have [beer] tapped and broke open the window through which Luykas Pietersz jumped in first; that Marcelis fetched his sword to defend himself, but that he [Pietersz] remained inside by force and that thereafter Cors Boutsen and Herman Jansz also broke in and, coming inside, tapped in spite of the tavernkeeper beer from a half barrel which they gave away there to others.

Cors Boutsen admits that he also climbed through the window and that the window was broken open, but he does not know exactly by whom.

Luykas Pietersz declares that seeing Marcelis standing there, he was the first of the three to climb through the window and further declares as above.

Herman Jansz declares that he also climbed through the window but that, contrary to the declaration of Luykas Pietersz, he did not see Marcelis standing before the window.

Uldrick Kleyn declares that he heard the breaking of the window and that he saw them break in, to wit, Luykas Pietersz, Cortsz and Marceles, whereupon and on all of this [evidence] it is decided to hold the persons of Cors Boutsen, Luykas Pietersen and Herman Jansz in custody in irons until further order.

Jacob from Loosdrecht asks for a lot. Deferred to the drawing of lots.

Joannes van Twiller requests permission of the court to have a door leading out of the fort. Decided to write about it to the Hon. General [170] and to submit the matter to his wise and superior judgment. Meanwhile, the court is of opinion that for the security of the fort it would be better and more suitable if he had [a door] on the west side, within the fort. However, they leave the matter to the pleasure of the Hon. General.

JOANNES DYCKMAN
JAN VERBEECK
JAN THOMASZ
FRANS BARENTSEN PASTOORS

Tuesday, November 3, 1654

Present:

J. Dyckman J. Thomasz Frans Barentsen Pastors
J. Verbeeck Sander Leendertsen

Jacob van Loosdrecht, plaintiff, against Maria Jans, being the wife of Steeven Jansz, defendant.

The plaintiff declares that the defendant sold brandy to the savages and that he saw it.

Maria Jans declares that she said to the plaintiff that she would not do it for fifty, or even one hundred guilders, and that she did not sell any brandy to the savages. She requests that the matter may be disposed of.

The officer having put the matter into the hands of the magistrates, it is decided not to enter into any agreement regarding it until the case of Uldrick Kleyn is taken up also.

Jan Roelofsz is chosen and appointed surveyor besides Herman Bastiaensen, and is bound hereafter to take the surveyor's oath.

Wednesday, November 25, 1654

Oath taken by Jan Roelofsz, surveyor, chosen and appointed by this court on the 3d of this month:

I promise and swear in the presence of Almighty God that without [favor or] prejudice to any one I shall do the surveying in the presence of [the two members of the] [171] committee of this honorable court. So help me God Almighty.

This day, on the date above written, Jan Roeloffsz, surveyor, has taken the surveyor's oath.

Claes Hrendricxsz, carpenter, requests to have a lot
Willem Jansz Stoll, [a lot]
Jan Labatie, a lot
Jan Lammertsz, soldier, a lot
Adriaen Claesz requests a lot
Jacob Adriaensz soo gemackelyck, [a lot]

JOANNES DYCKMAN

Tuesday, December 2, 1654

Present:
- J: Dyckman
- J: Verbeeck
- Sander Leendertsen
- Pieter Hertgerts

The honorable consistory here, plaintiffs, against Claes Ripsz, have requested in the presence of the defendant that the defendant may be examined on [interrogatories] as follows:

We, the undersigned, Gedeon Schaets, minister, Rutger Jacobsz, elder, and Anthony de Hooges, deacon, being appointed a committee by the honorable consistory, request that the honorable court of Fort Orange and Beverwyck may be pleased to have Claes Ripsen, summoned before the court at our instance, according to our duty, answer the following interrogatories and then to take into consideration our arguments.

First, whether Klaes Ripsz does not admit having had carnal conversation with the sister [of] the wife of Teunis Jacopsz?

Answer, Yes.

[172] Whether he promised to marry her or not?

Answer, Yes, that he would marry her.

Whether he has acknowledged that he is the father of the child of which the aforesaid woman was recently delivered, or not?

Answer, Yes.

Whether he has requested to have the banns of marriage proclaimed here, or not?

Answer, Yes.

Whether he was informed that it had already taken place, or not?

Answer, Yes, that he was so informed.

And for certain reasons he is asked whether he does not often sleep with her yet under one cover as man and wife?

Answer, Yes.

All this, or the foregoing, being admitted by Klaes Ripsz, he is asked whether he is willing to marry her, or not? When?

Answer, Yes.

Says, he expects news from his father, whom he has written about it.

Moreover, all excuses and subterfuges about this are very illogical for, seeing that man is mortal, it would be full of danger for them to depart [without being married];

First, because, although it may be argued that they are engaged, this is neither binding [173] nor legal, as long as they are not united in marriage in the customary way.

Secondly, because as a consequence thereof the aforesaid child would be illegitimate.

Thirdly, because of people who live together like man and wife one can never know when the woman will again be pregnant by him.

Therefore, in view of the inevitable results and consequences above mentioned, we come to the positive conclusion that in order to avoid all scandal, to prevent further mischief, to promote good order, to maintain justice and finally to fulfil our bounden duty, Klaes Ripse must be united with the aforesaid person at the first opportunity. Whereupon we expect the judgment of the honorable court aforesaid. Thus done in Fort Orange, the first day of December 1654. Was signed: Gedeon Schaets, *pastor in loco*, Rutger Jacopsz, elder, and Anthonius de Hooges, deacon.

The honorable court having heard the arguments and debates on both sides, condemn the defendant to marry the aforesaid person even this day, and as the aforesaid woman is sickly and can not well take the trouble [to go out], the Reverend Gedeon Schaets is requested to [perform the marriage at her house]. Otherwise, if he, Claes Ripsz, refuses to do so, he shall immediately be put in irons, until he marries her. Which being proposed to him, it was found that he had nothing but frivolous excuses to offer and therefore was put in irons.

[174] Tuesday, December 1, 1654

Present:

J. Dyckman	Sander Leendertsen
J. Verbeeck	Frans Barentsen

Andryes de Vos, plaintiff, against Claes Gerritsz, Cornelis Pietersz and Jan Andryesz, defendants, to give testimony to the truth, whether it is not known to them when Mr Rensselaer, [either himself] or through Jan Barentsz Poest, took possession of the farm of Jan Barentsz Poest. They declare that they were there at that time and heard, to wit, Claes Gerritsz, that the taking out of the grain by Andryes de Vos was refused and that he was forbidden to have further access to the barn, such being done by them jointly, or as the deponents declare by Jan Barentsz Poest, offering to confirm this on oath.

Baeffgen Pieters, plaintiff, against Maria Jans, defendant, in a dispute about a water pail.

Maria Jans claims that the pail aforesaid was given to her.

Baeffgen Pieters, plaintiff, against Aert Otterspoor, defendant, about a tavern debt of fl.19 or fl.20.

Defendant's first default.

Mr Johan de Hulter having come into court has exhibited a certain letter written to Cristoffel Davitsz by the Hon. General. It is decided to have the same copied and in addition to notify him, Christoffel Davits, that he must give the aforesaid gentleman peaceful possession [of the land] in response to his complaints and if he sees fit have the case argued by his competent [attorney].

Maria Jans, plaintiff, against Abraham Crowaet, defendant. The defendant's third default and he is ordered to satisfy the plaintiff before his departure, on pain of arrest for debt.

[176][38] Pieter Bronck, being subpoenaed by the court, declares that he took out of the hand of Jacob Flodder and broke a pair of dividers which he held while in dispute with Hendrixsz, deceased, but whether he, Flodder, intended to do any harm with them he does not know.

Master Jacob, surgeon, declares that Jan Gouw cut Piet Bout across the hand.

Jan van Hoesem has brought into court fl. 80:–, in addition to the fl. 40:–, making together one hundred and twenty guilders, in payment in full by Jan Fransz van Hoesem for the lot of Willem Juriaensen, according to the judgment [against him] by this court, dated the 25th of November last.

JOANNES DYCKMAN
JAN VERBEECK
FRANS BARENTSEN PASTOORS

Tuesday, December 15, 1654

Present:

J. Dyckman   Jan Thomasz   Frans Barentsen Pastoors
J. Verbeeck   Sander Leendertsz

Maria Jans, plaintiff, against Abram Crowaet, defendant, for fl. 17:10:– and sixty guilders heretofore disbursed for convening the court in extraordinary session, and that he shall not depart from here until he has paid sixty guilders on account and in part payment of the sum of fl. 138, with costs.

Whereas Maria Jans, the wife of Steven Jansz, defendant, on the third of November last acknowledged before this court that she sold brandy to the savages, it is decided that the honorable magistrates shall send her a sealed memorandum stating

---

[38] In numbering, page 175 has been omitted.

what she therefor and on that account ought to pay to the officer; that she must comport herself according to their good advice, with further warning not to do so any more in the future, on pain of arbitrary correction.

[178][39] Cornelis, who lives with Poest, has been assigned lot No. 5.

JOANNES DYCKMAN
JAN VERBEECK
JAN THOMASZ
FRANS BARENTSEN PASTOORS

Tuesday, December 22, 1654

Present:

J. Dyckman   San: Leendertsz
J: Thomasz   Pieter Hertgertsz

Interrogatories on which this honorable court, at the request of Andryes de Vos, is to examine Ryck Rutgertsz from Bunnick and Goosen Gerritsen

Whether the witness, to wit, Goosen Gerritsen, does not admit having been some time ago with the plaintiff on the farm of Jan Barentsz Poest to trade together in regard to some dry boards and that they agreed about the purchase?	He admits that he heard [what was said].
Whether he, Andryes de Vos, did not then go out of the door and among other things complain that against his will he had been forcibly deprived by Jan Barentsz of the use of	Answers, Yes.

[39] In numbering, page 177 has been omitted.

the barn, for the threshing of both oats and pease, and that he had thus far been unable to get a copy of the contract, so that he did not know at all how he must govern himself?

Whether he, Andryes de Vos, did not send him, Goosen Gerritsen, to go to the honorable secretary, Anthonius de Hooges, to ask for a copy of the contract about the purchase of the [179] wheat and that the plaintiff, Andryes de Vos, would get it two days later when he came to the fort?

Answers, that upon this request he went to Anthonius de Hooges.

Also, whether Secretary de Hooges did not reply then that Mr Rensselaer had the contract and had locked it in his desk and that therefore he could not do so?

Answers, Yes, that he asked for it, but received for answer that Mr Rensselaer had locked it in his desk. This declaration he has confirmed by oath.

Whether Ryck Rutgertsz was not present on the farm and whether he acknowledges that he was present in the barn when Mr Rensselaer and Monsr Adriaen vander Donck and a servant came there while they were busy putting the wheat in the barn as they were not allowed to put it in the stacks?

Answers, Yes.

Whether he, Ryck Rutgertsz, does not acknowledge

Declares, that Mr Rensselaer said that he was entitled to

that he then did not know that Mr Rensselaer had forbidden to put it in there because the summer wheat had to be put in there and that he was entitled to the barn as well as Andryes de Vos, as buyer of the grain, as he had bought his wheat on the same condition? the use of the half of the barn and that he would have the use of it.

Which declaration Ryck Rutgertsz with uplifted fingers has confirmed by oath.

[180] Tuesday, December 22, 1654

Present:

J. Dyckman
J. Thomasz
Sander Leendertsen
Pieter Hertgerts

Jan Thomasz, plaintiff, against Willem Jansz Schut, defendant.

The plaintiff declares that the defendant has again hired himself out for a year at fl.240 and free washing.

The defendant denies it and says that he would rather leave than serve out the aforesaid time.

The court, having heard the arguments and pleadings on both sides, forbid the defendant to leave, or to hire himself to any one in this jurisdiction during the aforesaid time, and order him to serve out his time with the plaintiff, on pain of banishment, the defendant being further ordered to regulate himself according to the [contract].

Roeloff Jacopsz, plaintiff, against Hans Inckluis, defendant, for fl. 23:8:–.

The defendant admits the aforesaid debt and promises to pay it within the time of six weeks.

Roeloff Jacopsz, plaintiff, against Merten, the mason, defendant, for fl. 5:8:–.

The defendant agrees to pay this at the first opportunity.

Luykas Pietersz, being summoned to appear in court, has with uplifted fingers declared under oath that he is not guilty of the breaking open of Marcelis's window.

Cors Boutsz's defense having been heard, he is ordered to deliver 40 boards to the plaintiff.

Jan van Aecken, plaintiff, against Carsten Meyndertsen, defendant, about some hardware for which they sent beavers to Holland for joint account.

Defendant's first default.

Jacob Hendrixsz Maet has brought into court fl.160:– in seawan, in payment of the first term of the lease of the excise, [181] which is entered here for future use.

JOANNES DYCKMAN
JAN THOMASZ
PIETER HARTGERTS

Extraordinary Session, Wednesday, December 23, 1654

Present:

J. Dyckman   Pieter Hertgerts
Sander Leendertsen Frans Barentsz

Jan van Aecken, plaintiff, against Carsten Fredrixsz, defendant, about some beavers sent for joint account to Holland to obtain hardware, which has now arrived and is in the hands of the defendant.

The court, having heard the arguments and debates on both sides, order the defendant to deliver to the [plaintiff] the goods sent over and to settle all accounts even this day, if it is possible, and the defendant is ordered to pay the costs of this extraordinary session, amounting to fl. 28:10:–.

JOANNES DYCKMAN
PIETER HARTGERTS
FRANS BARENTSEN PASTOORS

Tuesday, January 13, 1654 [1655]

Present:

J. Dyckman   Sander Leendertsz   Jan Thomasz
J. Verbeeck   Pieter Hertgers   Frans Barentsz

Evert Pels requests this honorable court that whereas by balance of accounts fl.276:7:– is due him from Jan van Bremen, the latter's effects at Katskill may remain attached until he first and before all [others] shall have been paid.

There being likewise due to the Hon. Pieter Hertgerts from the said Jan van Bremen the sum of fl. 270:–, he requests that he may be promptly paid as soon as Evert Pels shall have been paid.

And there being due to Willem Fredrixsz Bout from the aforesaid Jan Dirrixsz van Bremen about three hundred guilders, he requests that the first two persons being paid he may and shall then, upon production of proper proof, be paid for one-third.

Which requests being approved, they are communicated to Jan Dirrixsz van Bremen by letter, to regulate himself accordingly in paying the persons who had his property attached.

JOANNES DYCKMAN
JAN VERBEECK
JAN THOMASZ
PIETER HARTGERS
FRANS BARENTSEN PASTOORS

[183] Tuesday, January 26, 1654 [1655]

Present:

J. Dyckman   J. Thomasz   Pieter Hertgerts
J. Verbeeck   Sander Leendertsz   Frans Barensz

A petition was read of Jacques Thysz, requesting permission to have the use of the lot granted to Master Jacob, the surgeon, situated next to the lot of Commissary Dyckman. It is decided to state in an apostil that for certain reasons, instead of the aforesaid lot, another lot, on the hill, has been granted to the petitioner, but if his wife and children should in addition need another lot for themselves, he may in that case again apply to this honorable court.

Upon the request of Jacob Jansz Stoll of the one part and Claes Hendrixsz from Wtrecht of the other part about the [exchange of] said first party's two houses standing in this fort and the other party's [house] standing at the Manathans, at present occupied by . . . . , the commissary and officer here, together with the Hon. Sander Leendertsz and Pieter Hertgerts, are appointed by this honorable court to have said parties come before them this morning to legally convey [said houses] to one another as they sold them in accordance with the contract of sale.

Klaes Ripsz, being summoned by the court and once more questioned in regard to the declaration made by him on the second of December last, has again persisted in said declaration, but there being read to him the declarations made on the 4th instant at the request of the commissary and officer by the Reverend Domine Gidiony Schaets and Adriaen Jansz from Leyden, as shown by the said documents, [184] the aforesaid defendant, Klaes Ripsz, has suddenly denied the testimony given by him and declared that he knows nothing as to the substance thereof. It being thereupon decided to summon the Reverend Domine Gidiony Schaets and Adriaen Jansz aforesaid to appear as witnesses in the presence of the defendant, the said witnesses, who deserve full credence, have made their former testimony seem conclusive, whereupon the officer has demanded sentence.

Having stood outside and being sharply examined in regard to the offenses committed by him in word and deed, the defendant has confessed his guilt, admitted that he acted wrongly and prayed for forgiveness, which is granted with the understanding that the first time he is again heard to utter such words, he shall

be punished as an example to others and that he must pay fifty
guilders to the commissary and officer.

> JOANNES DYCKMAN
> JAN VERBEECK
> JAN THOMASZ
> PIETER HARTGERS
> FRANS BARENTSEN PASTOORS

[185] Tuesday, February 2, 1655

Present:

J: Dyckman   San: Leendertsz   Frans Barentsen Pastoors
J. Thomasz   Pieter Hertgerts

At the funeral of the child of Hendrick Jochemsz, Claes Gerritsz said that Cornelis Vos had given the houses the [nick]names that are in circulation, which Hendrick Jochemsz overheard in the presence of Jacob Hap.

A written statement was read, signed by the Hon. Anthonius de Hooges and Adriaen Jansz from Leyden, of this date, regarding the matter of Cornelis de Vos and Claes Gerritsz, in general as to the well-known accusation that Cornelis Vos and Claes Gerritsz had a hand in giving the names that are in circulation, together with a declaration of each, as may be seen more fully from the statement.

Jacob Hendrixsz Maet, plaintiff, against Pieter Bronck, defendant, for   fl. 129: 14:—
                                                23: 2:—
                                         ─────────────
                                         fl. 152: 16:—

Of the old account of the farmer [of the excise], fl.274 must [be credited] to his account toward payment of the second term, on account of wages earned by Abram Jacobsz, deceased, on the new Company's house, leaving fl. 93:18, which Pieter Bronck must pay in addition to what the farmer receives.

Jochem Becker declares that Cornelis Vos gave the [nick] names and that he heard so from the mouth of Claes Rotterdam, his servant, at the harvest feast of Oom Dirrick.

Jochem Becker and Jan van Hoesem request that as the old captain's house is no longer fit for occupation, the same may be put in proper repair.

Before any repairs are made, fearing that an accident may take place, it is decided to have a further inspection made at a convenient opportunity.

[186] Claes Gerritsz being summoned by the court and being asked whether he knew who was guilty of bestowing the [nick] names that are in circulation, declares that some time ago, sitting in the evening at the house of Cornelis Vos, he heard out of his own mouth that he had given the following names:

First, the house of Jan Thomasz, "The Cuckoo's Nest" (*het Koeckoeck Nest*)

Goosen Gerritsen's house he gave the name of "Concord" (*de Eendracht*)

Rut Jacopsz' house "The Whistling Wind" (*Soesende Wint*), to the best of his knowledge

The house of Jan van Aecken, "The Finch's Nest" (*het Vinckenest*)

The house of Andryes Herpertsz, "The House of Ill Manners" (*'t Huys Onbeschoft*)

The house of Philip Pietersz Schuldert, "Fly like the Wind" (*Vliegende Wint*)

Evert Wendel, "The Griffin" (*de Vogel Grijp*, literally, the Grasping Bird)

The house of Gerrit Jansz, "The House of Discord" (*Haspel in de Sack op het Dack*)[40]

---

[40] Literally: Spool in the bag on the roof. The word *Haspel*, which means a spool, is used figuratively in the sense of an awkward, incompetent person. Of persons who frequently quarrel or disagree, it is said that they get along like *haspels in een zak*, like spools in a bag. The expression as a whole, however, as it occurs in the text, is obscure.

The house of Dirck Jansz Kroon, "The Savingsbank" (*de Spaerpot*)

He also declared having heard the house of Mr de Hooges mentioned, but that the exact name had escaped him.

Mother Bogaerdus's house, "The Vulture World" (*de Gierswerelt*)

The house of Volckert Jansz is called "The Bird Song" (*de Vogelsanck*)[40a]

Mr Rensselaer's house, "Spoiled early" (*Vroegh bedorven*)

Pieter Hertgerts's house, he named "The little sparrow" [*het Huysmusgen*, used figuratively for a home body, a stay at home]

Claes Gerritsz has with uplifted fingers confirmed the foregoing on oath.

A petition was read of Adriaen van Ilpendam, schoolmaster, praying for the exclusive right to keep day and night school and that the other schoolmaster who begins to keep night school may be enjoined from doing so. It is decided to note in the margin that the honorable court can for the present not find sufficient reasons for forbidding said schoolmaster to do so.

J: Dyckman
Jan Thomasz
Pieter Hartgers
Frans Barentsz Pastoors

[40a] In the city of Gouda, *de Vogelenzang* was a street assigned to women of ill fame. The word may be used here in some such opprobrious sense.

[187] Tuesday, February 23, 1653 [1655]

Present:

J. Dyckman   J. Thomasz   Pieter Hertgerts
J. Verbeeck   San: Leendersz Frans Barentsz Pastoors

Upon the complaint of Grietgen Jacop's daughter that Cors Boutsz had assaulted her on the public street and annoyed her, it is decided that the officer shall gather further information about the circumstances and that meanwhile Cors Boutsen shall be released from his provisional confinement on [promise] to reappear and defend himself.

Eldert Gerbertsz requesting that he may be allotted a garden in connection with his lot, the matter is postponed for certain reasons until the river is open.

Jacob Hendrixsz Maet being summoned to appear in court and the charges against him having been read to him in regard to the things committed and done by him late last Sunday evening, he is ordered to submit his counter evidence on the next court day.

Willem Fredrixsz being summoned to appear in court declares that Symon, the baker, and he, being at the house of Willem Fredrixsz, heard it stated that Claes Gerritsz had named the eating house "Seldom satisfied" (*Selden satt*) and the house of Cornelis Vos "The Finch's nest" (*het Vinckenest*).

Symon, the baker, being subpoenaed declares as above, to wit, like Willem Fredrixsz.

Grietgen Jacop's daughter declares that Cors Boutsen last evening pulled her apron by force from her body and that she was forced to leave it in his hands and that it was kept by him, Cors Boutsen, although, as Grietgen Jacops declares, she was not then asked for any payment. [Thus declared] in the presence of Adam Dingeman, to whose testimony she, Grietgen Jacop's daughter, [188] refers and who may be further examined in regard to it.

JOANNES DYCKMAN
JAN VERBEECK
JAN THOMASZ
PIETER HARTGERS
FRANS BARENTSEN PASTOORS

Thursday, February 25, 1655

Present:

J: Dyckman   J: Thomasz   Pieter Hertgerts
J: Verbeeck   San: Leendertsz Frans Barentsz Pastoors

There was read a written petition of Pieter Adriaensen Soo Gemackelyck, stating that the impost master, Jacob Hendrixsz Maet, last Sunday caused to be attached two and a quarter barrels of good beer and also had them removed without first having notified him, notwithstanding the beer was brewed of his own grain, and excusing himself on the ground of former usage and custom in the matter.

Whereupon the honorable court have decided to give for answer that the petitioner was not unacquainted with the fact that he was not allowed to export any strong beer, wine, or distilled liquors out of this jurisdiction without having first secured a proper certificate from the impost master. Concerning which, in order the better to convince him thereof, he is hereby reminded of the ordinances of the Hon. General and the Supreme Council published and posted to that end for several years and at different times, from which the petitioner had sufficient and definite knowledge on the subject and therefore was not allowed to do so on pain of the penalty thereto provided. Although he maintains that the beer was brewed from his own grain, the honorable court, knowing that the aforesaid ordinances were not published and posted without his knowledge, judge, according to the custom of the fatherland, that no strong beer may be removed from one place or jurisdiction to the other, [189] on pain of confiscation of the same, which being a custom of the fatherland, according to whose laws and regulations they must govern themselves in this country, they declare the aforesaid beer confiscated and furthermore, for good reasons, [condemn the petitioner] to pay the sum of fifty guilders to the impost master.

Interrogatories on which at the request of the commissary and officer here is to be examined Henrick Jansz Reur, court messenger of the colony of Rensselaerswyck.

First, whether before or about the time of the freshet he was at the house of Steeven Jansz, whose wife is called Maria?

Answer, Yes, that he was there at that time.

Whether Herman Jansz van Valckenburgh was there, or came into the house?

Answer, he was in the house at that time.

Whether at that time he did not in a violent outburst say in the presence of the bystanders that the last time he was in irons he had seen the wife of the aforesaid commissary have carnal conversation and commit adultery with other persons, indicating the size of the horns that were put on the commissary?

Declares, Yes.

Who else were present?

Supposedly, Jacob Loosdrecht.

Whether the deponent did not upbraid him and said: "You should keep still, for if the husband hears of it, he will fight with you?"

Answer, Yes.

Whether he has anything else to say regarding it?

Answer, No.

On the 26th of February, Hendrick Jansz Reur has with uplifted [190] fingers confirmed these interrogatories by oath.

Interrogatories on which this honorable court at the request of Commissary Joannes Dyckman is to examine Jacob Hendrixs Maet, he to answer categorically, yes, or no

First, how old he is and where born? — Says, About 24 years and born at Loosdreght.

Whether before or about the time of the late freshet he was at the house of Steeven Jansz, the wife named Maria, and when? — Says, He does not know.

Whether at that time Harman Jansz van Valckenburgh, commonly called "Scheele Herman" (Cross-eyed Herman) was not sitting there, drinking? — Says, He saw him drinking.

Whether he did not hear him relate and declare that when he was last in irons he, Herman Jansz van Valckenburgh, aforesaid, saw the wife of the commissary aforesaid have carnal conversation and commit adultery with others, showing with outstretched arms the size of the horns which were put on the said commissary's head? — Answers and declares, Yes.

With offer, if need be, to confirm the foregoing by oath, this 26th of February 1655.

Whether he has anything more to say and what? — Answers, No.

[191] Thursday, February 26, 1654 [1655]

Interrogatories on which Loys Jacobusz is examined in court
Present:
  Ut supra

First, how old he is and where born?	About 22 years and born at Herentaels.[41]
Whether some time ago, and how long, at the house of Adriaen Jansz from Leyden, in the hallway, he did not reveal to Mr de Hooges the scandalous name that was given to him, or his wife?	Answers, Yes.
Secondly, he is asked from whom he heard it?	Declares, That he heard it from Susanna de Truy, the wife of Evert Wendel, the tailor.

Loys Jacobusz has offered, if need be, to confirm this, his declaration, by oath, and it is decided to subpoena both persons, the wife of Evert Wendel as well as Loys Jacobusz, to appear on the next court day.

JOANNES DYCKMAN
JAN VERBEECK
JAN THOMASZ
PIETER HARTGERTS
FRANS BARENTSEN PASTOORS

---

[41] Herenthals, a city in the province of Antwerp, Belgium.

Friday, February 26, 1654

Present:

J. Dyckman   J. Thomasz   Pieter Hertgerts
J. Verbeeck San: Leendersz Frans Barentsz Pastoors

The written demand and conclusion drawn up by the officer against Herman Jansz van Valckenburgh on account of various serious crimes committed by him having been examined, sentence in the matter is postponed until tomorrow.

[192] Saturday, February 27, 1655

Present:

Omnes

The written demand and conclusion of Joannes Dyckman, commissary and officer here, against Herman Jansz van Valckenburgh, at present in custody, being read and reread, the following sentence is pronounced on account of the crimes committed by him:

Sentence

Herman Jansz van Valckenburgh, at present in custody on account of various crimes committed by him, has, after being confronted with all the evidence, voluntarily confessed that he committed them.

First, the prisoner, some time ago, of his own accord, together with his accomplices broke open the window of Marcelis Jansz, of which complaint was lodged with the honorable court by the officer, and which, he confesses, was done by him out of pure mischief. Then, after the window was broken open, he climbed into the house and according to the complaints of Marcelis Jansz assaulted and molested him in his own house; scattered the fire over the floor in starting a fire on the hearth of the inside room, without allowing the woman or the man of the house to come into the inside room to extinguish the fire which had commenced to burn one of the doorposts and the floor; until finally the aforesaid Marcelis was assisted by the officer, who upon his complaint about assault went with him and found the conditions as described [193] and caused the fire to be extinguished; without which to all appearances the house would have suffered considerable damage from the fire that was started, yes, would have been totally ruined.

Furthermore, secondly, he has confessed that lately when they were riding the goose, he, on the public street, (be it said without disrespect) befouled the servant, or one of the men of Mr de Hulter commonly called Voogel, which he publicly confesses in accordance with the testimony thereof secured by Adriaen Claesz; therefore violating and disturbing the peace on the public highways and streets.

Last Monday evening, coming to the house of Steeven Jansz, he threatened to beat him, Steeven, in his house, whereupon [the said Herman] taking off his coat, he, Steeven, was forced to turn [for help] to the officer, who took him into custody, first asking the witnesses who were present whether it was true, who declared [it to be] absolutely [true], as may be seen more at large by the declarations.

About the time of the last freshet, sitting at the house of Steeven Jansz with his feet in irons, he declared openly that he had seen the wife of Commissary or Officer Dyckman commit adultery with several persons, showing with outstretched arms the size of the horns which he saw put on the commissary, according to the information and sworn interrogatories procured thereof, which being read to him, he has publicly denied the same and declared that he knew nothing about it, the prisoner declaring that he was drunk that evening and that the next day he was informed by others that he had said so, but that he knows nothing about the aforesaid [194] person but what is consistent with honor and virtue.

Furthermore, he has here and there made much noise and created many disturbances by fighting, etc., which he must admit himself.

The Honorable Court having heard these and other complaints and the same having been proved by his own confession, have condemned the prisoner, as they do condemn him on the demand made by the officer upon due evidence, pronouncing sentence in the name and on the part of the High and Mighty Lords the States General, his Highness the Prince of Orange, the Honorable Directors of the West India Company and the Honorable General and the Supreme Council of New Netherland, as follows:

Herman Jansz van Valckenburgh shall be brought to the place where it is customary to execute justice and be put in the flogging iron, with a few rods hanging from the post above his head and on his breast a sign with the words " False Accuser." Furthermore, the prisoner shall be banished from this jurisdiction for the period of six consecutive years, upon the sole condition that if the prisoner hereafter commits any further offenses, the old charges and the new shall be dealt with together as they deserve, the Honorable Court being moved to mitigate and reduce the sentence to this extent in the hope that he may improve his conduct, although the crimes committed by him demand greater and severer punishment.

Thus done and sentenced the 26th of February and executed on the 27th of this month of February, in full view of the people who were present.

JOANNES DYCKMAN
JAN VERBEECK
JAN THOMASZ
PIETER HARTGERS
FRANS BARENTSEN PASTOORS

[195] Tuesday, March 2, 1655

Present:

 J. Dyckman   J. Thomasz   Pieter Hertgertsen
 J. Verbeeck   San: Leendertsz

Herman Jacopsz, plaintiff, against Claes Hendrixsz, defendant, about one month and six days' house rent which the plaintiff claims is due him from the defendant. The respective parties being heard, it is decided to refer them, as is done hereby, to referees and arbitrators, to wit, Andryes Herpertsz and Rem Jansz, smith, to agree if they can.

Jan Barentsz Wemp, plaintiff, against Claes Gerritsz, defendant, about a wagon which is broken and which was loaned by the plaintiff for the use of the defendant. It is decided that the plaintiff, if he considers his cause just, may prosecute the matter further.

Cornelis Vos is given a copy of the deposition about the missing tub of butter, to file his answer thereto on the next court day.

        JOANNES DYCKMAN
        JAN VERBEECK
        JAN THOMASZ
        PIETER HARTGERS

[196] Tuesday, March 16, 1655

Present:

 J. Dyckman   J. Thomasz   Pieter Hertgertsz
 J. Verbeeck   San: Leendertsz

Jacob Hendrixsz Maat, plaintiff, against Steeven Jansz, carpenter, defendant, about one hundred boards according to the note signed by the defendant.

The defendant admits the aforesaid debt and agrees to satisfy the plaintiff as required one month before the departure of the ships from this country for *Patria*.

The honorable schout of the colony of Rensselaerswyck, plaintiff, against Claes Hendrixsz, carpenter, defendant, about certain interrogatories read to the defendant on account of the wounding of Evert Pels and Gysbert Cornelisz, as appears more fully from the document which is returned to his honor, together with the confession.

Jan Barent Wemp, plaintiff, against Claes Gerritsz, defendant.

Jan Thomasz, as attorney for the plaintiff, alleges that the wagon loaned by the plaintiff was broken by the defendant, but the defendant says that he did so in the service of Andryes de Vos.

Ordered that the plaintiff may summon the defendant, or Andryes de Vos, on the next court day to answer his complaint.

Wybregh Jacob's daughter, plaintiff, against Aelgen Jan's daughter, defendant, on account of some opprobrious words said to the plaintiff at her house.

The defendant admits having said them, but appeals to the testimony of Hester, the wife of Herman Bastiaensen, whom the plaintiff may cause to be subpoenaed on the next court d

[197] Cornelis Vos, being summoned to appear in court, is ordered and notified on the next court day promptly to clear himself of the charge of having given the familiar nicknames; also to explain the meaning of the words and to declare what induced him thereto and who advised him to do so and whether he did it alone, or who helped him with it.

Rem Jansz, smith, requests a lot on the hill for his brother-in-law, Michiel de Karreman,[42] which is granted him on the same conditions that are granted to others, the gardens to be assigned afterwards by lot.

Jan van Hoesem and Jochem Becker request that the old captain's house, which is unfit to be used any longer as a bakery, may be put in a proper state of repair. They are notified that before any one undertakes to bake in it, it must first be properly repaired, in order that no dreaded fire may break out there in the future.

---

[42] Michiel, the carter.

And as to the charge that some bakers, who are freemen, bake without having taken the oath, it is decided to issue further resolutions on the subject, as elsewhere no one is allowed to exercise a trade who has not taken the burgher oath.

Upon the request of Ysbrant Eldersz to have a lot near the third kill, it is decided that an inspection thereof shall be made.

[198] Hendrick Gerritsz, tailor, and Rem Jansz, smith, having appeared before the honorable court, Hendrick Gerritsz aforesaid acknowledges that he is satisfied and paid by Rem Jansz for a certain house and lot, standing and situated in Beverwyck, as he, Hendrick Gerritsz, bought the same lately from Rut Arentsz, tailor, deceased, bounded on the south by a wagon road, on the west by a plain, and on the east by Lourus Jansz, or whoever bought the house of him; hereby completely conveying and transferring said house and lot to the purchaser, Rem Jansz, from now on forever, without the grantor retaining any further right or interest in the same, just as it was granted and conveyed to him, Hendrick Gerritsz, by the curators appointed to administer the estate of the aforesaid Rut Arentsz, tailor, deceased; requesting that this conveyance made this day before the honorable court may be held and remain inviolate and that extracts from this register may be issued to the parties to serve them in the future. Which request being granted, copies will be issued as required.

Upon the written demand and conclusion of Joannes Dyckman, commissary and officer here, against Jacob Hendrixsz Maat, defendant, on account of deeds committed by him at the house of Steeven Jansz, both within and outside of the door, according to the evidence thereof, and also on account of drawing his knife on the 21st of February aforesaid, in the evening, and his own confession in the matter, it is decided to condemn the defendant to pay [199] a fine of one hundred and fifty guilders for the benefit of the aforesaid officer, with costs, payable promptly within forty-eight hours, without any exemption.

       JOANNES DYCKMAN
       JAN VERBEECK
       JAN THOMASZ
       PIETER HARTGERTS

The same date.

Given and granted to the honorable magistrates five lots on the hill, marked No. 1 to No. 5.

Sander Leendersz, No. 1, on the west side of Philip Pietersz.
Frans Barensz, No. 2, on the west side of Sander Leendertsz.
Pieter Hertgerts, No. 3, on the west side of Frans Barentsz.
Jan Thomasz, No. 4, on the west side of the guardhouse.
No. 5, on the west side, adjoining it.

       JOANNES DYCKMAN
       JAN VERBEECK
       JAN THOMASZ
       PIETER HARTGERTS
       FRANS BARENTSEN PASTOORS

[200]   Tuesday, April 27, 1655

Present:

J. Dyckman J. Thomasz   Frans Barentsz Pastoors
J. Verbeeck Pieter Hertgertsz

Joannes Dyckman, commissary and officer here, plaintiff, against Abraham Pietersz Vosburgh, defendant.

First, in the matter of a note in the sum of two hundred and fifty guilders in favor of the plaintiff, given by way of compromise for the crimes committed by the defendant, on which, in the presence of his referees, Rutger Jacopsz and Goosen Gerritsz, he promised to pay one half within six weeks and the other half three months later, according to his own request and that of his referees, but which has not yet been paid. The defendant appearing before this honorable court, he is for the reasons alleged by him given additional time to make payment within three weeks from this date, on pain of peremptory execution.

Secondly, the defendant is notified that in so far as he extended his lot contrary to the orders and regulations, he must draw in his lines within forty-eight hours, as otherwise the officer in his official capacity, by order and command of this honorable court, shall have to do so. However, he is warned once more and, if unwilling, [the officer is] to proceed with the execution of the first as well as the second order at the expiration of the periods aforesaid.

Joannes Dyckman, commissary and officer, plaintiff, against Cornelis Vos, defendant.

The defendant, appearing, hands in his defense, stating that he is not guilty of nicknaming the houses and persons, in direct contradiction to the oath of Claes Gerritsz. Whereupon it is decided that the officer must bring in his replication in legal form on the next court day, for the purpose of examining the parties with reference thereto.

[201] Grietgen Nanningh's daughter, plaintiff, against Jan Witmont, defendant, on account of a pewter can with brandy which was stolen, [the plaintiff] requesting the return of her can.

Whereupon it is decided to notify her that this honorable court shall at the first opportunity take care that the aforesaid can be returned to her.

Claes Jacobsz promises to make the payment on account of his lot on the hill within forty-eight hours.

The commissary and officer here, plaintiff, against Jochem Becker, defendant, on account of a pail of good beer found some time ago among the savages in going the rounds, referring to the testimony and declarations of Willem Jansz Stoll and Marcelis Jansz.

Jan Thomasz, plaintiff, against Willem Jansz Schut, defendant.

The plaintiff refers to the testimony and declarations of Arent the Noorman and Marcelis, but during the session of this honorable court the defendant has agreed to serve the plaintiff for two months, a week or two more or less, which will begin on the first of May next.

The honorable magistrates, Jan Verbeeck and Pieter Hertgerts, are appointed and chosen treasurers of this honorable court to receive the excise moneys of the impost master as well as the moneys for the lots which have been granted.

Evert Pels, plaintiff, against Pieter Bronck, defendant, because Pieter Bronck, in spite of the attachment of the property in the hands of Jan van Breemen, has not paid but removed the grain that was attached.

The defendant, that is to say, the plaintiff, refers to the testimony of Arent the Noorman and Marcelis Jansz, who were present in Katskill and whom the plaintiff may cause to be subpoenaed on the next court day.

[202] Femmetgen Albert's daughter, plaintiff, against Jacob Willemsz de Wolff and Gerrit Sleghtenhorst, defendants, the defendants being absent, about a bolting chest which was delivered to the defendants and which she needs and which she delivered to the defendants only at the leasing of the house.

The commissary and officer agrees to notify the defendants that they must return the chest free of costs and charges as they received it and do so immediately.

Maria Jans, wife of Steeven Jansz, is notified that she must promptly pay for the bed sold to the Hon. Pieter Hertgerts, with her consent and notwithstanding the attachment, or else deliver the bed to his honor within the time of three weeks.

The foregoing two pages are by mistake incorrectly entered and are therefore rewritten as follows:

Grietgen Nanning's daughter, plaintiff, against Jan Witmont, defendant, about a pewter can with brandy, which was stolen. Requests that the aforesaid can be returned.

Whereupon it is decided to notify her that this honorable court will at the first opportunity take care that the aforesaid stolen can be returned to her.

Claes Jacobsz promises within forty-eight hours to make the required payment for his lot on the hill.

The commissary and officer here, plaintiff, against Jochem Becker, defendant, about a pail of good beer, found some time ago among the savages by [the guard going] the rounds.

The defendant refers to the testimony and declarations of Willem Jansz Stoll and Marcelis Jansz, who are to be further examined about it.

Jan Thomasz, plaintiff, against Willem Jansz Schut, defendant, about a renewal of contract of service by the same, the defendant [203] to swear to the truth [of his statements]. Said service is alleged to be for the period of four months, commencing at the opening of the trade.

Parties thereupon agree and the defendant promises by hand clasp that he will serve the plaintiff for the period of two months, commencing the first of May next, or a week or two later, provided that he shall receive reasonable wages.

The honorable magistrates, Jan Verbeeck and Pieter Hertgerts, are chosen and appointed treasurers of this honorable court to receive the excise moneys of the impost master as well as the money that is promised and due for the lots that have been granted.

Evert Pels, plaintiff, against Pieter Bronck, defendant, because Pieter Bronck, notwithstanding the three attachments that were issued against the grain in the possession of Jan van Bremen, has not paid, but removed the grain thence. The plaintiff refers for corroberation of his statements to the testimony of Arent Andries and Marcelis Jansz, who being absent, but having been with the plaintiff at Katskil, may again be summoned to appear on the next court day to give further testimony in the matter as is proper.

Femmetgen Albert's daughter, plaintiff, against Jacob Willemsz de Wolff and Gerrit Slechtenhorst, defendants.

Defendants' first default, on account of a bolting chest, delivered to the defendants and which she needs, being delivered by the plaintiff only at the leasing of the house.

The commissary and officer agrees to notify the defendants that they must return the aforesaid bolting chest free of costs and charges as they received it, namely, immediately and as is proper.

[204] Maria Jans, wife of Steeven Jansz, is notified that she must promptly pay within three weeks for the bed sold to the Hon. Pieter Hertgerts, with her consent and in spite of the attachment which was issued, or in default thereof deliver the bed to his honor at the expiration of the aforesaid time.

Extraordinary Session, Tuesday, May 1, 1655 [43]

Present:

| J. Dyckman | J. Thomasz | Frans Barentsz |
| J. Verbeeck | Pieter Hertgerts | Volckart Jansz |

Volckart Jansz, appearing in court, protests against the way they now begin to set off the lot of the poorhouse and requests that a plot may be made thereof upon further inspection.

Pursuant to a letter sent to the honorable court by the honorable supreme council of New Netherland under date of the 11th of April last past, showing that his honor, Volckart Jansz, has been chosen by the honorable supreme court of New Netherland as a magistrate of this court and as associate justice of this bench of justice, in the stead of Jacob Jansz Schermerhoren, who has gone to Holland, [the said Volckart Jansz,] being summoned and the aforesaid order and letter having been read to him, has with some exceptions taken the following oath as magistrate of this honorable court. The oath of Volckart Jansz reads as follows:

---

[43] May 1, 1655, came on a Saturday.

I, Volckart Jansz, chosen by the honorable supreme council of New Netherland as magistrate of this honorable court, to fill the place which has become vacant, promise and swear that as a good and faithful magistrate I shall to the best of my knowledge help this honorable court to administer law and justice, as required. So truly help me God Almighty.

On the date hereof Volckart Jansz took his seat as magistrate of this honorable court and was wished much success therewith.

Jacob Jansz Flodder being arrested for some slanderous words spoken about this honorable court, is notified that next Tuesday at nine o'clock he must take care to appear and at the same time hear the demand and conclusion which the commissary and officer shall make and institute in regard thereto.

Femmetgen Alberts again requesting the return of her bolting chest, she is told that she may have her opponents summoned to appear on Tuesday next.

Rut Jacopsz requesting how much shorter he must make his garden on the west side, he is told that the court when it adjourns shall make a further inspection thereof and show him.

Herman Bastiaensz, surveyor, requests that he may be discharged from his office of surveyor, or properly sustained therein, complaining [206] among other things that Willem Teller has anew moved out his palisades and that others had done likewise.

[The court decides that] he shall be upheld in his capacity of surveyor and that Willem Teller shall be notified that he must before Tuesday next move back the newly set palisades of his garden, on pain of having the honorable court provide therein and have the aforesaid extension taken off.

Abraham Pietersz Vosburgh, appearing before this honorable court, requests that upon paying the fine for which he gave a note to the officer in the sum of fl.250:–, he may be exempt from the obligation to move back the fence of his lot, which is granted him on certain conditions, he to appear before this honorable court on Tuesday next, when, if the court approve of it, the piece of ground that has been added shall be granted anew, if it seems advisable and the court is satisfied therewith.

[207] Tuesday, May 9, 1655 [44]

Present:

J. Dyckman   J. Thomasz   Frans Barentsz
J. Verbeeck   Pieter Hertgerts   Volckert Jansz

A petition was read of Herman Jacobsz of Amsterdam, praying that he may be qualified as beer carrier. Whereupon it is decided to note in the margin that the brewers' helpers thus far perform this work themselves and that for this reason it can not be taken away from them. And as for delivering the bread grain, that there is already a carter to do this.

Joannes Dyckman, commissary and officer here, has delivered to the court a certain replication to the answer filed by Cornelis Vos, which it is decided to place in the hands of the opponent to file his rejoinder thereto on the next court day, to justify himself if he can.

A petition was read of Hendrick Jochemsz, requesting restitution of the one hundred guilders which he advanced to the Hon. General and the honorable members of the Supreme Council, the same to be applied with others toward the payment of duties. Whereupon it is decided that the commissary and officer shall at the first opportunity when he goes to the Manathans take the aforesaid petition with him to promote the restitution through one merchant or another, or else and especially, as he bought therewith some goods of Theunis Tempelier, to promote the settlement or payment thereof, to wit, of the aforesaid one hundred guilders.

And as to his request for permission to build a room as an extension to his house, the commissary and officer shall be given orders to promote that as much as possible.

[208] A petition was read of the bakers of Beverwyck, requesting in the first place that the weight of bread be regulated. Whereupon it is decided to write in the margin that this honorable court will do so at the first opportunity.

---

[44] The date should be May 11, 1655.

As to the abuse that some bakers continue to bake without having taken the oath, this will be prevented as much as possible.

And as to the request that they may form a guild, the honorable members of this court consider this for the present for certain reasons not advisable.

Pieter Bronck, being summoned, is enjoined from tapping strong beer, for the reason that he brews the same, in whatever manner it may be, and on acting contrary hereto he shall the first time forfeit 25 guilders, the second time forfeit 50 guilders and the third time receive arbitrary correction, provided that he shall be permitted to draw the wines which he has now in the cellar according to the gage.

Rut Jacobsz, plaintiff, against Femmetgen Alberts Geverts, defendant, about the sum of about fl.400 which are due to the plaintiff by the defendant according to the account rendered thereof and of which the plaintiff demands payment.

The court having heard the statements and arguments on both sides, order and condemn the defendant, Femmetgen Alberts, to pay the plaintiff each half year, in part payment of the account, the sum of one hundred guilders, promptly, on pain, etc.

Pieter de Vlamingh [the Fleming] requests lot No. 5, toward the hill, of which a further inspection will be made.

[209] Marcelis Jansz and Arent Andriesz, being summoned to appear in court, declare at the request of Evert Pels that they heard from the mouth of Jan van Bremen that [Pieter Bronck] promised to pay Evert, but as the aforesaid person, being here, hid himself, it is decided that in returning from the Manathans they shall, if they please, in passing bring the aforesaid Jan van Bremen with them, in order that he may give an account of himself here before the honorable court.

Claes Jansz, carpenter, and Willem Jansz Stoll declare that they heard Ryndert Pietersz say that he heard from the mouth of Dirrixsz van Bremen that Pieter Bronck had promised to pay Evert Pels, for which reason Evert Pels requests that Jan Dirrixsz van Bremen be summoned to come here at his own expense, if in the wrong, to appear before this honorable court to justify himself, which is granted.

Geurt Hendrixsz, plaintiff, against Philip Pieters Scheuler, defendant, about an interest in a drag net which the defendant bought of Geurt Hendrixsz, whereupon it is decided that in order to learn the truth he may have those who entered the partnership and had an interest in the drag net summoned to appear on the next court day, when the parties will be further examined.

Maria Jans, wife of Steeven Jansz, being summoned by the officer on account of a pewter pint measure which she sold to the Hon. Pieter Hertgerts and which was stolen and given [210] to Jan Witmont and which belonged to Giertgen Bouts, she is notified that she must turn over to the Hon. Pieter Hertgerts what she received therefor in order that the missing pint may be returned free of costs and charges to Giertgen Bouts.

Jan Gauw requesting that he may have the lot which was heretofore granted to Carsten living in the Grenen Bosch and which was not built upon within the proper time, this is granted him on condition that he agree with the officer and satisfy him with regard to the fine to be paid because the lot was not built upon within the stipulated time.

Hendrick Jochemsz is granted permission to have the burghers shoot the target[45] provided he keeps good order and takes care that no accidents occur or result therefrom.

---

[45] *Den papegay te laaten schieten*; a method of target shooting which is described by George McCall Theal, in his *History and Ethnography of Africe south of the Zambesi*, vol. 2, p. 316, as follows: "A figure resembling a parrot, and hence called a *papegaai*, was fixed upon a pole in the center of a circle with a radius of eighteen metres. The marksmen chose their position upon an arc of this circle in the order in which they paid the subscription fees, which were — to residents of Stellenbosch one shilling, and to all others four shillings. They fired in the same order, standing and without rests for their guns. The small prizes were — for knocking off the head four shillings, the right wing two shillings, the left wing one shilling and sixpence, the tail one shilling, and a splinter sixpence. The great prize was given to him who knocked off the rump and by doing so destroyed the whole figure. It was five pounds in cash from the honourable company and whatever subscription money was in hand. The winner was escorted home in state by the whole body of shooters, and had the title of King of the Marksmen until some one else wrest it from him."

Steeven Jansz, plaintiff, against Jan Jansz, defendant, about some money due him for tavern expenses.

The defendant is ordered to pay the plaintiff one-half now or within a month and the other half two months later, promptly, without any exceptions.

Maria Jan, wife of Steeven Jansz, is ordered by this honorable court to suspend tapping in this fort for the period of two weeks from this date, precisely.

The commissary and officer is ordered to pay within the space of forty-eight hours [211] to Jacob Jansz Flodder the sum of fifty-six guilders, being the [half?][46] of what the officer received from the hands of the aforesaid Flodder on account of the late Hendrixsz, but the officer retains nevertheless entire his cause of action on account of his misbehavior in the public street on Saturday last in calling the honorable commissary and some magistrates of the court here bloodhounds and tirants steeped in liquor, for which he may proceed against him when time and opportunity offer themselves.

The court of the colony of Rensselaerswyck learning that the result and outcome of the fight between Steven Jansz and Jacob Hendricksz Maat offers and furnishes them good reasons and motives for being vigilant and watchful with respect to the proper administration of justice according to their bounden duty, the fact in the case being that Steven Jansz was wounded and struck by the aforesaid Jacob Jansz with a knife in his left side in such a way that he is in peril of losing his life and considering that the aforesaid fight took place within the district and jurisdiction of the aforesaid colony, they therefore propose and submit the matter to the honorable court of Fort Orange and Beverwyck with the friendly request, if Jacob Hendricksz above mentioned should happen to stay or sojourn in their honors' jurisdiction, that they would be pleased by legal process to deliver him into the hands of their officer in order that he may take full charge of the case [212] and proceed against his person as shall be

---

[46] The Dutch text has: *tselt.*

found proper according to law, the equity hereof being founded on the reciprocal duty to accommodate [the court of Fort Orange and Beverrwyck] in case a similar situation should present itself on their side, their honors being well aware that this is a mutual obligation resting upon all, especially associated, courts. Whereupon they expect a speedy resolution and answer, since there may be *periculum in mora*. Done at the session of their honors of the aforesaid colony, this 2d of July 1655.[47] Below was written: By order of the same, (signed) A: de Hooges, secretary.

Tuesday, June 8, 1655

Present:

| J: Verbeeck | Sander Leendersz | F^r. Barentsz |
| J: Thomasz | P^r. Hartgers | V^t. Jansz |

Rem Jansz, smith, plaintiff, against Willem Hap, defendant, about the final payment of 550 guilders in beavers, which the defendant still owes on the house bought of the plaintiff, standing in Fort Orange.

The court, having heard the arguments and pleadings on both sides, order the defendant to satisfy and pay the plaintiff the aforesaid sum of 550 guilders acording to the contract of sale within three weeks, or at the latest at the end of the month of June, promptly, without any exception.

Andries de Vos, appearing, requests a copy of the testimony and interrogatories secured and drawn up some time ago by the honorable court.

[213] The impost master, Jacob Hendricksz Maat, being summoned by the honorable court to turn over to the court the third and last payment or term of the amount bid by him at the farming out of the excise here, has done so on his appearance in court, so that he has paid in full what he owed for the excise on wine and beer, from the first term to the last.

---

[47] Thus in the original record. Perhaps a mistake for June 2, 1655.

Same date

Maria Goosens, wife of Steven Jansz, charged with and having confessed to the sale of some brandy to the savages, is ordered to pay a fine of 300 guilders and prohibited from coming into this place for a year and six weeks, and this by way of pardon and intercession in her behalf on the part of the magistrates.

Tuesday, July 13, 1655

Present:

J. de Deckere [48]	S. Leendertsz	F^s. Barentsz
J. Verbeecq	P^r. Hartgers	V^t. Jansz
J. Tomasz		

Johan de Deckere, commissary and officer here, ex officio plaintiff, against Juriaen Jansz, defendant.

The plaintiff states and the truth is that the defendant on the 7th of this current month of July has not hesitated in the presence and hearing of the honorable magistrates, P^r. Harties and Frans Barentsz Pastoor, to denounce in scandalous, villanous and contemptuous terms the ordinance against going into the woods to trade, published on the first of July last, and to speak of it in such a way as if the magistrates of this court were thereby trying to reserve the entire trade to themselves; also, to make the aforesaid gentlemen, and hence the entire court, [214] out to be and to call them so to speak before the whole world asses, who were incapable of carrying out the provisions of their placards and ordinances against those who violated them, all of which are matters of serious consequence in a well regulated country where justice and government prevail, which ought not to be suffered, but severely punished.

---

[48] Johannes de Deckere was appointed on June 21, 1655, presiding commissary at Fort Orange, *vice* Joannes Dyckman, in accordance with a resolution of the Director General and Council of New Netherland of June 16, 1655. See *New York Colonial Manuscripts*, vol. 6, p. 57 and 59.

Therefore, the plaintiff, in his capacity aforesaid, demands that the defendant shall be condemned to withdraw his statements here in court and furthermore, bareheaded, with folded hands and on bended knees pray God and the court and the aforesaid two honorable magistrates for forgiveness, declaring that he is heartily sorry and promising that he will nevermore in the future do the same, nor anything like it, and that in addition he shall be condemned to pay for the benefit of the plaintiff the sum of six hundred guilders, with costs, or such other amount, etc.

The honorable members of this court having heard the verbal testimony of the defendant, condemn him to declare publicly that he spoke ill and that he is heartily sorry about it and further condemn him to pay for the benefit of the officer the sum of eighty guilders, to be paid within twenty-four hours, on pain of being apprehended. One-third hereof is set aside for the poor.

[215] Idem, plaintiff, against Willem Bout, defendant.

He demands condemnation in a fine of [blank] guilders because the defendant on the fourth of July last, on Sunday evening, after the ringing of the bell, continued to serve and tap liquor, etc.

Remitted.

Idem, plaintiff, against [blank]

He demands ut supra, because the defendant after the aforesaid time sat drinking.

Ut supra.

Idem, plaintiff, against [blank]

He demands ut supra because ut supra.

Ut supra.

[216] Tomas Clabbort, plaintiff against The[u]nis Jacobsz, defendant.

He demands condemnation in the sum of fl.2270:–, on account of the purchase of certain grain, less the amount that has been paid, etc.

The honorable court having heard the parties and also Andries de Vos, who interposed and undertook to carry on the defense for the defendant, and having taken into consideration all that is to be considered in the matter, condemn the aforesaid defendant and Andries de Vos, each *in solido* to tender and pay the aforesaid sum of fl.2270:–, less the amount that has been paid, provided that one paying, the other shall be released, without prejudice to the cause of action for damages which the defendant and the interposer think they have against Mr Renselaer and his associates, for various reasons, Actum ut supra.

[217] Marcelis Jansz, plaintiff, against Corn. Pot, defendant, for the sum of fl.1101:2:–, for tavern expenses.

The magistrates condemn the defendant to pay the amount asked within the space of fourteen days.

Marcelis Jansz, farmer of the wine excise, jointly with the officer, plaintiffs, against Daniel Verwegen, defendant.

He demands that the defendant be condemned to pay a fine of five hogsheads of wine, or the value thereof. Also that a certain hogshead of wine, which on the 23d of May last was removed by the defendant without a permit, be declared confiscated, or [the defendant be condemned] to pay the value thereof, or other penalty, etc.

The court, having heard the parties on both sides and taken everything into consideration, declare the hogshead of wine, which according to his own confession was removed by the defendant on the 23d of May last, confiscated, provided that the defendant may redeem the same for the sum of eighty guilders. The second demand is denied.

Volkert Jansz and P^r. Hartgers, magistrates, cause it to be noted in connection with the aforesaid sentence that it was decreed against their advice, it being on the contrary their opinion that the defendant ought to be absolved, provided he declare that the aforesaid hogshead is the same as that which he entered on the 15th of May aforesaid at the farmer's office.

[218] Theunis Jacobsz, plaintiff, against Andries de Vos, defendant.

He demands that the defendant be condemned to indemnify him, the plaintiff, with reference to the judgment heretofore demanded by Tommas Clabbort against the plaintiff.

The defendant agrees to carry on the defense for the plaintiff.

Whereas it is said that Gerrit Banker through a certain savage let some other savages with their beavers come into his house, and Rut Jacobsz, Jacob Teunisz, Evert Wendel and Philip P^{rsz}. were then near there, they, being subpoenaed to testify to the truth for the benefit of the commissary and officer here, in his official capacity, have deposed and declared as follows:

Ruth Jacobsz declares that he asked of the said savage, and Philip P^{rsz}. and Jacob Teunisz that they heard [him ask], whether the said savage had traded with certain savages, whereupon the aforesaid savage said, Yes.

The aforesaid Philip P^{rsz}. and Evert Wendel declare in addition that the said savage came out of the house of the said Philip P^{rsz}. and that the said savage spoke to them and picked up a certain package of beavers belonging to them and went away with it, whereupon all the other savages speaking to the first savage followed him and together were seen to enter the house of Gerrit Banker.

[219] Interogatories upon which at the request of Johan de Deckere, commissary and officer here, are to be heard and examined under oath Tomas Paulw, Willem Teljer and Symon Leen, all being summoned to testify to the truth.

First, to ask the deponents' ages.

Tomas Paulw declares that he is 54 years old; Willem Teljer 39, and Symon Leen 34 years.

Secondly, whether on Wednesday last, the 7th of this month of July, they did not

They declare, Yes.

hear and see that a dispute and quarrel arose between Jochim, the baker, and Gerrit Slechtenhorst, about the piling up of some wood?

Likewise, whether immediately after the said persons did not each pick up an ax and take hold of it to hack each other and whether this was not prevented and stopped by the intervention of the deponents?

They declare that the said persons each took up an ax, but that they were stopped and prevented [from using them] and that Jochim, the baker, was the first to take up the ax.

Fourthly, whether he, Jochim, the baker, after the said separation, did not run home and returning with a naked sword in the hand made for the aforesaid Slechtenhorst?

They declare, Yes.

[220] Fifthly, whether the said Slechtenhorst, seeing this, did not retreat to the house of the aforesaid Tomas Paulw, but was followed into the said house and whether the said Jochim, being seized by the said Tomas Paulw, let him take the sword, or gave it to him, or both?

Tomas Paulw and Symon Leen declare, Yes. Willem Hil says that he knows nothing about it.

Sixthly,[49] whether the said Slechtenhorst, seeing the said Jochim without sword, did not begin to fight with the said Jochim in the house of the aforenamed Tomas Poulw and whether the said Jochim in the

Symon Leen declares that things took place as stated.

Tomas Poulw declares that he saw the said persons fight in his house.

Willem Teljer declares that he knows nothing about it.

---

[49] The original has "Fifthly," by mistake.

course of the struggle and while the said Slechtenhorst lay underneath did not tear at his male organs in a scandalous way, causing him to yell and scream?

Whether the said Jochim, being threatened by Symon Leen to have his hand cut off if he did not stop tearing at the aforesaid improper place, was not somewhat frightened and disturbed thereby, got up and ran home through the bakery, out of the back part of the house?

[221] Whether they, the witnesses, did not also see that the said Slechtenhorst then also ran home and returned with a naked cutlass, challenging the aforesaid Jochim to fight with him to the death, or to see who would be the bravest?

And what else followed after that?

Symon Leen declares as stated.

Tomas Paulw declares that he saw the said Jochim run away.

Willem Teljer declares that he knows nothing about it.

Symon Leen and Tomas Poulw declare as stated.

Willem Teljer declares that he saw the said Slechtenhorst come with a naked sword.

They declare that Jochim, the baker, then ran away and the said Slechtenhorst returned home.

Thus done and deposed on the date above written.

There appeared before the honorable magistrates Claes Gerritsz and declared that in satisfaction of a certain judgment of the honorable court given under date of the 12th of May 1654 in favor of Rut Jacobsz for the restitution of the 20 beavers belonging to Brant van Slechtenhorst which are in his custody, he specially binds his house and lot and furthermore his person and property, nothing excepted, submitting them to the control of all courts and judges. Actum ut supra.

[222] There was read a petition presented by Jochim, the baker, Jacob Willemsz, Tomas Paulw and Daniel Ringhaut, bakers, on which was entered and given the following apostil:

The magistrates hereby prohibit and forbid the petitioners to put any sugar, currants, raisins, or prunes in any bread which they bake and hence to sell the same, on pain of forfeiting fifty guilders for the benefit of the officer. Actum ut supra.

Wednesday, July 14, [1655]

Present:

Omnibus.

Johan de Deckere, commissary and officer here, ex officio plaintiff, against Jochim, the baker, defendant.

The plaintiff says and declares it to be the truth that the defendant on the 7th of July last tried to attack and wound the person of Gerrit Slechtenhorst with an ax, and being prevented from doing so, ran after him and pursued him with a naked sword into the house of Tomas Paulw; also that he fought with him there and tore at the male organs of said Slechtenhorst in a very scandalous way, trying to mutilate and ruin him, being only prevented from so doing by threats, whereby, in addition to disturbance of the public peace, also private injury and violence has been committed against the person and in the house of the aforesaid Tomas Paulw;

The plaintiff, therefore, in his capacity aforesaid, demands that the defendant [223] be condemned to pay a fine of one thousand guilders.

The defendant requests a copy of the demand together with a copy of the interrogatories.

The same, plaintiff, against Gerrit Banker, Herman [Vetter?].[50]

---

[50] Harmen Vedder?

The plaintiff says that it is the truth that the defendant lately, though a certain savage, has not hesitated to entice some other savages to come with their beavers into his house, contrary to the ordinance issued against it.

The plaintiff, ex officio, as above, therefore demands that the defendant be fined three hundred guilders and in addition be suspended from the exercise of his trade for the period of one year, all in accordance with the ordinance aforesaid, or [that the court impose such] other penalty [as it may see fit].

The magistrates having given the defendants the privilege to deny the charges upon oath and they remaining thus far in default, have nevertheless granted them time until the next court day to take the oath, on pain of being condemned to pay the fines and penalties provided by the ordinance. Meanwhile the defendants are prohibited and enjoined from carrying on any trade or barter with the savages until Tuesday next.

[224] Jacob Hap, appearing before the court, requests an apostil on his petition presented heretofore, namely, praying for permission and consent to purchase of the native Indians a small piece of land situated [blank].

It is decided to postpone the matter until the return of the honorable general and to notify him that in case consent is given, he shall be the first and next person.

Monsieur Jan de Hulter appearing before the court requests letters of recommendation to the honorable council in New Netherland, in order that they may be pleased to pass and to cause to be published a certain ordinance to inhibit, restrain and control the insolence, opposition and disobedience of his servants in particular and others in general.

It is decided to communicate and recommend this to the honorable council.

[225] Tuesday, July 20, 1655

Presentibus omnibus
preter Sander Leendertz

Interrogatories on which at the request of Johan de Deckere, commissary and officer here, ex officio, are to be heard and examined under oath Rut Jacobsz, Jan Daret, Philips P^{rsz}., Goosen Gerritsz and Andries Jacobsz, all subpoenaed by the court to testify to the truth.

First, whether they, the deponents, on Friday last, did not hear a certain savage acknowledge, confess and affirm that without any previous gift [on his part] he had received as a present from Catelyn Sanders, wife of Sander Leendertsz, a piece of cloth, then shown by him and thrown around his body? — They declare accordingly.

Whether the said savage did not declare also that he still had all his beavers and that before [leaving] he would first trade with the said Catelyn? — Declare as above.

Whether the said savage did say also that he would receive some more presents and what they were? — They declare as above and that he would receive in addition to the piece of cloth a piece of linen and stockings.

[226] What else they can testify to in this matter? — They declare that they know nothing more about it.

Johan de Deckere, commissary and officer here, ex officio plaintiff, against Catelyn Sanders, wife of Sander Leendertsz, defendant.

He demands that the defendant be fined three hundred guilders and suspended from her business for a year and six weeks, in view of the fact that she has recently, or last week, undertaken to give or donate a piece of cloth to a certain savage, contrary to the ordinance issued against the making of presents, or such other penalty, etc.

The defendant admits that she gave the savage a piece of cloth, but that she received from him first two beavers and then a lynx coat.

The plaintiff persists in his demand by way of replication.

The defendant persists by way of rejoinder.

The plaintiff asks that the defendant make oath.

The magistrates order the defendant to declare under oath that she received as present from the aforesaid savage first two beavers and then a lynx coat and that in return therefor she gave the said savage a piece of cloth.

The defendant took the oath.

[227] The same, plaintiff, against Jacob Backer, defendant and prisoner.

The plaintiff says and the truth is that the defendant last Friday did not hesitate to declare openly and in so many Dutch words that the sentence, meaning and referring to the sentence passed last Tuesday against Daniel Vervelen, was a false sentence; and whereas this is an intollerable wrong and flagrant insult to the honorable magistrates of this court, whom the plaintiff in virtue of his office ought to and is bound to defend;

Therefore, the plaintiff demands that the defendant and prisoner be condemned to make honorable and profitable amends for this wrong; honorable [amends], by appearing in court and there, bareheaded, with folded hands and on bended knees praying God and the court for forgiveness and acknowledging that the said words thoughtlessly escaped him and consequently, that he is heartily sorry; and profitable [amends], by paying for the benefit of the plaintiff the sum of six hundred guilders, or some other amount.

The defendant denies the charges.

The plaintiff persists.

The same, plaintiff, against Jochim, the baker.

The defendant to reply.

The defendant answers promptly in writing.

The plaintiff persists by way of replication.

The defendant by way of rejoinder requests copies of the plaintiff's evidence.

Pieter Ryverdingh, plaintiff, against Huybert Jansz, defendant, for payment of the sum of fl. 53:3:— on account of the purchase of a barrel of Holland beer.

The defendant admits the debt and requests eight days' delay.

The court gives judgment for the plaintiff and grants the requested delay.

Johan de Deckere, commissary and officer here, ex officio plaintiff, against Gerrit Banker, to testify in accordance with the order made on the last court day.

The defendant refuses to make oath.

The plaintiff therefore demands that he be condemned to pay the fines and penalties provided by the ordinance.

The court allows the defendant eight days' time to make the said declaration under oath, on pain as stated in the previous order. Meanwhile, the defendant is prohibited from doing any trading or bartering with the savages.

[229] There was read a petition of Teunis Corn[elisz] van Vechten, praying that he might be authorized and have the privilege to drive the cart, to the exclusion of others.

It is decided to defer the matter until the home coming of the honorable general and, in case the going around with the cart be granted to any one in particular, to procure that he shall be the first one in line for the position. Done, the 20th of July 1655.

Tuesday, July 27, 1655

Johan de Deckere, commissary and officer here, ex officio plaintiff, against Gerrit Slechtenhorst, defendant.

The plaintiff says and declares it to be the truth that the defendant on the 7th of July last ventured first to pick and start a quarrel with Jochim Wesselsz, the baker, then to threaten him with an ax, and afterwards to fight with said Jochim, the baker, in the house of Tomas Paulw, and on being separated from him by others, to pursue the said Jochim with a naked cutlass in his hand and to strike with the said cutlass against the transom bar of the door of the said Tomas Paulw, thereby, in addition to the public disturbance committing private injury and violence against the person and house of the aforesaid Tomas Paulw;

Therefore, the plaintiff demands that the defendant be condemned to pay a fine of six hundred guilders, or some other penalty, etc.

The defendant obtains a copy of the demand.

Idem, plaintiff, against Jochim Wessels, baker, defendant, to produce his evidence and desist from producing [further testimony].

The defendant agrees to submit all his evidence on the next court day and then to desist from further production [of evidence].

Idem, plaintiff, against Gerrit Bancker, defendant, to take the oath in conformity to the order of the preceding session of the court, on pain as stated therein.

The defendant says that as yet he is not willing to take the oath.

The plaintiff requests consequently that defendant be condemned to pay the fines and penalties provided by the ordinance referred to and mentioned in the aforesaid order.

The magistrates, seeing that the defendant not only remains in default, but openly in court refuses to take the oath, condemn the defendant to pay a fine of three hundred guilders and prohibit the defendant from doing any trading or bartering with the savages for the period of an entire year.

Idem, plaintiff, against Marcelis Jansz, defendant, because the defendant on Sunday last served or continued to serve drinks during divine service.

Demands that the defendant be fined six guilders in accordance with the ordinance.

The magistrates condemn the defendant to pay a fine of four guilders.

[231] Idem, plaintiff, against Willem Jansz Stoll. Demands that the defendant be fined three guilders because he sat drinking last Sunday during divine service at the house of Marcelis Jansz.

The defendant admits having been at the house of Marcelis Jansz aforesaid, but denies that he was drinking. Agrees voluntarily to pay the fine, which, however, for certain reasons will be refunded to him.

Robbert Vastrick, plaintiff, against Abram Pietersz, defendant, for the sum of sixty guilders and six stivers, according to his note. Demands therefore that the defendant be ordered to pay the amount.

The defendant admits the debt.

The plaintiff requests judgment against the defendant.

The magistrates condemn the defendant to pay the amount asked in beavers, according to the note and his admission made in court.

Abram Pietersz Vosburgh, plaintiff, against Pouwels Lammertsz, defendant, requesting that the defendant be ordered to serve the plaintiff six consecutive days, commencing on this date.

The magistrates, having heard both parties, condemn the defendant in the sum of twenty-four guilders, or otherwise, at his choice and option, to the aforesaid six days' service, to commence tomorrow.

Steven Jansz, plaintiff, against Willem Hofmeyer. Default.

Idem, plaintiff, against Claes Wip, defendant. Default.

Idem, plaintiff, against Jan Gou, defendant. Default.

Appeared before this honorable court, Frans Barentsz Pastoor, our fellow servant, and declared that he offered himself as surety for Pieter Bronck for the benefit of Ca[r]sten and Meyndert, the smiths, for the recovery of eleven and a half beavers, belonging to them and in the custody of Louris Jansz, he, the surety, promising to release the said Ca[r]sten and Meyndert from all damage and claims, binding therefor his person, etc. Done on the date above written, in the presence of the undersigned magistrates.

FRANS BARENTSZ PASTOORS

[233] Tuesday, August 24 [1655]

Present:

| J. de Deckere | Sander Leendertsz | Frans Barentsz |
| Rutger Jacobsz | Andries Herpertsz | Volkert Jansz |

According to the notice received from the honorable general and the honorable supreme council, upon the nomination made by this honorable court, there were chosen, in the place of the retiring magistrates, Jan Verbeeck and P^r. Hertgers, whose term has expired, Rutger Jacobsz, Andries Herpertsz and Dirck Jansz Croon as extraordinary magistrate, of whom the two ordinary magistrates (Dirck Jansz Croon being away from home, or absent), after being summoned by the court, have taken the following oath of fidelity before the commissary:

We, the undersigned, in the capacity of chosen magistrates of the bench of justice of Fort Orange and Beverwyck, promise and swear hereby that together with our fellow magistrates we shall help to administer law and justice between man and man and according to the best of our knowledge and ability help to maintain and execute the same; also in all respects to conduct ourselves loyally and faithfully toward the honorable States General of the United Netherlands, the honorable directors and patroons of this New Netherland province and the honorable general and council residing in New Amsterdam. So truly help us God Almighty.

On this date the oath was taken by Rutger Jacobsz and on the 26th by Andries Herpertsz and they were wished much success.

And on the 20th of September the oath was taken by Dirck Jansz Croon.

[234] Johan de Deckere, officer here, ex officio plaintiff, against Gerrit Slechtenhorst, defendant, to make answer.

The defendant promptly makes answer in writing.

Idem, plaintiff, against Jochim Wesselsz, baker, defendant, to submit all his evidence in accordance with the promise made on the last court day, and to desist from introducing further evidence.

Default.

Thursday, August 26, [1655]

Present:

R. Jacobsz   S. Leendertsz   V. Jansz
Andries Herpertsz   Frans Barentsz

Johan de Deckere, commissary and officer here, ex officio plaintiff, against Gertruyt Nanninghs, defendant, about the fine of 6 guilders because the defendant served liquor on the day of prayer.

Default. Fine remitted.

Pieter Ryverdingh, messenger, coming before the court, requests that he may draw and receive the sum of fifty guilders out of the excise money.

The request being approved, it is decided to give him an order or the farmer of the excise.

[235] Tuesday, November 23, 1655

Presentibus omnibus
preter R. Jacobsz

Pieter Lokermans demands of Claes Hendrixse restitution of ten beavers promised by him for a certain lot and consequently release from the obligation to purchase the same.

The defendant says that he is not bound to return the beavers, as it was unnecessary for him to deliver the ground brief to the plaintiff as soon as the river was open.

The court, having heard the parties, denies the plaintiff his demand and orders the defendant to fulfil his promise.

A petition is read of Ludovicus Cobes, requesting permission to keep day and evening school.

The petitioner's request is granted.

Upon the request of Jochim, the baker, presented in the form of a petition, namely, that the straw roof of the house of Willem Juriaensz may be condemned and he be ordered, on account of the danger involved, to cover the same with boards instead, the petitioner's request is granted and it is furthermore decided that the aforesaid Willem Juriaensz shall be ordered and urged to effect the same within eight, or at the longest within fourteen days.

After deliberation it is decided, in default of a sufficient supply of money, to take out of the excise money the sum of two hundred guilders to be used in this juncture of time for necessary purposes.

Tuesday, November 30, 1655

Johan de Deckere, commissary and officer here, ex officio plaintiff, against Jochim, the baker, defendant, to present as yet his evidence and to waive the right to produce further testimony.

The defendant submits his evidence.

The court orders the witnesses to be reexamined.

Idem, plaintiff, against Gerrit Slechtenhorst, defendant, to proceed with the case. The parties rest and submit no further evidence, requesting decision and sentence.

The court condemns the defendant to pay a fine of twenty-five guilders and costs.

The defendant states that he intends to appeal.

[236] Idem, plaintiff, against Jacob Hap, defendant.

He demands that the defendant be fined 300 guilders for

having now about three weeks ago ventured to injure and wound the person of Dirk van Hamel severily in the head with a mug.

The defendant admits the charge brought against him by the plaintiff.

The plaintiff asks that sentence be pronounced.

The court condemns the defendant to pay a fine of thirty guilders.

Idem, plaintiff, against the same defendant.

He demands that a fine of one hundred guilders be imposed because the defendant recently threw a knife, wounding his servant, Isaack Floris in the shoulder.

The defendant says that the act was committed in haste.

The court condemn the defendant to pay a fine of twenty guilders.

Idem, plaintiff, against the wife of Willem Bout,[51] defendant.

He demands that she be fined six guilders for having last Sunday served liquor or entertained company during divine service, contrary to the ordinance issued against it.

The court condemn the defendant to pay the fine requested.

Volckert Jansz asks to have it noted that the aforesaid sentence was passed contrary to his advice.

Pieter Ryverdingh, plaintiff, against Jan Gou, defendant.
Default.

Idem, plaintiff, against Poulus the Noorman.
Default.

Johan de Deckere, commissary and officer here, appears and declares that he appeals from the above sentence pronounced against Jacop Hap to the honorable director general and council of New Netherland, serving notice that he will submit his grievances and prosecute his appeal there and in such way as he shall see fit.

[237] Johan de Deckere, commissary and officer here, ex officio plaintiff, against Jannitge Jans, wife of Adriaen Dircksz Vries, at present a prisoner, defendant.

---

[51] Geertruyt Nanninghs.

The plaintiff says that it is the truth that the prisoner has not hesitated on the 26th of September last, being Sunday, to sell brandy to a certain savage, contrary to the placard and ordinance issued against it.

He demands therefore, in the name of the supreme authorities of this province, the honorable director general and council of New Netherland, that the prisoner shall be brought to the place where it is customary to execute justice and that she shall there be publicly exposed at the whipping post and be punished with the rod; furthermore, that all her property shall be declared forfeited for the benefit of the officer, that she shall be forever banished from this country and be condemned to pay the costs and expenses of the trial.

The court, having heard the confession of the prisoner, administering justice and preferring leniency to the rigor of justice, condemn the prisoner to be publicly exhibited at the whipping post, the rod being suspended above her head; declare her property, if she has any, forfeited for the benefit of the officer, and order her, as soon as the river is open, to leave this province forever, on pain of incurring heavier punishment, and condemn her to pay the costs and expenses of the trial. Thus passed on the sixth of November in the presence of all the magistrates and pronounced on the first of December following; present, the commissary and all the magistrates.

J. DE DECKERE
1655
SANDER LENRSENE
FRANS BARENTSZ PASTOORS
VOLCKART JANSZ
ANDRIES HERBERTS
DIRCK JANSEN CROON

[238] Tuesday, December 7, 1655

Presentibus omnibus
preter Volkert Jansz

Johan de Deckere, commissary and officer here, ex officio plaintiff, against Hendrick Jochimsz, defendant.

He demands a fine of fl. 12:0: because the defendant on Sunday last, in the fore and after noon, has entertained company, contrary to the ordinance issued against it.

The court, having heard the parties on both sides, condemn the defendant to pay the fine asked.

Idem, plaintiff, against Herman Bamboes, defendant.

He demands a fine of fl.6:0, for reasons as above.

The court *ut supra*.

Appeared in court Jacob Willemsz, baker, and Willem Jansz Schut, being subpoenaed to testify to the truth, and declared under solemn oath at the request of Johan de Deckere, commissary and officer here, that it is true that they, in the month of July last, were present at the house of Tomas Paul, when Jochim, the baker, and Gerrit Slechtenhorst were fighting and that they consequently saw that the said Jochem several times tore at the male organs of the said Slechtenhorst and that he, Jacob Willemsz, forced said Jochim's hand away from the said place and that they afterwards heard the said Jochim say that he would have torn them, meaning the said instrument with its appendix, from his body, if he had not been prevented therefrom. So truly may Almighty God help the deponents. *Actum ut supra*.

Idem, plaintiff, against Jochem, the baker, defendant, requesting sentence, the order of the last court day being complied with.

The court, having heard the arguments and defense on both sides, having examined the documents respectively submitted and having taken into consideration all that is to be considered, condemn the defendant to pay a fine of one hundred guilders and costs.

[239] Appeared in court Tomas Paul, Jacob Willemsz and Hans Coenraets, and declared at the request as above, by true words, in the place of an oath, that it is true that on Saturday last, to the house of the aforesaid Jacob Willemsz came the wife of Carsten the Noorman, having in her hands two round sugar cookies and saying, on being asked, that she had obtained or bought them at the house of Jochim, the baker; also, that some time thereafter there came out of the house of Jochem, the baker, a certain savage, carrying an oblong sugar bun, which he said he had likewise obtained or bought at the house aforesaid. All of which they offer, if need be and required, to confirm by oath. *Actum ut supra.*

Marcelis Jansz, plaintiff, for the attachment of certain house rent amounting to the sum of about fl. 130:–, in the custody of Claes Hendrixse, belonging to Jacob Adriaensz, wheelwright, defendant.

He demands security in the amount of fl. [blank], for tavern expenses and beer furnished, etc.

The court decrees the attachment.

J. DE DECKERE
1656
FRANS BARENTSEN PASTOORS
RUTGER JACOBSZ
ANDRIES HERBERTS
DIRCK JANSEN CROON

[240] Tuesday, December 14, 1655

Presentibus omnibus preter V. Jansz

Johan de Deckere, commissary and officer here, plaintiff, against Claes Hendrixse, defendant, for the fine of fl. 1:10:–, because the defendant eight days ago in the evening, after the ringing of the bell, was found sitting in the tavern of Herman

Bamboes, contrary to the ordinance made about this, for which see.

The court condemn the defendant to pay the fine and costs.

Domine Gedeon Schaets requests in the name of Paulus Schrick payment by Gerrit Slechtenhorst of the sum of fl. 100:–, belonging to Femmitge Aelbrechts, for which he offers to give security.

The court, having heard both parties, orders Gerrit Slechtenhorst to turn over and pay the requested one hundred guilders to Domine Schaets, under security for their restitution if it should be found to be proper.

Goossen Gerritsz, plaintiff, against Herman, the brewer,[52] defendant. Default.

Dirck Bentsingh, plaintiff, against Michiel Ryckertsz, defendant.

He demands the restitution of fl. 250:–, received by the defendant on account of the sale of a certain lot, which the defendant is now unable to deliver in accordance with the provisions of the contract.

The court order the defendant to return the requested fl.250:– to the plaintiff.

Johan de Deckere, ex officio plaintiff, against Jochem, the baker, defendant, for a fine of fl. 50:–, because the defendant last Saturday sold to a certain savage a sugar bun, contrary to the ordinance passed on that subject.

The defendant is willing to pay the fine, provided the charge be proved.

The plaintiff agrees to prove the same.

[241] There appeared in court Domine Gedeon Schaets and declared that he offered himself as surety and principal for the restitution of the one hundred guilders which Gerrit Slechtenhorst has heretofore been ordered to pay for the benefit of P. Schrik,

---

[52] Harmen Harmensen Gansevoort?

promising to release the said Slechtenhorst from all further claims, binding himself thereto as by law provided.

GIDEON SCHAETS
J. DE DECKERE
1656
FRANS BARENTSEN PASTOORS
RUTGER JACOBSZ
ANDRIES HERBERTS
DIRCK JANSEN CROON

Tuesday, January 18, 1656

Presentibus omnibus

Jan Hendrixse, plaintiff, against Jan Baptist van Renselaer, defendant.

He requests compensation for a certain sow run over by the defendant's horse, valued at the sum of four beavers, or so much more or less as the magistrates or honest people shall consider proper.

The court refers the parties to Goosen Gerritsz and Philip P^{rsz}. Schuyler, referees.

Tomas Chambers, plaintiff, against Jacob Hap, defendant. Default.

Roelof Jacobsz, plaintiff, against Maerten, the farmer, defendant and prisoner.

He demands payment of the sum of fl. 11:2:— due for tavern expenses.

Default.

Johan de Deckere, commissary and officer, demands a fine of sixteen guilders for violation of the ordinance against sleighing.

The court holds the matter under consideration.

[242] Johan de Deckere, commissary and officer here, ex officio plaintiff, against Willem Teller, defendant.

He demands that the defendant be arbitrarily mulcted for having fought a week ago last Sunday with Tierk Claesz.

The defendant agrees to compound with the officer. The officer accepts.

Idem, plaintiff, against Jan van Housen, defendant. Default.
Idem, plaintiff, against Tierk Claesz, defendant. Default.
Idem, plaintiff, against Jan van Bremen, defendant. Default.
Idem, plaintiff, against Piet Bont, defendant. Default.

Frans Barentsz, our fellow member of the board, having shown to us that except at his great discomfort, loss and inconvenience he is no longer able to attend to and take up the monthly collection ordered by the Honorable Director General Petrus Stuyvesant, he requests therefore that with respect to said duties in connection with his office of deacon he may now be relieved and that such other person as the court shall deem fit may be appointed and substituted in his place.

The court, having weighed the reasons of the aforesaid Pastoor, order and hereby request the person of Evert Wendel to take up the aforesaid collection in the stead of the said Frans Barentsz, together with Willem Tellier, and to allow himself to be employed therein. *Actum ut supra.*

J. DE DECKERE

1656

[243] At the request of Thomas Chambers, he is granted and ceded a lot for a house, in width, front and rear, ten rods and eight feet; in length, twelve rods and eleven feet; adjoining to the north Abram Pietersz Vosburch, to the south Claes Hendrixse, and to the west the wagon road; therefore, a lot for two gardens is included herein.

Frans Barentsz Pastoor asks to have a note made in connection herewith that he does not approve of granting the aforesaid request any further than to the third post of the lot and fence of Abram Vosburch.

> J. DE DECKERE
> 1656
> FRANS BARENTSEN PASTOORS
> VOLCKART JANSZ
> RUTGER JACOBSZ
> ANDRIES HERBERTS
> DIRCK JANSEN CROON

Tuesday, February 1, 1656

Presentibus omnibus
preter S. Leendertsz

Tomas Chambers, plaintiff, against Jacob Hap, defendant.

He requests that the defendant according to his promise made on the last of December last past before the members of both the courts, take the oath.

The defendant requests eight days' time in order meanwhile to gather additional testimony.

Arent Vogel, plaintiff, against Jan van Bremen, defendant.

He demands the sum of fl. 1800:— as compensation for damages which the plaintiff suffered through the defendant's failure to haul logs for him, the plaintiff, according to his promise and verbal agreement, or at least, to haul as many as the defendant agreed to and was bound to haul.

The parties agree to get together their evidence.

[244] Pieter Ryverdingh in the capacity of attorney of Steven Jansz, plaintiff, against Jacob de Looper, defendant.

He demands and requests condemnation in the sum of fl. 34:18, due for tavern expenses according to the book.

The defendant admits the debt and requests that execution be deferred for three weeks.

The court orders the defendant to pay the fl. 34:18 demanded and defers the executions according to the request.

Idem, plaintiff in the capacity aforesaid, against Jan Gou. He demands payment of the sum of fl.35:4:— for expenses as above.

The defendant admits the debt and agrees to pay within the time of two months.

The court gives judgment for the plaintiff and allows six weeks delay.

Idem, plaintiff, against Willem Hofmeyer, defendant. Demands judgment for fl. 20:16, by balance of accounts, on account of expenses as above.

The defendant claims that he settled with Mary Goossens and therefore does not owe as much. He agrees to prove it.

Idem, plaintiff, against Poulus Maertens, defendant. Default.

The officer demands a fine of sixteen guilders for violation of the attachment. The court takes the matter under advisement.

Idem, plaintiff, against Abram Pietersz Vosburch, defendant. Default.

[245] Frans Barentsz Pastoor, plaintiff, against the same defendant. Default.

Johan de Deckere, ex officio plaintiff, against Tierck Claesen, defendant.

He demands that the defendant be fined sixteen guilders for having fought last Sunday with Willem Tellier and killed a goat of Sander Leendertsz.

The court, having heard the defendant's confession, condemns him to pay a fine of two and a half beavers.

Idem, plaintiff, against the same defendant, for having been found last Sunday in the company of the Lutherans, performing divine service, contrary to the ordinance issued against it. Demands therefore that he be fined fl. 6.

The court, having heard the confession of the defendant, condemns him to pay the fine demanded.

Idem, plaintiff, against Hendrick Jochemsz, defendant.

He demands that the defendant be fined six guilders for having Sunday a week ago continued to serve liquor during divine service.

The court, having heard parties on both sides, condemn the defendant to pay the fine asked.

Idem, plaintiff, against Jan van Bremen, defendant. He demands that the defendant be fined fl. 300, for having in the month of May last past wounded the person of Hans Vos with a carving knife.

The court refer the parties to two referees, one to be chosen by each.

[246] Idem, plaintiff, against Jochem, the baker, defendant, to proceed with the case.

The defendant persists in his former statement that he is satisfied to pay the fine, provided the crime be proved.

The plaintiff agrees to do so.

Idem, plaintiff, against Jacob Hap, defendant. He demands that the defendant be fined fl. 100 for having last week scandalously beaten and wounded his wife and thrown firebrands at her, so that the sparks or embers flew through the partition door into the plaintiff's residence.

The defendant acknowledges that he beat his wife and drew blood.

The court are of opinion that the defendant is not punishable for it as it happened between man and wife.

Idem, plaintiff, against Hendrick Jansz, the cowherd, defendant.

He demands that the defendant be put in irons and arbitrarily punished, because the defendant is suspected of having made and distributed some notorious lampoons, or pasquils.

The defendant admits having composed or helped to compose a lampoon or little verse, without having, as he says, injured any one's honor or reputation.

The court order the defendant to be provisionally put in irons and held for further examination.

Jochem, the baker, has promised in court to satisfy the officer at the latest before Easter in regard to the fine of one hundred guilders which he was condemned to pay on the 7th of December 1655.

[247] Resolved that on Thursday next every one must bring in his account as to what is due him on account of wages and materials furnished for the fort, the block house and its appurtenances, as well as to what was contributed by him toward presents for the Indians and the ransom of prisoners from the Esopus. Also that on the date aforesaid the building and completion of the aforesaid block house and the appurtenances thereof will be publicly let to the lowest bidder.

The commissary and officer, Johan de Deckere, requests that for so far as he is exercising the duties of secretary here, he may on that account and for the keeping of the minutes or court proceedings receive for each part of the work a reasonable salary and this provisionally.

The foregoing request being examined, it is flatly rejected by Rut Jacobsz and Volckert Jansz and laid aside by the other members of the court until the arrival of Mr Stuyvesant.

J. DECKERE

1656

SANDER LENRSE
FRANS BARENTSZ PASTOORS
VOLCKART JANSZ
RUTGER JACOBSZ
ANDRIES HERBERTS
DIRCK JANSEN CROON

Tuesday, February 8, 1656

Presentibus omnibus

Pieter Bronck, plaintiff, against Claes Teunisz. Default.

Maritge Dyckmans, plaintiff, against Abram Pietersz Vosburch, defendant, requesting a new writ of execution upon a judgment of this honorable court dated the 27th of April last.

The court, having heard the defendant, grants the requested writ of execution and orders the defendant to pay the sum of fl. 100:— within 14 days, putting off the further execution for the time of six weeks.

[248] Frans Barentsz Pastoor, plaintiff, against Abraham Pietersz Vosburch, defendant, demanding payment of the sum of fl. 214:6:— in beavers for beer delivered, according to balance of accounts. Also that the defendant be condemned to pay in addition the sum of fl. 60:— for so much advance [in price] on thirty beavers not included, for which the plaintiff has been obliged to accept and receive fl. 243:16 in seawan, at eight guilders the beaver, all according to the contract thereof.

The defendant, admitting the aforesaid debt of fl. 214:6:— says nevertheless that he is not held to pay the same otherwise than for one third part in beavers, which he agrees to do, claiming that this is sufficient and that in case of refusal and in virtue of the said offer he is not further or otherwise liable and demanding that all further claims and the fl.60:— demanded [by the plaintiff] be denied.

The plaintiff persists in his demand. The defendant likewise in his.

The court, before rendering a decision in the matter, refer parties to Goossen Gerritsen and Willem Bout, referees.

Johan de Deckere, commissary and officer here, plaintiff, against Tomas Paul. Default.

Idem, plaintiff, against Hans Coenraets. Default.

Idem, plaintiff, against Jochem, the baker, to proceed with the case.

The defendant offers to declare under oath that he did not

sell any sugar bun to the savage, as stated by the plaintiff, nor that he has any knowledge that such took place at his house.

The case is dismissed.

[249] Idem, plaintiff, against the same defendant, demanding that the defendant be fined fl. 12:— because a week ago today a lightweight loaf was found at the defendant's contrary to the ordinance made with reference thereto.

The court, having heard the defendant, condemn him to pay the fine demanded.

Idem, plaintiff, against Daniel Ringhout, defendant, on account of the same offense.

The court fine him as above.

Idem, plaintiff, against Hendrik Jansz, the cowherd, defendant in detention.

Whereas the defendant, or person in detention, acknowledges that he wrote and made a lampoon, which being read is found to be slanderous and defamatory, the plaintiff persists in his conclusion or else demands that the defendant be condemned to pay a pecuniary fine.

The court condemn the defendant to pay a fine or penalty of 20 guilders and in addition 6 guilders for jailer's fee and other expenses.

Idem, plaintiff, having attached certain house rent and a house standing here in the fort, belonging to Aelbert, the Noorman, in regard to which the defendant [53] makes complaint.

He concludes that the attachment, as being duly and lawfully made, shall hold good until the termination of the case. Furthermore, that the defendant shall be condemned to pay first a sum of fifteen times six guilders and in addition a sum of twenty-five guilders, all because the defendant on Sunday a week ago together with fifteen other persons were found holding separate

---

[53] *Overgedaechde*, meaning a defendant who is summoned to appear before a court other than that to whose jurisdiction he would ordinarily be subject. In this case, Albert Andriessen Bradt, the Noorman, being a tenant of the patroon, apparently claimed that the court of Beverwyck had no jurisdiction over him.

divine service at the house of Willem Juriaensz, contrary to the ordinance passed against it.

Default with decree granting the attachment.

[250] Tomas Chambers, plaintiff, against Jacob Jansz Stol, defendant, to make oath as requested.

The defendant, having taken the requested oath, declares that he and Johanna de Hulter, in regard to the expense of having their grain thrashed at the Esopus, had agreed with the aforesaid Chambers on the following conditions, namely, that as soon as each of the three received his or her grain, or the same was thrashed, each party was to pay his own expenses, but that nothing was said or agreed upon as to each of them bearing, share and share alike, the total expense of thrashing the grain, except that it was agreed upon that the cost of shipping would be borne and paid by each in proportion to the quantity of his grain. So help him God.

Interrogatories upon which, at the request of Johan de Deckere, commissary and officer here, is to be heard and examined Lambert van Valckenburch, sergeant of the burgher company, being summoned by the court to give testimony to the truth.

Whether he, the witness, yesterday, a week ago, in the evening, was not molested on the public highway because he, as sergeant, by order of his captain, wanted to take one Willem Hap to the guard house?

Answer, Yes.

Who the aforesaid persons were and how many there were of them?

Declares that he saw but one person, without knowing who he was or being acquainted with him, only, that he heard that it must have been a certain tailor, the brother-in-law of Dirk Bentsingh.

Whether he, or they, did not come for him with bare knives, intending to attack him, in order to wrest the said Hap from his hands?

Declares that the aforesaid person did as stated in the question.

Who else were present there, what else happened in connection with the said molestation and how the same ended?

Declares that of the persons who were present he does not know a single one and that he took the said Hap to the guard house.

Thus done and declared on the date above written. *Presentibus ut supra.*

J. DE DECKERE
1656
SANDER LENRSEN
FRANS BARENTSEN PASTOORS
VOLCKART JANSZ
ANDRIES HERBERTS
DIRCK JANSEN CROON

Tuesday, February 15, 1656

Presentibus omnibus

Marcelis Jansz, plaintiff, against Daniel Ringhout, defendant, about payment of fl. 19: 4:— for the excise on three half aams of brandy on account of tapsters' excise.

The court, having heard the parties, denies the plaintiff's demand.

[252] Frans Barentsen Pastoor, plaintiff, against Abram Pietersen Vosburch, defendant.

Default.

Tierck Claesz, plaintiff, against Tomas Paul, defendant.

The court, having heard the parties, refers them to Jan Tomasz and Cornelis Teunisz Bos, to reconcile parties if possible.

Jacob Jansz Schermerhoorn, having order and power of attorney from Cornelis Boon, residing at Dordrecht in Holland, and in that capacity plaintiff against Jacob Loserik, defendant, about payment of the sum of fl. 1065:6:–, in satisfaction of the second payment on the house bought of the said Boon by the defendant in the month of July of last year, 1655.

The defendant requests delay to recover the amount from Steven Jansz.

Granted by the court.

Jacob Loserik, plaintiff, against Steven Jansz, defendant. Default.

Sander Leendertsz, plaintiff, against Tierk Claesz, defendant, about payment of fl. 25:– in compensation for a goat killed by the defendant.

The court refers the parties to Jan Verbeecq and Jan Tomasz, referees.

[253] Johan de Deckere, commissary and officer here, ex officio plaintiff, against Hendrik Jansz, cowherd, defendant, demanding that the defendant be fined fl. 100 for having this day a week ago drawn a knife on the person of Jacob Loserik.

The defendant admits having drawn a knife, but [says] that he wounded no one.

The plaintiff demands sentence as above.

The court takes the matter under advisement.

Idem, plaintiff, against Willem Hap, defendant. Default.

Idem, plaintiff, against Jacob Loserik, defendant, demanding that he be fined three hundred guilders for having this day a week ago attempted to hurt the person of Hendrik Jansz, cowherd, with a knife, in such a way that the stab made two holes and broke the knife, which was left in the coat of the aforesaid Hendrik Jansz, and that furthermore he threw him backwards into the water.

The defendant denies the deed but requests nevertheless a copy of the plaintiff's charge.

The plaintiff agrees.

Idem, plaintiff, against Aelbert, the Noorman, defendant,[54] to have the second default entered against him.

The plaintiff, in view of the defendant's failure to appear, requests the second default.

The court grants the request.

[254] Rut Jacobsz, our fellow member of the court, having requested permission to make or suspend a water wheel for a small mill in the kill behind his dwelling house, his request is granted.

Volckert Jansz and Jan Tomasz, representing also Pieter Hertgers, having requested that the five or six feet of ground of the public road included within the inclosure of the lot on which their brewery stands, which have been provisionally granted to them by Commissary Johan de Deckere and Rutger Jacobsz, may be confirmed [to them] by the court as a body, their request is unanimously granted until further order to the contrary.

Upon the remonstrance and petition of Jochem, the baker, that the resolution heretofore passed in condemnation of the thatched roof of Willem Juriaensz and the order given for its removal may be executed, it is upon further examination of the matter and in consideration of the lack of means of the aforesaid Willem Juriaensz decided to delegate the Hon. Commissary Johan de Deckere, together with Frans Barentsz Pastoor and Dirk Jansz Croon, magistrates, to persuade and request the neighbors of the aforesaid Willem Juriaensz to make a voluntary loan and contribution in money, as much as each one is pleased to give, to replace the condemned thatched roof by one of boards, in order thereby, as far as possible, to prevent all danger of fire. The persons who contribute any money shall as security for the restitution thereof have a mortgage on the house or its improvement, the contributors after the death of the said Willem Juriaensz to be reimbursed from time to time out of the house rent in proportion to their respective contribution and in case the

---

[54] Albert Andriessen Bradt.

present owner of the lot of the aforesaid house, or the person who may acquire his title, [255] should wish to tear down the said house after the death of the aforesaid Willem Juriaensz, he shall be holden to reimburse them as aforesaid.

The aforesaid proposition having been made by the said delegates to the aforesaid persons, they have promised to contribute to the aforesaid purpose as follows:

Jochem, the baker, has promised to furnish thirteen boards and the roof timbers
Sander Leendertsz, 12 boards and eight guilders' worth of nails
Rutger Jacobs, 5 boards
Andries Herpertsz, 8 boards
Jacob, the baker, 10 guilders
Jan van Housen, 25 boards
Jan Tomasz, privately, 12 boards
The same, jointly with Volckert Jansz and Pieter Hertgers, 15 guilders
The deacons [blank]

For the restitution of all of which aforesaid moneys the commissary and magistrates, by virtue of their authority, bind and mortgage the aforesaid house and the improvements thereof for the benefit of the aforesaid persons.

The three ordinances sent by the Hon. General and the Supreme Council of New Netherland to the Commissary and the magistrates and received by them on the 9th of this current month of February, being read and examined, it is decided to publish two of them relating to the combination and concentration of the separate dwellings and the farming of the fur trade. The third, relating to the excise, or the payment of the 20th penny on slaughtered cattle, hogs, sheep and goats, it is for pregnant reasons considered inadvisable to publish or post, it being apparent that at this juncture of time and on account of the excessive expense [256] to which the community is put in repairing the fort, the block house and other works thereabout, and in ransoming the prisoners, it would only cause complaint, opposition and friction, which at the first opportunity when the river is open will be submitted and brought to the attention of the aforesaid Hon. General and Supreme Council.

Interrogatories on which at the request of Johan de Deckere, commissary and officer here, Jan Gou and Willem Berck are to heard and examined under oath, they being legally summoned to give testimony to the truth.

First, whether they, the witnesses, on Tuesday last were not at the house and tavern of Baefge Pieters, and whether there were not also present Jacob Loserik and Hendrik Jansz, cow herd?

They declare in conformity [with the question].

Whether some dispute did not arise between the aforesaid Loserik and Hendrik Jansz and about what?

They declare, Yes, and that the dispute arose because he, Hendrik, touched the said Loserik's body, at least that they saw no other cause or reason.

Also, whether the aforesaid quarreling persons did not draw their knives and attempted to hurt or wound each other and whether the said Hendrik Jansz in the course of the fight did not receive a cut in his thumb and afterwards a stab in his coat, in such a way that the knife of the said Loserik broke into pieces?

They declare that the said Loserik first went out of the door and was immediately followed by the said Hendrik; that they both drew their knives and that the said Loserik thrusting at his opponent struck his leather coat and that the knife broke into pieces, but that they do not know how, nor in what way, the said Hendrik received the cut in his thumb.

[257] Finally, what else they have to testify in regard to this? They declare that the said Loserik, on delivering the thrust, ran up to the said Hendrick and pushed him backwards into the water.

Thus declared and deposed on the date above written.

J. de Deckere
1656
Sander Lenrsen
Frans Barentsen Pastoor
Volckart Jansz
Rutger Jacobsz
Andries Herberts
Dirck Jansen Croon

Tuesday, February 22, 1656

Johan de Deckere, commissary and officer here, ex officio plaintiff, against Willem Jansz Stoll, defendant, about the fine of one hundred guilders, because the defendant yesterday three weeks ago, being the last of January, drew a knife on the sergeant of the burgher guard.

The defendant says that he has no knowledge of his drawing the knife.

The plaintiff agrees to prove the same.

Idem, plaintiff, against Aelbert Andriesz, defendant, to answer the complaint and conclusion brought against the defendant on the 8th of this month.

The defendant admits the substance of the complaint and offers to pay twenty-five guilders, but refuses the further demands.

The plaintiff refuses the offer and persists in his complaint and conclusion.

The court having heard the defendant and his plea and examined the ordinance, condemn the defendant to pay the demanded fine [258] of fl.115:–, declaring the attached house and house rent subject to execution as security for the fine.

Volckert Jansz has a note made of the fact that he does **not** concern himself with the aforesaid case or sentence.

Idem, plaintiff, against Jacob Loserik, defendant.

The plaintiff persists in his demand by way of replication.

The defendant agrees to secure evidence.

Jacob Loserik, plaintiff, against Steven Jansz, defendant in regard to security.

He demands that the defendant be ordered to guarantee him against all loss and damage and release him from all costs which may result from the suit brought against him, the plaintiff, on the last court day by Jacob Jansz Schermerhoorn.

The defendant requests an adjournment of eight days or until the river is open.

Granted by the court.

Pieter Bronck, plaintiff, against Claes Teunisz, defendant, requesting execution of a certain judgment in the sum of fl.201:– given by the court of the colony of Rensselaerswyck, declining settlement.

The court grants the desired execution, but at the defendant's request nevertheless suspends the same for six weeks.

[259] Pieter Ryverdingh, plaintiff, against Jacob Adriaensz, wheelwright, defendant.

Default.

J. DE DECKERE
1656
SANDER LENRSEN
FRANS BARENTSEN PASTOORS
RUTGER JACOBSZ
ANDRIES HERBERTS
DIRCK JANSEN CROON

Tuesday, March 14, 1656

Presentibus:

 J. de Decker   Andries Herp'sz
 Rutger Jacobs   V. Jansz

Johan de Deckere, commissary and officer here, plaintiff, against Claes Jansz, defendant, about the fine of fl.6:— because the defendant on Sunday two weeks ago was found sitting in the tavern of Herman Bamboes, drinking.
Default.

Idem, plaintiff, against Frans Pietersz for the same cause.
The court condemn the defendant to pay a fine of fl.3:— and 12 stivers for costs.

Idem, plaintiff, against Poulus Lambertsz, defendant, as above. Default.

Idem, plaintiff, against Claes Ribse, defendant. Default.

Idem, plaintiff, against Hendrik Jansz, cow herd, defendant, asking that the court give its opinion.
The court condemn the defendant to pay a fine of fl.20:— to the officer and ten guilders for the bench.
The plaintiff protests against the above sentence as far as the ten guilders are concerned.

[260] Idem, plaintiff, against the wife of Jan with the beard. Default.

Idem, plaintiff, against Annitge Lamberts. Default.

Jacob Jansz Flodder, plaintiff, against Margariet Slechtenhorst, to show cause why the defendant caused plaintiff's tiles to be attached, or else, to have the attachment vacated.
Default.

         J. de Deckere
         1656
        Sander Lenrsen
        Frans Barentsz Pastoors
        Rutger Jacobsz
        Andries Herberts
        Dirck Jansen Croon

Tuesday, April 4, 1656

Presentibus:

| J. de Deckere | F. Barentsz | A. Herpertsz |
| S. Leenderts | R. Jacobsz | V. Jansz |

Johan de Deckere, commissary and officer here, plaintiff, against Baefgie Pieters, because the defendant last Sunday a week ago treated him, the plaintiff, very badly and by closing her door interfered with and impeded him in the exercise of his office, wherefore the plaintiff demands that the defendant be condemned to pay a fine of fifty guilders for the benefit of the poor and that in addition she be enjoined from exercising her trade for the space of six weeks and [condemned to pay] the costs.

The court, having heard the defendant, condemned her to pay a fine of fl.25:– within twenty-four hours.

Idem, plaintiff, against Poulus Lambertsz, defendant, about the fine of fl.6:– because on Sunday February 21 he was found during divine service in the tavern of Herman Bamboes.

The court having heard the confession of the defendant condemn him to pay a fine of fl.3:12:–

Idem, plaintiff, against Claes Jansz, as above.

The defendant agrees to pay fl.3:–

[261] Idem, plaintiff, against Jan Maertens, *alias* Wever. Default.

Idem, plaintiff, against Herman Bamboes. Default.

Idem, plaintiff, against Willem Jansz Stoll. Default.

Idem, plaintiff, against Annetge Lamberts, about the fine of fl.12:– because the defendant has spoken and acted very badly toward him, the plaintiff.

The court, having heard the defendant, condemn her to pay a penalty or fine of fl.4:4:–

Idem, plaintiff, against Jacob Loserik. Default.

Idem, plaintiff, against Piet Bout, defendant.

The plaintiff says that it is the truth that the defendant last Saturday a week ago at the house of Herman Bamboes committed great insolence, disturbance and violence, drew his knife and challenged and dared every one, especially the aforesaid Bamboes, to thrust and cut in such a way that the said Bamboes was forced to complain about it to him, the plaintiff, as officer, wherefore the plaintiff demands that the defendant be condemned to pay a fine of two hundred guilders.

The defendant says that he was pestered and teased by every one and requests to have a copy of the complaint.

The plaintiff accepts the aforesaid confession in his favor, but grants nevertheless the requested copy.

P^r. Colebrantsz, plaintiff, against *Moy* Aeltgie.[55] Default.

[262] There appeared in court Cornelis Barentsz Slecht, hereby certifying at the request of Joffrou Johanna de Hulter, widow of the late Johan de Hulter, that it is true that he, the appearer, during the late troubles with the savages on the part of the aforesaid Joffrou has delivered on account and for the behoof of Tomas Chambers, first, 150 lb. of butter, five schepels of flour and four traces. Also that with one Pieter Bruynen, also a servant of the said Joffrou, he has attended and served at the house of the aforesaid Chambers, as is confirmed and corroborated by the aforesaid Bruynen, also appearing here, and that he served in the capacity of a cook at the house aforesaid. May God Almighty help him, the appearer. Done on the date above written.

SANDER LENRSEN
FRANS BARENTSEN PASTOORS
RUTGER JACOBSZ
ANDRIES HERBERTS
DIRCK JANSEN CROON

---

[55] Fair Alida.

Tuesday, April 18, 1656

Presentibus omnibus
preter A. Herpertsz

We, the undersigned, declare hereby that we offer ourselves as sureties and principal debtors for the payment of such sums of money as have been agreed to by the honorable court of this fort for the building of the block-house church and the wages thereof, binding ourselves therefor according to law. Done as above.

Herman Bastiaensz, plaintiff, against Claes Jacobsz, defendant, about payment of wages earned.

The court, having heard the parties, refer them to Stoffel Jansz and Claes Jansz, referees.

A petition being read of the bakers, requesting permission to charge and receive 18 stivers for an ordinary wheaten loaf of eight pounds and five stivers for a white loaf of one pound, their second request is granted.

[263] There appeared Pieter Hertgers and Cornelis Teunisz Bos, who declared that they offered themselves as sureties for the performance and fulfilment of all the conditions on which Stoffel Jansz and Jan Roelofsz, in accordance with the specifications and by public bid have agreed to build the block-house church, binding themselves thereto according to law. Done as above.

We, the undersigned, hereby declare that we offer ourselves as sureties and principal debtors for the payment of such sums of money as the honorable court have promised to Stoffel Jansz and Jan Roelofsz for building the block-house church and the wages thereof, binding ourselves thereto as by law provided. Done as above.

SANDER LENRSEN

Jan Verbeecq, Jan Tomasz, Jochem Keteluyn, Auckes Bruynsen and Arien Jansz from Leyden are ordered to build on their vacant lots within one month, or at least to put them in such shape that the work can to all appearances not be stopped but must necessarily proceed, on pain of being deprived of their lots which shall be placed at the disposal of the court, to which end an inspection will then be made. All this without prejudice to the rights already acquired or to be acquired by the officer. It is furthermore decided that all those who this day have not registered their lots in conformity with the order brought to every one's knowledge by the notices that have been posted, shall be and remain deprived and divested of the same. Done as above.

Tjerck Claesz requests permission to have the lot of Jacob Jansz Flodder. Granted.

[264] We, the undersigned, promise hereby, each in his own capacity, that we shall indemnify and hold the aforesaid sureties, Sander Leendertsz and Philip P^{rsz}. Schuyler harmless in regard to all costs and damages resulting from their surety bond inserted above. Therefore we submit ourselves as counter sureties, binding therefor our properties and those of our inhabitants, none excepted, submitting the same to the control of all courts and judges. Done as above.

                J. DE DECKERE
                1656
            FRANS BARENTSZ PASTOORS
            RUTGER JACOBSZ
            ANDRIES HERBERTS
            DIRCK JANSEN CROON

Extraordinary Session, Wednesday, April 19, 1656

Presentibus omnibus

P^r. Hertgers, Jan Tomasz and Volckert Jansz, plaintiffs and parties arresting, against Herman Bamboes, defendant and person arrested.

They demand that the arrest, etc. and furthermore that the defendant be condemned to pay the sum of fl.1408:—, one-third part to be paid in beavers or grain, on account of the delivery of beer, according to the tally kept thereof, declining settlement.

The defendant admits the debt, except what he paid on it, and requests that payment of the balance may be delayed until the coming month of June, offering meanwhile to leave as a pledge and deliver into the hands of the plaintiffs the sum of one thousand guilders, upon condition that if he, the defendant, does not make any payment before that time, they, the plaintiffs, shall be at liberty to satisfy themselves out of the aforesaid money and that in case he make payment meanwhile, they, the plaintiffs, shall be bound to deliver to him, the defendant, one hundred beavers in lieu of the aforesaid one thousand guilders.

[265] The plaintiffs accept the offer as it stands, provided that the thousand guilders be this day delivered into their hands.

The court accordingly condemn the defendant to pay the sum demanded, provided that he may deduct therefrom what he shall prove having paid thereon. Furthermore, they order him to deliver this day the thousand guilders offered by him into the hands of the plaintiffs, under the conditions specified and aforementioned, and condemn him to pay one-half of the costs of this court. *Actum ut supra.*

J. DE DECKERE
1656
SANDER LENRSEN
FRANS BARENTSZ PASTOORS
RUTGER JACOBSZ
ANDRIES HERBERTS
DIRCK JANSEN CROON

Tuesday, April 25, 1656

Presentibus omnibus
preter V. Jansz

Johan de Deckere, ex officio plaintiff, against Juriaen, the glazier. Default.

Idem, plaintiff, against Willem Tellier, defendant.

The plaintiff says and it is the truth that the defendant in the week before Easter did not hesitate to close and fence off at both ends with boards and palisades a certain common or public road, alley, or foot path, situated opposite the house of Abram Pietersz Vosburch, going to the river, whereby the same was made useless, notwithstanding the fact that the defendant, through the court messenger was forbidden and prohibited from doing so by the said Vosburch, as the party most directly concerned. Also that upon inspection by this honorable court and survey made by the surveyor it was found that the aforesaid defendant had inclosed within the fence of his garden about four and a half feet of ground of the aforesaid foot path or public road from the wagon road to the river and consequently lessened its width [266] aside from the fact that the defendant has encroached at least a foot or two along the public road outside of the old palisades and thereby narrowed the public wagon road. All of which being seen and considered by this honorable court and the ground brief of the defendant's garden being also examined, it clearly appeared therefrom that the defendant had unjustly taken possession of the aforesaid four feet and a half of land as well as the one or two feet of ground and added them to his garden in bad faith. The surveyor being thereupon, with the advise and consent of the magistrates who were present, ordered by the plaintiff to saw off and tear down the fence or boards at the end of the defendant's garden, according to the tenor of the ground brief, the defendant began to address and assail not only the plaintiff but also the magistrates in very angry, abusive and threatening terms, saying in particular that it would end in killing, putting himself with an angry face not only in a posture of defense, but actually becoming agressive, trying either to break the saw or by force or violence to wrest it from the hands of the surveyor and thereby as much as was in his power to prevent the carrying out of the order and command given to the surveyor, and openly notifying the court that force and violence were used against him by the said sawing and that he would complain thereof. To this must be added that the defendant some time ago has not hesitated to state even in court that the building of the block-house, or certain proceedings by the court concerning it, would cry to Heaven for vengeance; all of which things were spewed out, spoken, or attested in the face of the court, or in the face or presence of the plaintiff and the magistrates while they were exercising their functions and therefore representing the supreme authorities of this province, and consequently in the highest degree injurious, intolerable and of evil consequence. The plaintiff, in the capacity above mentioned, demands therefore [267] that the defendant shall immediately and without the formality of a regular trial, as in this matter there is no need of any evidence or testimony and no further investigation is required, be condemned to pay a fine of fl.600:—

The defendant gave for answer that he did not care anything about the aforesaid matter and thereupon left immediately.

The plaintiff persists in his complaint and demand.

The defendant having again come into court has openly accused and told the president, Johan de Deckere, that he had forcibly deprived him of the aforesaid foot path or alley and given it to another person.

The president protests against this slanderous charge and demands honorable and profitable reparation, intending otherwise to bring suit and to prosecute it where and in such way as he shall see fit.

The court order the officer to furnish the defendant with a copy of the aforesaid complaint.

Fop Jansz, carpenter, plaintiff, against Rutger Jacobsz, defendant, about payment of the sum of fl.42:— for ten a half days' wages at ½ beaver a day.

The court, having heard the parties, condemn the defendant to pay the sum of fl.42:—

Rutger Jacobs, Goossen Gerritsz and Teunis Dirxse, appointed by order of the court curators of the estate and property of the late Rut Arentsz, and in that capacity plaintiffs against Johannes Dyckman, in charge of the administration of the effects, moneys and income of the said estate, defendant, about payment of the sum of fl.261:4:— which he, Dyckman, according to his own statement and account spent less than he received.

The wife of the aforesaid Dyckman, appearing for him on account of his disability, says that she has no knowledge of the matter or of the money and therefore can not make answer.

[268] The plaintiffs persist in their demand.

The court having examined the list or account in the aforesaid Dyckman's own handwriting, from which it appears that there was a balance of fl. 261:4:— left, condemn him to pay the sum demanded.

Johan de Deckere, commissary and officer here, ex officio plaintiff, against Jacob Loserik, defendant, to have him present his evidence and to have sentence pronounced.

The court taking the matter under advisement, meanwhile refer the parties to referees, each party to choose one.

Frans Barents Pastoor, having power of attorney from Marcelis Jansz, excise master, plaintiff, against Jacob Loserik, former farmer of the excise, defendant, about payment of the sum of fl. 183:— on account of some remnants of wine, beer and brandy which at the expiration of the defendant's term of service were found in the cellars or houses of the tapsters according to the gager's certificates.

The court, having heard the parties, holds the matter under advisement.

Teunis Slingerlant is at his request granted a garden.

J. DE DECKERE

1656

[269] Extraordinary Session, Monday, May 1, 1656

In the place of the retiring magistrates, Sander Leendertsz, Frans Barentsz Pastoor and Volckert Jansz, according to the copy of the resolution of the Hon. Director General and Council of New Netherland, Jacob Schermerhoorn and Philip P[rs]. Schuyler, of the double number nominated, have been chosen and confirmed as ordinary magistrates and Goossen Gerritsz as extraordinary magistrate, who, being summoned by the court, have taken the following oath of fidelity before the commissary, except Goosen Gerritsz, who with various excuses, such as they were, declined to do so.

We, the undersigned, being chosen magistrates of the bench of justice of Fort Orange and Beverwyck, promise and swear in the presence of God Almighty and our fellow members, that we shall help to do true equity and justice between man and man and furthermore cause to execute and help to promote all matters relating to justice or administration according to the best of our knowledge, and in all respects conduct ourselves loyally and faithfully toward the Lords States General of the United Netherlands, the Honorable Directors of the Chartered West India Company and the Hon. Director General and Council of New Netherland, with the further promise that we shall help to maintain here the Reformed Religion according to God's Word and the regulations of the Synod of Dordrecht and not publicly tolerate any sect. So help us God Almighty.

After having been congratulated the aforesaid Schermerhoorn and Philip P[rs]. have this day taken their seats.

[270] The retiring magistrates are released from their oath and thanked for their faithful services and the performance of their official duties, with promise that with respect to their honorarium of fl.150:— a year, their claims will when the time is convenient and the treasury supplied with funds be taken into consideration together with those of the present and future magistrates and be paid.

After deliberation it is decided and concluded that the magistrates who retire at the end of each year shall for the space of one year after the expiration of their term of office be exempt and relieved from attending the usual burgher watch, but that nevertheless, in case of need and when commanded, they shall be bound and liable to take part in all extraordinary rounds and do guard duty the same as other burghers. This resolution will be communicated and made known to the military council in order that they may hereafter govern and regulate themselves accordingly. *Actum ut supra.*

On the second of May Goossen Gerritsz has taken the aforesaid oath of fidelity before the Commissary.

[56] The above resolution, providing that the retiring magistrates, both the ordinary and extraordinary ones, shall for the space of one year be free and exempt from the usual rounds and guard duty (except under pregnant circumstances when the public welfare and need require it), is confirmed and approved by us, so that the captain and lieutenant and the lower officers of the burgher company are hereby ordered to let them enjoy this exemption. Given over our own and usual signature, this day, the 8th of November 1656.

P. STUYVESANT

[271] Tuesday, May 2, 1656

Johan de Deckere, commissary and officer here, ex officio plaintiff, against Jacob Loserik, defendant, requesting a decision.

The court, having heard the parties on both sides and having examined the evidence submitted by them, condemn the defendant to pay a fine of seven and a half beavers, to be paid within twenty-four hours.

---

[56] The following lines are in the handwriting of Peter Stuyvesant.

Interrogatories on which at the request of Johan de Deckere, commissary and officer here, made ex officio, is to be heard and examined Juriaen Jansz, glazier, being summoned by the court to give testimony to the truth.

Whether he, the witness, on the 25th of March last was not at the house or tavern of Herman Bamboes and whether there was not also present there one Piet Bont, who sought to make trouble and to revive an old dispute with him, the said P^t. Bont saying: "It cost me once nine beavers and I shall not stop even if it should cost me ten beavers more?"

Declares, Yes.

Who else were present there?

Declares that among others Hendrik Jansz, the cowherd, Jan Roelofsz and Jacob Loserik were present there.

Whether he, Piet Bont, did not draw a knife and wanted to cut him, the witness, with it?

Declares, Yes.

Fourth, whether he, the witness, when the said P^t. Bont tried to hurt him and was stabbing at him, did not draw back and retreat to the back room and whether Jan Roelofsz thereupon did not say to said Bont: "You act like a rascal." Also whether he, P^t. Bont, then did not try to

Declares, Yes, but as to the questions in regard to Roelofsz, he did not see what took place but heard about it.

attack the said Jan Roelofsz and if the said Jan Roelofsz, picking up a wood ax and hacking in the direction of P^t. Bont's body, did not strike the door post?

There appeared Herman Bamboes, who after the above questions had been read to them, declared that he agreed with the statements made therein and that they were in all respects in accordance with the truth.

Thus done and declared on the date above written.

Idem, plaintiff, against Jan Roelofsz, defendant. Default.

Idem, plaintiff, against Hendrik Jansz, cowherd, defendant. Default.

Frans Barentsz Pastoor, plaintiff, against Jacob Loserik, defendant, to request that judgment be pronounced.

The court refers the parties to referees, one to be chosen by each party.

Barent Aelbertsz is granted a garden behind the fort, marked No. 16, in with 4 rods, in length 8 rods.

Jan van Housen, appearing before the court, requests a lot on the hill to build thereon a house.

After deliberation his request is granted and a lot shall be assigned to him, for which he is to pay to the court, for the benefit of the public, the sum of sixty guilders.

[273] Tuesday, May 30, 1656

Johan de Deckere, ex officio plaintiff, against Jan, the weaver, defendant. Default.

Idem, plaintiff, against Willem Tellier, defendant, requesting sentence.

The defendant requests that the plaintiff be ordered to sign the complaint which he caused to be delivered to him.

The plaintiff, declining the aforesaid request as being irrelevant and impertinent, again requests that sentence be pronounced, the more so as he can produce no other witnesses than the members of the court themselves and the case therefore is not of a nature to follow the ordinary course of proceedings, much less to be held up and kept pending by reason of the aforesaid frivolous request.

The court order the defendant to present all his evidence (if he thinks he has any) on the next court day, in order that the court may then make such disposition in the matter as it shall judge proper; in default whereof judgment shall be rendered *de plano*.

Idem, plaintiff, against Jan Roelofsz, defendant. Default.

Idem, plaintiff, against Willem Telier, in a case of atrocious slander.

The plaintiff says and it is the truth that the defendant has not hesitated on Tuesday, the 25th of April last, to cast in his teeth in open court the very villainous, hateful and slanderous accusation that he had forcibly deprived him, the defendant, of and given to another person a certain alley or foot path, which the court in the week before Easter in accordance with the description in the defendant's own ground brief had decided not to belong to him, but to be a common alley or foot path; which is [274] so wide of the truth that he, the plaintiff, turning the aforesaid accusation around, can in accordance with the aforesaid decision of the court state on good authority that on the contrary he, the defendant, in contempt and disobedience of his lawful superiors has in the most unjust, violent and forcible way tried to possess himself of the said foot path and in bad faith to fence off and use the same, in regard to which he, the plaintiff, has instituted a special action in this honorable court. The plaintiff, therefore, considering himself in the highest degree injured, affronted and wounded in his honor, reputation and office by the aforesaid false and impudent libel, slander and accusation, and being consequently forced for the sake of reparation to resort to and make use of the means and ways of justice;

Demands that the defendant shall be condemned to make honorable and pecuniary reparation for the aforesaid villainous and false slander, namely, honorable reparation by appearing in court and there bareheaded and with folded hands and on bended knees praying God, the court and the plaintiff, if he desires to be present, for forgiveness, confessing that he has unjustly and contrary to the truth made the aforesaid accusation and that he knows nothing of the plaintiff but what is honorable and virtuous and that he has in the aforesaid particular exercised his functions correctly and therefore that he is heartily sorry about it all, but promises never to do the like again; pecuniary reparation, by paying to the plaintiff, to be distributed by him among the poor, the sum of six hundred guilders, he, the plaintiff, being satisfied to declare under solemn oath that he would not care to suffer the said or similar insult again for the aforesaid or any larger amount, [275] demanding costs or other [penalty].

The defendant persists in his previous statement.

The plaintiff asks that sentence be pronounced.

The court [decides] as in the other case preceding this.

Jacob, the baker, plaintiff, having attached certain eighteen beavers belonging to Jan Gou, and at present in the custody of Jochem, the baker, defendant,

He demands that the attachment [be sustained] and furthermore that judgment be given in the sum of fl.48:— for the recovery of money loaned.

Default and attachment sustained.

Goossen Gerritsz, plaintiff, against Abram P[rsz]. Vosburch, defendant. Default.

Arien Symonsz, plaintiff, against Herman Bamboes, defendant, about the payment of 50 beavers, being the balance of a larger sum due for the purchase of certain wines and other goods, according to the account thereof, the plaintiff being ready, upon the payment aforesaid, to restore to the defendant the seawan that was left with him as security.

The court, having heard the confession of the defendant, give judgment for the number of beavers demanded.

Herman Bamboes, plaintiff, against Margriet Clabborts, defendant, about payment of the sum of fl. 82:17:– for beer and other [liquors] fetched [at his tavern], according to the account thereof.

The court, having heard the parties on both sides and also the solemn declaration of the plaintiff, give judgment against the defendant for the sum of fl. 71:17:–

[276] Idem, plaintiff, against Willem Hofmeyer, defendant. Default.

Idem, plaintiff, against Carsten, the Noorman, defendant, about payment of the sum of fl. 11:19:–

The defendant admits the debt and requests a delay of four weeks.

The court consequently gives judgment, granting the delay requested.

Idem, plaintiff, against Daniel Ringhout, defendant. Default.

Pr. Ruyverdingh, plaintiff, against Jan de Cuyper. Default.

Jan Peeck, plaintiff, against Maria Dyckmans, for the payment of fl. 1627:– on account of the purchase of certain two houses standing here in the fort, with a garden thereto belonging, bid on and bought by the defendant's husband at public auction, declining settlement. Otherwise, the plaintiff asks permission again to take possession of the aforesaid two houses and to offer and sell the same at public auction to the loss or benefit of the aforesaid [defendant's] husband and his sureties.

The court, having heard the parties on both sides, grants the plaintiff permission to take possession of the aforesaid two houses and garden and to sell them at public auction to the loss or benefit of the aforesaid Dyckman and his sureties.

Jacob Loosdrecht, plaintiff, against Steven Jansz. Default.

[277] Cornelis Teunisz Bos, having power of attorney from Jacob Adriaensz, plaintiff, against Cornelis Segersz, defendant,

for the sum of fl. 537:— by balance of account of the purchase of a certain house.

The defendant admits the debt and requests delay until fall.

The court orders the defendant to pay the sum demanded, delaying execution for the space of six weeks.

P^r. Bronck, plaintiff, having attached a certain sum of money in the custody of Frans Barentsz, belonging to Jan van Bremen, defendant.

The wife of the defendant asks for adjournment until her husband's return.

Upon the petition of a number of burghers and inhabitants of Beverwyck, praying that the corral or palisades in front of their houses may be removed, the following marginal note is entered:

The court, having taken the petitioners' or remonstrants' request into consideration, [favors it] to the extent [of promising] that, as soon as the church shall have been erected, due regard will be had to it, the court to make such disposition in the matter as the circumstances of the time will then allow.

Philip P^{rsz}. Schuyler is granted and allowed an addition to his lot on which his house stands, at present surveyed as follows: Adjoining on the south the wagon road, in length 9 rods, 5 feet; on the west side the hill, in width 5 rods, 11 feet; on the north side P^r. Hertgers, in length 9 rods, 7 feet; and on the east side Sander Leendertsz, in width 6 rods and 2 feet.

There was read a petition of some bakers, praying that they and all other bakers, present and future, be prohibited from baking any sweetmeats to be sold to the savages.

Whereupon the following apostil is given: It is left to the choice and option of the petitioners and all other bakers to bake and use the specified sweetmeats, or not. Done the 9th of June 1656.

[278] The officer and commissary, Johan de Deckere, notifies Dirk Bentsingh that he will institute his action against him on account of the very abusive and villainous terms used by him about the court before all the world, namely, that they were a

pack of rascals, villains and dogs, where and in such way as he shall see fit.

> J. DE DECKERE
> RUTGER JACOBSZ
> ANDRIES HERBERTS
> JACOB SCHERMERHO[ORN]
> DIRCK JANSEN CROON

Tuesday, June 27, 1656

Johan de Deckere, commissary and officer here, ex officio plaintiff, against Jochem, the baker, defendant.

First default.

Idem, plaintiff, against Daniel Ringhout, defendant, for payment of the fine of fl. 24:— because the defendant on the first of this current month of June baked light weight white bread, contrary to the ordinance, and asking also that he be condemned to suspend his trade for the space of six weeks.

The court orders the payment of the fine and the suspension of his trade, respectively, as demanded.

Idem, plaintiff, against Willem Hofmeyer, defendant, for payment of the fine of fl.12:— on account of the matter before mentioned.

The court orders the payment to be made.

Idem, plaintiff, against Tomas Paul, defendant.

First default.

[279] Idem, plaintiff, against Cornelis Cornelisz, defendant, to pay the fine of fl.6:— for some fighting.

The court condemns the defendant to pay the fine of four guilders.

Idem, plaintiff, against P^r. Bont, defendant, to submit his evidence, and furthermore requesting judgment.

The court refer parties to Frans Barentsz and Jan Verbeecq, referees.

Anna de Hulter, plaintiff, against Tomas Chiambers, defendant. The plaintiff requests that the defendant be ordered to institute his action for any claims which he may have against her, *simul et semel*, on pain of having judgment given against him by default.

The defendant requests adjournment until next week.

Goossen Gerritsz, plaintiff, against Abram P^rsz. Vosburch, defendant.

The plaintiff demands payment of the sum of fl.439:3, according to his note of hand, to be paid with 10 beavers and the balance in seawan.

The defendant admits the debt and offers to pay 100 guilders a week.

The court orders the defendant to pay the sum demanded as agreed to by him.

Jannitge Jans, plaintiff, against Hendrik, the baker, defendant. First default.

Cornelis Cornelisz, plaintiff, against Willem Hofmeyer, defendant, about payment of the sum of fl.75:— for tavern expenses.

The court, having heard the confession of the defendant, orders him to pay the sum demanded.

[280] Idem, plaintiff, against Claes Uylenspiegel, defendant. First default.

P^r. Bronk, plaintiff, having attached the sum of fl.283:3, in the custody of Frans Barentsz, belonging to Jan van Bremen, against said van Bremen, defendant.

He demands that the attachment be sustained and furthermore that the defendant be ordered to pay the aforesaid fl.283:3, on account of the delivery of some goods.

The court gives judgment for the plaintiff and declares the money attached to be security for the debt and subject to execution.

Maria Dyckmans, plaintiff, having attached a certain sum of fl.84:— in the custody of and belonging to as above, on account of house rent, to be paid in grain, beavers, or the value thereof.

The defendant *ut supra*.

The court *ut supra*.

Poulus Cornelisz, plaintiff, against Claes Cornelisz van den Berch, defendant, about payment of three beavers, according to his note.

The court refers parties to referees, each party to choose one.

P^r. Ryverdingh, plaintiff, against Herman Bamboes, defendant, about payment of 28 beavers and 3 guilders, 9 stivers, for the delivery of some goods.

The defendant admits the debt. The court gives judgment for the plaintiff.

[281] Herman Bamboes, plaintiff, against Jochem, the baker. First default.

Idem, plaintiff, against Daniel Ringhout, defendant, about payment of the sum of fl.42:— for tavern expenses.

The defendant admits the debt and agrees to pay within six weeks. The court gives judgment accordingly.

Idem, plaintiff, against Willem Hofmeyer, defendant, about payment of the sum of fl.27:— for tavern expenses.

The defendant admits the debt. Judgment for the plaintiff.

Idem, plaintiff, against Dirk Bentsingh, defendant, for payment of 5 beavers for canceling the purchase of a house.

The court gives judgment for the plaintiff.

Idem, plaintiff, against Willem Hap, defendant. First default.

[57] Salomon La Chair, plaintiff, against Abraham van Linthout, defendant, whose goods he caused to be attached, for payment of the sum of fl. 328:— by balance and settlement of accounts, at least by provisional judgment.

The defendant says that he has a counter claim, but he can not present it at this place and time.

The court grants the provisional judgment asked and declares the goods attached to be security therefor and subject to execution, without prejudice to the defendant's right in the principal matter at issue.

---

[57] Salomon La Chair and Jacob van Couwenhoven were sureties for the payment by Abraham van Linthout of the purchase price of a yacht. See *Records of New Amsterdam*, 1653-74, 2:82,100.

[282] Extraordinary Session, Thursday, June 29, 1656

Johan de Deckere, commissary and officer here, ex officio plaintiff, against P^t. Bont, defendant, asking that judgment be given.

The court condemn the defendant to pay a fine of four beavers.

Idem, plaintiff, against Jochem, the baker, defendant.

He demands that the defendant be condemned to pay a fine of fl. 24:— and in addition be suspended for six weeks from exercising his trade, all because the defendant on the 7th of this current month baked light weight white bread, contrary to the ordinance.

The court, having heard the defendant, condemn him to pay the fine demanded and suspend him for six weeks from the exercise of his trade.

Idem, plaintiff, against Tomas Paul and his wife, defendants, first, to pay a fine of fl. 12:— for cause as above, and in addition fl. 25:— because the defendant's wife called the plaintiff and the members of the court as they were making the inspection a pack of extortioners and devils.

The court condemn the defendant and his wife to pay the sum of fl. 22:— within twenty-four hours.

Idem, plaintiff, against Geertruy Haps. Default.

[283] Tuesday, July 4, 1656

Johan de Deckere, commissary and president of the bench of justice, plaintiff ex officio, against Willem Telier, defendant, to produce his evidence, if he has any, and asking that judgment be given accordingly.

The court, having taken everything duly into consideration, order the defendant to pay the sum of one hundred guilders for the benefit of the plaintiff.

Idem, plaintiff ex officio, against the same defendant, all as above.

The court as above order the defendant to pay a fine of fl. 50:- for the benefit of the poor.

Andries Herperts causes a note to be made that the aforesaid sentence was rendered contrary to his judgment, his opinion being that the aforesaid defendant on the first count should have been condemned to pay the sum of fl. 150:- and on the second count a fine of 300 guilders and in addition be ordered to make honorable reparation.

Idem, plaintiff, against Marcelis Jansz, asking permission to levy on Abram P^{rsz}. Vosburch the sum of fl. 4:-, belonging to the defendant and attached in the hands of the said Vosburch.

The court orders Abram Vosburch to turn over the said four guilders to the plaintiff, against his receipt.

Idem, plaintiff, having attached certain moneys in the custody of Tomas Chiambers, belonging to Jacob Loserik, requesting as above permission to levy the money in his custody.

The court grants the request.

[284] Jacob Gerritsz, plaintiff, against Tomas Chiambers, defendant, about payment of the sum of fl. 382:- for wages earned in building a barn, mill and house, to be paid in beavers or grain.

The court, having heard the parties on both sides, order the defendant to pay the sum of fl. 382:-

Anna de Hulter, plaintiff, against Tomas Chiambers, defendant, to institute his action.

The defendant exhibits a copy of his account.

The plaintiff takes a copy thereof.

Andries de Vos, plaintiff, against P^r. Bronk, defendant, for payment of the sum of fl. 600:-, to be paid one third in seawan and the rest in beavers.

The defendant admits the debt.

The court therefore gives judgment for the plaintiff.

P^r. Bronk, by virtue of a transfer [of claim] from Christoffel Davidts, plaintiff, against Jacob Gerritsz, defendant, for payment of the sum of fl. 264:4:-, according to his note, payable in beavers or grain.

The defendant admits the debt.

The court gives judgment for the plaintiff.

Herman Jacobsz, plaintiff, against Jochem, the baker, defendant. Second default.

Idem, plaintiff, against Willem Hap, defendant. Second default.

[285] Cornelis Cornelisz, plaintiff, against Claes Uylenspiegel, defendant, for payment of the sum of fl.60:— for tavern expenses.

The defendant requests delay until the fall.

The court gives judgment for the plaintiff, granting delay of execution for six weeks.

Michiel Jansz, plaintiff, against Jan Michielsz, defendant, for payment of the sum of fl. 31:1:—, by balance of accounts adjusted in the year 1646.

The court, having heard the parties on both sides, order the defendant to pay the sum demanded, denying the defendant his counter claim.

There was submitted and presented a certain memorial of the honorable consistory of the village of Beverwyck, stating and setting forth that one Michiel Antonisz from Uytrecht, owing to a certain mistaken and untruthful report of a certain neighbor, who had lived in one and the same street next to one Grietge Jacobs, the aforesaid Michiel's first wife, that she, meaning instead of the wife, the mother, was dead and buried, had thereupon, mistaking the one for the other, married for the second time one Femmetge Aelberts, residing in Katskil; that since that time the first wife, the aforesaid Grietge Jacobs from Amsterdam, had also arrived here and revealed herself, whereupon the aforesaid Femmetge had declared that she wished no longer to live with the aforesaid Michiel Anthonisz, being of opinion that the said Grietge Jacobs, having the oldest papers, should have the priority and continue her marriage with the aforesaid Michiel Anthonisz, her own and lawful husband; that the same for the reasons aforesaid was also requested by the aforesaid Grietge

Jacobs; furthermore, that the aforesaid case, being not [286] only of an ecclesiastical but also of a political nature, is referred to the christian authorities to request their approval, the aforesaid consistory requesting finally that at the instance of the said Femmetge Aelbrechts she be granted letters of divorce.

The commissary and magistrates, having examined the aforesaid memorial and the request made therein and having summoned the said Michiel Anthonisz and Grietgen Jacobs to appear before them and confronted them with each other and heard their respective prayers and requests, have after mature deliberation considered, first, that the aforesaid case was contrary neither to the laws of God nor of man, the more so as the aforesaid Michiel Anthonisz had for nine years been out of the country and for a period of more than five successive years had heard or received no word or sign from the aforesaid Grietge Jacobs; also, that all marriages by mistake are *ipso jure* null and void, and finally, that the aforesaid Femmitge Aelberts has renounced her aforesaid matrimonial rights and relinquished them in favor of the aforesaid parties who were first joined in marriage. They therefore approve the aforesaid memorial and ordain, order and consent that the said Michiel Anthonisz and Grietge Jacobs shall be and remain husband and wife and that the bonds of marriage between them are not dissolved by the second marriage with the aforesaid Femmitge, declaring the said Femmitge freed therefrom, restoring her to her former liberty and granting her the right at all times to marry again, where and whomsoever she pleases, without interference or objection by any one.

[287] Tuesday, July 17, 1656

Presentibus omnibus preter Philip P[rsz].

Johan de Deckere, commissary and officer here, requests an interpretation of a certain order issued by this honorable court on the 18th of April last, in regard to certain persons who had and have thus far failed to build on their vacant lots and consequently whether Arien Jansz from Leyden was not then or is not now subject to a fine of fl. 25:–?

The court, having examined the aforesaid request, declare that they were then and are still of opinion that the aforesaid Arien Jansz from Leyden is liable and they therefore condemn him hereby to pay a fine of fl. 25:–, on pain of forfeiting the lot, and this regardless of the provisions of the aforesaid order.

Daniel Ringhout, plaintiff, against Juriaen Teunisz, defendant, for payment of 21 beavers for the purchase and delivery of some brandy.

The defendant admits the debt and promises to pay the plaintiff before his departure for the fatherland.

The court accordingly gives judgment for the plaintiff.

Juriaen Teunisz, plaintiff, against Baefge Pieters, defendant, for payment of 28 beavers for brandy delivered.

The defendant admits the debt.

The court accordingly gives judgment for the plaintiff.

Jan van Housen, plaintiff, against Hendrik Gerritsz, defendant. Default.

Dirk Jansz Croon, plaintiff, against Symon Groot, defendant. Default.

[288] Idem, plaintiff, against Cornelis Vos, defendant, for payment of the sum of fl. 464, by balance of a larger amount for some merchandise delivered, payable in beavers with the interest thereon, according to the custom of the trade, or other arrangement.

The defendant admits the debt.

The court orders the defendant to pay the sum demanded within the space of 14 days, on pain of execution.

Idem, plaintiff, having attached certain 3½ beavers in the custody of Meyndert, the smith, and also 1½ ditto, in the care of Rem Jansz, belonging to Moy Aeltie,[58] the wife of Huybert . . . , against the said Moy Aeltie, defendant.

Default, with order sustaining the attachment.

---

[58] Fair Alida.

Pieter Bronck, plaintiff, against Jan, the weaver, defendant. Default.

Appeared in court Mr Abram Staets and Sander Leendertsz, in charge of the receipt and disbursement of a certain contribution heretofore ordered and levied on property owners for defraying the cost of the bridge and other expenses, who exhibited their account and turned over the balance of the money, amounting to fl. 7:3:–. The same being accepted and the account being verified, the court has expressed its satisfaction therewith and thanked them for their trouble, releasing them hereby from all claims for the money received.

Commissary Johan de Deckere has turned over to Rutger Jacobsz and consigned to him the sum of fl. 93:5:–, heretofore in his custody on account of Jacob Adriaensz.

[289] Wednesday, October 4, anno 1656 [59]

The honorable officer, plaintiff, against Henderick Henericksen, baker, defendant.

The officer says that the defendant was fined by the court twenty-four guilders for having baked light weight bread and ten guilders for using abusive language, which sentence he has refused to comply with and to satisfy. Also, that on account of his refusal he was prohibited from baking, which order in contempt of the court he has also refused to obey.

[The defendant gives] for answer that he has never baked bread for the Christians that was found short of weight, but as to the savages, he declares that he did not know that it was forbidden.

Whether he was not fined thirty-four guilders by the court? [Answers], Yes.

---

[59] Of the remainder of this volume, covering the minutes from October 4 to December 12, 1656, a copy is in part 2 of volume 16 of the New York Colonial Manuscripts, calendared in *Calendar of Historical Manuscripts*, edited by E. B. O'Callaghan, part I, Dutch Manuscripts, 1630–1664, p. 312–13.

Whether the first and second time that notice was served on him, he refused to comply with and satisfy the sentence?

Answers, that he put it off until the arrival of the officer.

Whether, upon further refusal, he was not enjoined by the court from baking for the space of six weeks?

Answers, that the court messenger served notice on him to that effect, but that he gave the court messenger for answer, "Why should I stop baking? My money is ready."

[290] The court messenger being thereupon personally examined and the writ returned by him being inspected, his report is that the defendant answered: "I must nevertheless go on and await what will come of it."

Being asked further whether he has been obedient and stopped baking? Answers, No.

The officer demands that he be fined the double amount and be suspended from the exercise of his trade for the period of three months and remain under arrest until the fine is paid.

A vote being taken, the defendant is by a majority of those present condemned to pay the fine demanded and as an example to others suspended for the space of six weeks, or else ordered to compose with the officer.

[P. STUYVESANT
RUTGER JACOBSEN
ANDERIES HERBERTSEN
JACOB JANSSEN SCHERMERHOORN
PHILIP PIETERSEN][60]

[291] Whereas Egbertjen Egberts, innkeeper in the village of Beverwyck, in contempt and disregard of the ordinances and placards of the Director General and Council and in violation of the express prohibition of the commissary and magistrates of

---

[60] The signatures, which are cut from the record, are supplied from the copy in part 2 of volume 16 of the New York Colonial Manuscripts in the State Library.

the aforesaid village, has not hesitated to sell beer to the savages or, as she herself declares, to give it to them for some *tapoesjens*, according to her own confession made without being subjected to pain or duress, therefore the officer, in his capacity of plaintiff, for the maintenance of the aforesaid ordinances and placards, in accordance with the published and frequently renewed ordinances, has demanded that the aforesaid Egbertje Egberts be fined five hundred guilders and moreover as an example to others be subjected to arbitrary corporal punishment and correction and be banished from this country, as the very sad and dangerous accidents resulting from the tapping, selling, or giving of wine or beer to the savages indeed require that on account of the aforesaid disregard and violation of the original and more than once renewed ordinances and the sad accidents resulting from the drunkeness of the savages, the aforesaid Egbertjen Egberts as an example to others receive arbitrary corporal punishment therefor and be banished from this country. Nevertheless, the Director General and the magistrates of this court, taking into consideration the voluntary admission of guilt by the said Egbertje Egberts and being for the present inclined to show leniency instead of rigor (on which, however, in the future no one is to rely), have [292] sentenced and condemned the aforesaid Egbertjen Egberts, as they sentence and condemn her hereby, to pay a fine of three hundred guilders, she to remain under civil detention until the judgment is satisfied or satisfactory security is given; the further demands of the officer being denied.

Thus done, sentenced and condemned at the session of the Hon. Director General and the Magistrates of the village of Beverwyck, this 6th of October Anno 1656.

> P. STUYVESANT
> RUTGER JACOBSZ
> ANDRIES HERBERTS
> JACOB JANSEN SCHERMERHO[OREN]
> PHILIP PIETERSEN

[293] Whereas Willem Hoffmeyr, born in Brazil,[61] aged about twenty years, in notorious disregard and contempt of the well meant ordinances and placards of the Director General and Council of New Netherland and in violation of the orders and directions of the commissary and magistrates of Fort Orange and the village of Beverwyck, has not hesitated to sell and peddle beer to the savage barbarians, as he without pain or duress confesses and admits that he, Willem Hofmeyer, at present in custody, once with two half barrels in a canoe and afterwards, on the 22d, 23d and 24th of July last past, with five half barrels of good and small beer mixed together, sailed up the river and sold and peddled the beer among the savages (notwithstanding the strict prohibition of the Director General and Council) and what is worse, had it sold and peddled for him by one savage to other savages; and whereas, furthermore, in further contempt of court, the said prisoner, while he was being examined on account of the said offense and released on bail, has not hesitated the same day to admit 28 drunken savages to his house and contrary to the express prohibition and warning of the court to pour out or sell beer to them, which disobedience, disregard, yes, contempt of good order and justice, as well as his frequent violations and transgressions of the well meant ordinances and placards of the Director General and Council of New Netherland issued and repeatedly renewed against the dangerous and harmful sale of [294] beer or wine to the savages, are matters of very evil and injurious consequences which in a land of justice, as an example to others, can and ought not to remain unpunished; therefore, the Director General together with the magistrates of Fort Orange and the village of Beverwyck, in the name and on the part of the High and Mighty Lords, the States General of the United Netherlands and the Honorable Directors of the Chartered West

---

[61] His name does not appear in "Doopregister der Hollanders in Brazilië," 1633-54, published in *Algemeen Nederlandsch Familieblad*, 1888-89, vols. 5 and 6, but under date of January 9, 1647, is recorded the baptism of Sigismundus, son of Harman Hoffmeyer and Joanna Hoffmeyers.

Minutes of October 6, 1656, in the handwriting of Peter Stuyvesant

India Company, administering justice in the case, upon the complaint and demand of the officer and in view of his own free and voluntary confession, sentence and condemn the aforesaid Willem Hoffmeyer, now in custody, as they sentence and condemn him hereby, to pay a fine of five hundred guilders and to be banished from this country for the space of three years, he to remain in strict confinement until the judgment is satisfied. Thus done and sentenced at the session of the Director General and the magistrates of Fort Orange. This day, the sixth of October 1656.

    P. STUYVESANT
    RUTGER JACOBSZ
    ANDRIES HERBERTS
    JACOB JANSEN SCHERMERHOOR[EN]
    PHILIP PIETERSEN

[295] Whereas Dirckie Harmense, innkeeper in the village of Beverwyck, in disregard and contempt of the ordinances and placards of the Director General and Council and contrary to the express prohibition of the commissary and magistrates of the aforesaid village, has not hesitated to sell, or, as she herself declares, to give, beer to the savages for some *tapoesjens*, according to her own confession made without pain or duress, whereupon the officer, in his capacity of plaintiff, for the maintenance of the aforesaid ordinances and placards, in accordance with the provisions of the aforesaid and repeatedly renewed ordinances, has demanded that the aforesaid Dirckje Harmens be fined five hundred guilders and furthermore that as an example to others she receive arbitrary corporal punishment and correction and be banished from this country, as the sad and dangerous accidents resulting from the tapping, selling or giving of wine or beer to the savages indeed demand that in view of the aforesaid disregard and violation of the aforementioned and more than once renewed ordinances and the sad accidents resulting from the drunkeness of the savages the aforesaid Dirckje Harmens, as an example to others, receive arbitrary and corporal punishment

and be banished from this country. However, taking into consideration the voluntary confession of the aforesaid Dirckjen Harmens, the Director General and the magistrates of this court are for the present inclined [206] to show leniency instead of rigor (on which, however, no one should rely in the future) and have sentenced and condemned the aforesaid Dirckjen Harmens, as they sentence and condemn her hereby, to pay a fine of three hundred guilders, she to remain in civil detention until the satisfaction of the judgment or until she shall have furnished satisfactory security, the further demands of the officer being denied. Thus done, sentenced and condemned at the session of the Director General and the magistrates of the village of Beverwyck, this 6th of October Anno 1656.

P. STUYVESANT
RUTGER JACOBSZ
ANDRIES HERBERTS
JACOB JANSEN SCHERMERHO[OREN]
PHILIP PIETERSEN

The 12th of October the officer arrested a certain drunken savage, committing insolence, and brought him on a brewer's wagon to the fort where he was placed in confinement.

[297] The 13th of October Anno 1656, at the request of the officer of Fort Orange, the savage named Macheck Sipoeti, a Mahican, was examined by Jan Tomassen, well acquainted with the Mahican language, in the presence of the Hon. J. B. Rencelaer, director of the colony of Renselaerswyck, and the Hon. Ruth Jacobsen and Anderies Herbertsen, magistrates of the court of Fort Orange and the village of Beverwyck.

He was asked first where he had been drinking, whereupon he answered, in an Indian house, situated near the Gojer's kill.[62]

He was then asked where the savages had obtained the brandy, whereupon he answered, on the east side of the river, from the Dutch, who lived there.

---

[62] Near Schodack. See *Early Records of Albany*, 2:131.

Thirdly, he was asked the names of the Dutch who had sold or given them the brandy, whereupon he answered that he did not know their names.

Finally, he was asked how large the cask was, whereupon he indicated the size in such a way that one was able to judge that it must have been an anker.

RUTGER JACOBSZ
ANDRIES HERBERTS
LA MONTAGNE

[298] Ordinary Session, October 17, 1656

Fredrick Hendericksz, skipper, plaintiff, against Henderick Jochimsen, defendant.

The plaintiff demands payment by the defendant of 37 whole beavers, due him on a note.

The defendant admits the debt.

The parties being heard by the court, the defendant is ordered to pay the plaintiff the number of 37 whole beavers, at once.

Jan Jansen van Ekel, plaintiff, against Abraham Pietersen. The defendant having failed to appear the second time, default is entered against him.

Gossen Gerritsen, plaintiff, having power of attorney from the widow of Reyer Stoffelsen, against Gillis Pietersen. The plaintiff, in his capacity, demands payment of the sum of 200 guilders, according to a note of hand which he exhibits in court.

The defendant admits the debt.

The parties being heard, the court orders the defendant to pay the aforesaid sum of 200 guilders within the space of two months.

Lowies Cobus, having power of attorney from Jan Peeck, plaintiff, against Claes Ripsen, defendant.

He demands payment of 50 guilders made over to the defendant, arising from a certain fine.

The defendant says that he satisfied the former officer Dyckman for the aforesaid sum.

The wife of the aforesaid Dyckman, in the absence of her husband, acknowledges that the aforesaid sum was paid to her husband. The defendant is discharged by the court from the plaintiff's demand.

[299] Gossen Gerritsen, attorney for the widow of Reyer Stoffelsen, plaintiff, against Christoffel Davids, defendant.

The plaintiff demands payment of 60 guilders in corn.

The defendant admits the debt and promises to pay, on condition that the note which he executed in favor of Reyer Stoffelsen be returned to him; also a silver beaker which he gave to Reyer Stoffelsen, deceased, to have it remodeled in Holland.

The parties having been heard, the defendant is ordered by the court to pay the said sum of 60 guilders in corn within the space of six weeks, provided that the note, if there is one, be at the same time returned to him. As to the beaker, he is to corroborate his claim by testimony.

Gossen Gerritsen, plaintiff, against Lambert van Valckenborch, defendant.

Owing to nonappearance of the defendant, default is entered against him.

Gossen Gerritsen, plaintiff, against Claes Teunissen, defendant. The defendant failing to appear, default is taken against him.

Isbrant Eldersen, plaintiff, against Leendert Philipsen, defendant. The plaintiff demands the return of a pair of black cloth sleeves given to the defendant to be altered.

The defendant admits that he received the half sleeves from the plaintiff, but claims that they were stolen from his house.

The parties having been heard, the defendant is ordered to restore the sleeves in question, or pay 8 guilders cash for them.

Jan Gouw, plaintiff, against Harmen Jacobsen, defendant.

For want of appearance, default is taken against the defendant.

[300] Tomas Poulussen, plaintiff, against Tjerck Claesen.

The plaintiff demands payment of 6 beavers.

The defendant admits the debt, but claims that 16 guilders is due him by the plaintiff for wages.

The plaintiff maintains that he does not owe as much.

The parties having been heard, the defendant is ordered to pay 4 beavers to the plaintiff within the space of six weeks, and meanwhile to settle the dispute in regard to the wages and after the liquidation to pay to the plaintiff the balance, if any there be, of the value of 2 beavers.

N. B. The time of payment expires on the first of December.

The officer, plaintiff, in a criminal case, against Jurriaen the glazier, defendant.

The officer says that the defendant in the night of the 11th of October, coming from the watch to the door of his house, knocked on said door and after it had been opened by his wife, drew his sword from the scabbard and struck with it his own wife, saying: "You d—— whore and rascal," at which noise Cornelis Pietersen Hoogenboom, then lying asleep on a chest, woke up and fled to the garret, where he was followed by the defendant, who held a candle and his naked sword in his hand and finally, without any altercation, cut and wounded Cornelis Pietersen in his right arm, as appears from the complaint of the said Cornelis Pietersen Hogenboom, the report of Mr Jacob de Hinsse, surgeon, and the testimony of Jan Barentsen, carpenter, Jan de Graef and Pieter, the baker, [301] examined by the honorable magistrates upon interrogatories.

The defendant says that on knocking at his door, he heard a noise of some one climbing into his garret, whereupon he conceived a suspicion of theft or other mischief, which caused him to visit his garret and finding there Cornelis Pietersen Hoogenboom hidden under a bedstead, he thought himself justified in attacking him in his own house as a thief or criminal, considering that the sun had set.

The magistrates, having learned from the report of the surgeon that the wound is not dangerous and heard from the witnesses the circumstances of the case, order, in consideration of the circumstances, that the defendant shall settle with the officer, provided however that he compensate Cornelis Pietersen Hoogenboom for maintenance, medicine and lost time.

Gommer Poulussen requests the court to grant him a place for a garden. The magistrates have taken the matter under advisement and will accommodate the petitioner according the situation of the place.

La Montagne
Rutger Jacobsz
Andries Herberts

[302] October 21, Anno 1656

Extraordinary session requested by Marceles Janssen

Marcelus Janssen, plaintiff, against Pieter Adriaensen, *alias* Soogemackelyck.

The plaintiff demands prompt payment of six hundred and twenty-five guilders, which the defendant promised to pay him within the space of fourteen days, which have now expired.

The defendant brings into court 386 guilders in strung and loose seawan, which the plaintiff accepts. He consents that the attachment against the defendant be vacated, but demands that he shall pay the costs of the extraordinary session.

The parties having been heard, the court orders that they shall each pay one half of the costs of the extraordinary session.

Lowies Cobus, plaintiff, against the wife of Jeles Fonda.

The plaintiff complains that the defendant without his knowledge or consent has taken an apron belonging to his wife hanging on the fence.

The defendant denies the charge and alleges that the plaintiff's wife gave her the said apron as a pledge for five and a half beavers, and the defendant being not satisfied with the apron as a pledge for the said sum, the plaintiff's wife gave her an under shirt in addition.

[303] The parties having been heard by the court, the court, seeing that they have neither proof nor witnesses, order the defendant to confirm her statement by oath, giving her time until the next court day to consider the solemnity of an oath.

Minutes of October 17, 1656, signed by Commissary La Montagne

Carsten Fredrickx, being summoned by order of the court to place a value on his lot which he must cede for the accommodation of this community to remove to the said lot a house leaning against the church, demands one hundred beavers, whereupon the court decides to take the matter under advisement.

La Montagne
Rutger Jacobsz
Andries Herberts

[Ordinance for the Sweeping of Chimneys][63]

[304] Whereas daily experience teaches us that in consequence of the foul and unswept condition of the chimneys, they often take fire and generally the houses also, yes, frequently the neighboring buildings, especially when they are covered with inflammable materials, whereby great damage is done not only to houses and goods, but — sad spectacle — to people also; therefore, the vice director and magistrates of this court, wishing as a matter of their official duty to prevent such accidents to the best of their ability, do hereby order all burghers and inhabitants of Fort Orange and the village of Beverwyck, and each one in particular, to keep the chimneys of the respective houses clean and free from danger of fire, on pain of forfeiture of one pound Flemish for every chimney which shall be found dirty and declared as such 15 days after the publication hereof.

Done in Fort Orange, the 24th of October 1656.

La Montagne
Rutger Jacobsz
Andries Herberts

---

[63] Printed in *Laws and Ordinances of New Netherland*, p. 257.

[305] Ordinary Session, October 24, Anno 1656

Johannes van Twillert, plaintiff, against Christoffel Davidts, defendant.

The plaintiff demands payment of the sum of 564 guilders, 8 stivers, according to the voluntary confession [of the defendant], whereupon judgment was given by the court of Rencelaerswyck and by virtue thereof an attachment secured against certain moneys in the custody of Jacob Janssen Stollen and Tomas Chambert.

The defendant admits the debt and agrees that the plaintiff shall receive from the hands of the aforesaid Jacob Janssen Stollen and Tomas Chambert the moneys attached, up to the amount of his debt due to the aforesaid van Twillert.

The magistrates, having heard the confession and the consent of the defendant, [give judgment for] the aforesaid sum of 564 guilders and 8 stivers and order that the property in the hands of Jacob Janssen Stollen and Tomas Chambert may be levied upon by the plaintiff to the amount of 564 guilders and 8 stivers.

Jan Janssen van Eeckel, plaintiff, against Abraham Pietersen Vosbergh.

The plaintiff requests execution of the judgment given against the defendant on the 29th of August last, whereby the defendant was ordered to pay twelve beavers within six weeks, which have now expired.

The wife of the defendant, appearing instead of her husband, offers to pay cash in seawan, or in beavers in the spring.

The plaintiff accepts the offer of payment in beavers on the first of June, provided the defendant give him one beaver by way of interest.

The magistrates, having heard the agreement between the parties, order the defendant to pay the sum in question to the plaintiff on the first of June Anno 1657, provided that the defendant shall pay the plaintiff one beaver as interest.

[306] Jan Janssen van Eeckelen, plaintiff, against Abraham Pietersen Vosburgh.

The parties being heard, it is ordered that the defendant, Abraham Pietersen, shall personally appear.

Evert Pries, plaintiff, against Jan van Aecken, defendant.

The plaintiff demands compensation for damage suffered by him on goods in his chest, which was entrusted to the care of the defendant and which damage occurred through the defendant's fault.

The defendant says that he did not have the care of the chest, but that it was left at his house by the plaintiff.

The magistrates order the parties each to choose a referee to adjust the matter.

Lowies Cobus, attorney of Jan Peeck, plaintiff, against Abraham Vosbergh, defendant.

The defendant failing to appear, default is entered against him.

Jan Gouw, plaintiff, against Harmen Jacobsen, defendant.

The plaintiff demands payment of 17 and a half beavers.

The defendant offers to make payment in seawan or grain.

The magistrates, having heard the parties, order the defendant to pay the number of 17 and a half beavers within the space of six weeks.

Frans Barentsen, plaintiff, against Abram Pieter Vosbrugh.

For want of appearance of the defendant, default is taken against him.

[307] Fop Barentsen against Cornelis Vos, defendant.

The defendant failing to appear, default is taken against him.

Cornelis Teunissen requests for Tomas Janssen Mingael a lot for a house, situated between Pieter Loockermans and Pieter Messen.

The honorable magistrates have taken the matter under advisement in order to accommodate the petitioner in all fairness.

Ultimo October Anno 1656

Ordinary session held in Fort Orange. Present: La Montagne, commissary and Rutgher Jacobsz and Andries Harperss:, magistrates.

Juffrouw Johanna Thullert,[64] plaintiff, against Harmen Jacobsen, defendant.

The defendant failing to appear, default is entered against him.

Juffrouw Johanna Thullert, plaintiff, against Govert Hendericksen, defendant.

The defendant failing to appear, default is entered against him.

Jochim, the baker, plaintiff, against Willem Hoffmeyr, defendant.

The parties having been heard, the court refers the case to referees chosen by the parties respectively, to settle the matter in an amicable manner.

Henderick Anderiessen, plaintiff, [308] against Henderick Gerritsen, defendant.

The plaintiff demands reparation for injury to his reputation done by the defendant.

The defendant denies that he has injured the plaintiff's reputation in any way.

The court orders the plaintiff to prove his charges.

Jan Janssen van Eeckelen, plaintiff, against Abraham Pietersen Vosbergen, defendant.

The plaintiff demands compensation for two hogsheads of French wine, the balance of three, put by the plaintiff in the defendant's cellar, which were spoiled through the defendant's fault, as the said defendant refused to sell them to some who tried to buy them.

The defendant maintains that the said damage is not his fault, as the wine was not placed in his care, but only put in his cellar with his consent by the plaintiff, who gave him permission to sell of it as much as he could, which he did, having sold one [hogs-

---

[64] Madam Johanna de Hulter.

head]. The remaining two hogsheads, which spoiled, he tried to improve with the help of Mr van Hamel, as the plaintiff afterwards also sought to do with the said Hamel's help.

The parties having been heard, the court orders the plaintiff to take back the wine in question. In regard to the damage, [309] the plaintiff's demand is denied and the defendant is discharged.

Jochim, the baker, requests the court to grant him a place for a garden.

The court will take the request under advisement and after inspection of the place requested, accommodate the said Jochim in all fairness.

The Honorable Anderies Herbertsen, magistrate, has declared before the court that the 27th of this month a Maquaes savage came quite drunk into his house and after committing many acts of violence left some goods in his house. Coming the other day to the said house to fetch his goods, he declared to the deponent that the wine which made him drunk was bought by three squas from Barent Pietersen, the miller.

November 7, Anno 1656

Ordinary session. Present: La Montagne, commissary; Rutgher Jacobsz:, Andries Harperss:, Jacob Schermerhooren and Philip Pieterss:, magistrates.

Juffrouw Johanna t'Hulter, plaintiff, against Tomas Clabbort, defendant.

The plaintiff demands payment of a certain account delivered to the defendant.

The defendant maintains that he satisfied her by means of a counter-claim delivered to the plaintiff.

The parties having been heard, it is ordered by the court that the plaintiff shall within the space of fourteen days state her objections to the defendant's account.

[310] Juffrouw t'Hullert,[65] plaintiff, against Govert Hendericksen, defendant.

---

[65] Madam Johanna de Hulter.

The defendant failing to appear, default is taken against him. N. B. Also default for the second and third times.

Harmen Jacobsen, plaintiff, against Jan Roeloffsen, Gerrit Hendericksen and Huybert Janssen, defendants.

The court orders the defendant, Huybert Janssen, to pay the admitted debt within the space of three months and orders default to be entered against Jan Roeloffsen and Gerrit Hendericksen.

Arent vanden Berch, plaintiff, against Henderick Gerritsen, defendant.

The defendant failing to appear, default is taken against him.

Cornelis Teunissen, plaintiff, in a case of slander against Abraham Stevensen Crawaet, defendant.

The defendant failing to appear, default is taken against him.

The officer, in a case of slander and insolence, plaintiff, against Tomas Chambert, *alias* Clabbort.

The plaintiff demands reparation for abusive remarks made in his presence and that of the entire court about the honorable directors, the director general and council and the entire court on the 6th of November last in the house of Willem Freedericksen Bout, where the [311] said court and the surveyors were met to decide some question regarding the survey.

The defendant excuses himself on the ground that he was drunk and does not know what he said or did, saying that he is sorry that he used offensive language to his superior authorities. He promises not to do it again and declares that he is ready to undergo such punishment as he deserves in case he should repeat the offense, craving pardon for the fault committed.

The court, observing the defendant's sorrow and his promises, and considering the condition he was in when he uttered the said abusive remarks, excuses him for the present from undergoing the merited punishment and, preferring leniency to rigor, condemn the defendant to pay a fine of one hundred and fifty guilders, to be paid within the space of six weeks.

N. B. the time will expire on the 20th of December.

November 22, Anno 1656

Ordinary session held in Fort Orange. Present: Rutgher Jacobss:, Andries Harperss:, Jacob Schermerhooren and Philippe Pieterss:, magistrates.

Frans Barentsen Pastoor, plaintiff, against Abraham Pietersen Vosborch, defendant.

The plaintiff demands payment of a balance of twenty-seven pieces of beaver at fl. 10 apiece, in seawan, which the defendant paid him in seawan at fl. 8 apiece, so that there is still due him fl. 54.

[312] The defendant maintains that he paid the twenty-seven beavers in full in seawan, at fl. 8 apiece.

The parties having been heard, the defendant is ordered to pay the plaintiff the sum of fl. 54 in seawan.

Frans Barentsen Pastoor, plaintiff, against Jan van Breemen, defendant.

The defendant failing to appear, default is taken against him.

Frans Barentsen Pastoor, plaintiff, against Jan Martensen, *alias* the weaver, defendant.

The defendant failing to appear, default is taken against him.

Lowies Cobus, as attorney, plaintiff, against Frans Barentsen Pastoor, defendant.

The plaintiff says that he had ten beavers attached in the hands of the defendant, which ten beavers the defendant paid in spite of the attachment.

The defendant says that he paid them by order of the court.

The plaintiff asks adjournment until the next court day, in order to have Pieter Brouwer subpoenaed.

The court consents to the adjournment.

Fop Barentsen, plaintiff, against Cornelis Vos, defendant.

The plaintiff demands payment of one hundred and fifty guilders loaned by him to the defendant some weeks ago.

The defendant denies that he owes the plaintiff any money.

[313] The court orders the plaintiff to prove the alleged debt on the next court day by written contract or testimony of witnesses.

November 28, Anno 1656

Ordinary session held in Fort Orange. Present: **R**utgher Jacobs:, Andries Harpertss:, Jacob Schermerhooren and Philippe Pieterss:, magistrates.

Juffrouw de Hulter, plaintiff, against Jan Gouw.

The plaintiff demands payment for 1200 tiles, amounting to seven and a half beavers.

The defendant denies that he owes the plaintiff the sum of fl. 64.

The parties having been heard, the defendant is ordered by the court to pay the plaintiff the sum of fl. 64 in beavers within the space of six weeks.

Cornelis Cornelissen, the younger, plaintiff, against Claes Vylens, defendant.

The defendant failing to appear, default is taken against him.

Foppe Barens, plaintiff, against Cornelis Vos, defendant.

The plaintiff, pursuant to the order of the court of the 22 of November last, produces Marcelus Janssen and Harmen Bastiaensen, as witnesses, who, appearing, testify that being requested by the parties to adjust their differences, the defendant's wife said that she would not speak of anything that happened before, as a result of which they, [314] the deponents, parted without having accomplished anything.

The court orders that a copy of the testimony of the witnesses shall be delivered to the defendant for his consideration and if he has any objections to make he is to submit them on the next court day.

Arent van den Berch, plaintiff, against Henderick Gerritsen, defendant.

The parties having been heard, the defendant is ordered to pay 3 beavers when called upon to do so.

The following persons are summoned to appear on account of their being found in the taverns after the ringing of the bell, contrary to the ordinance:

Harmen Jacobsen Bambus, tavernkeeper. **Paid.**
Jan Gauw } Default.
Harmen, the carpenter }
Jan Eeckelen. **Paid.**
Teunis Jacobsen. Default.
Albert, the carpenter, tavernkeeper. **Paid.**
Geurt Hendericksz } Default.
Gerrit Viesbeeck }
Daniel, the baker. **Paid.**
Henderick *Clootendraeyer* (ball turner) }
Henderick, the tailor, *alias* " Cordiael " } Default
Henderick, *alias* the " Styve Snyder " (stiff tailor) }

Jacob Janssen van Noortstrant requests the court to be appointed gager of the casks.

The court grants the request.

[315][66] Ordinary session held in Fort Orange on the 5th of December Anno 1656.

Present: Andries Harpartss:, Jacob Schermerhooren and Philippe Pieterss:, magistrates.

Anderies Herbertsen, as attorney of Goosen Gerritsen, plaintiff, against Claes Teunissen, defendant.

The plaintiff demands payment of a note of fl. 848:—

The defendant admits that he owes a certain balance of account and offers to pay it with his house, requesting that the plaintiff show his power of attorney.

The court orders the plaintiff to show his power of attorney on the next court day.

[316] Anderies Herbertsen, plaintiff in a case of slander, against the wife of Henderick, the baker, defendant.

The plaintiff says and complains that the defendant in his absence has called him a double thief who stole her meat out

---

[66] The upper half of the page is blank.

of the tub and her firewood out of her house, which he offers to prove.

The defendant denies having made such accusations, but admits that she said that the plaintiff as her accuser has been the cause of her husband being obliged to pay a fine of fl. 68, as a result of which they had to go without meat and wood.

The parties having been heard, the court orders the plaintiff to furnish the defendant with a copy of his complaint, to which she is to make answer on the next court day.

Jacob Schermerhoorn, plaintiff, against Christoffel Davids, defendant.

The plaintiff demands payment of 14 schepels of maize, being the balance of a note executed more than 10 years ago.

The defendant denies that he owes the amount, but declares that he is satisfied to pay it if the plaintiff swears to it.

The plaintiff having taken the oath, the court orders the defendant to pay the plaintiff two beavers in specie and 10 stivers in seawan.

Claes Hendericksz, plaintiff, against Gerrit Slechtenhorst, defendant.

The plaintiff demands the defendant's reasons for forbidding him to build on his own ground.

[317] The defendant says that the ground on which the plaintiff was busy building, belongs to him as lessee and he maintains that no one has a right to build thereon without his consent during the term of his lease.

The plaintiff exhibits a lease in the defendant's own handwriting, in the margin of which was written that the plaintiff was to have the use of the yard at present in controversy.

The defendant maintains that such use was granted to the plaintiff only to keep his woodpile there and to use the ground for bleaching purposes, offering to prove the same.

The parties having been heard, the court orders the defendant to prove on the next court day that he has granted the use of the yard to the plaintiff only for the purpose of piling up wood and of bleaching there.

Pieter Loockermans, plaintiff, against Matteus Abrahams, defendant.

The plaintiff demands payment of three and a half beavers.

The defendant admits the debt and offers to pay, provided that the three beavers in the hands of Jan Gauw, which the plaintiff has caused to be attached, shall be left at his disposal.

The court orders the defendant to pay the plaintiff the three and a half beavers. Meanwhile, the attachment of the three beavers is sustained.

Matteus Abrahamsen, plaintiff, against Jan Gauw, defendant.

The defendant failing to appear, default is taken against him.

[318] Foppe Barentsen, plaintiff, against Cornelis Vos, defendant.

The defendant submits his defense in writing, of which a copy is asked by the plaintiff.

The court orders the defendant to furnish the plaintiff with a copy of his defense, to which he is to file his answer on the next court day.

Albert Gysbertsen, wheelwright, requests a certain lot for a garden.

The court will first inspect the place so as to accommodate the petitioner according to its location.

Arent van Curler, having power of attorney from Adriaen Janssen from Leyden, tavernkeeper in the colony of Renselaerswyck, plaintiff, against Marcelus Janssen, formerly farmer of the excise on wine, beer and liquor sold by the tavernkeepers of Fort Orange, the village of Beverwyck and the dependencies thereof, defendant.

The plaintiff demands the return of an anker of brandy which the defendant about 13 months ago, on his own authority and without the knowledge of and consent of the officer of Fort Orange and the village of Beverwyck, unlawfully seized on the public street and highway and appropriated to himself, for which aforesaid [319] anker of brandy, the principal duly ordered and directed his servant to obtain a retail certificate from the aforesaid farmer, as was actually requested, according to the aforesaid affidavit filed herewith. The plaintiff requests therefore that the defendant be ordered to restore the aforesaid anker of brandy without loss or damage, all according to law.

Was signed: Arent van Curler.

The defendant requests a copy of the plaintiff's demand.

The court orders that a copy of the plaintiff's demands shall be delivered to the defendant.

December 12, Anno 1656

Ordinary session held in Fort Orange

Harmen Jacobsen, plaintiff, against Pieter Stevensen, defendant.

The plaintiff demands payment of fl.30, which the defendant owes.

The defendant admits that he owes fl.23:12, and no more.

The court orders the defendant to pay the acknowledged sum of fl.23:12.

Leendert Philipsen, plaintiff, against Tierck Claessen, defendant.

[320] The plaintiff says that the defendant, having hired a house from him, has without his knowledge sublet it to some one else and requests that the rent thereof be paid to him.

The defendant agrees to it.

The court orders that the plaintiff shall receive the rent of his own house.

Foppe Barentsen, plaintiff, against Cornelis de Vos, defendant.

The defendant asks for a copy of the plaintiff's demand.

The court orders the plaintiff to furnish the defendant with a copy of his demand, to file his answer thereto on the next court day.

Anderies Herbertsen, plaintiff, against Claes Teunissen, defendant.

The plaintiff exhibits his power of attorney.

The court refers the parties to the previously issued order.

Frans Barentsen Pastoor, plaintiff, against Jan van Bremen and Pieter Bronck, defendants.

The parties failing to appear, the second default is taken against Jan van Bremen and the first default against Pieter Bronck.

Claes Hendericksen, plaintiff, against Gerrit Slechtenhorst, defendant.

The defendant produces Jan de Ret [67] as a witness, who testifies that he was present when the copy [321] of the lease between the parties was changed or added to and that he heard the defendant simply grant the use of the yard in question to the plaintiff, but that he did not hear him give any consent to build thereon.

---

[67] Jan Dareth.

Finis

INDEX

Abeel, Stoffel Jansen, *see* Jansen, Stoffel

Abrahams, Matteus, 305

Adriaensen, Jacob, wheelwright, lot, 18, 187; to finish wagon, 72; house sold to Cornelis Segersen, 98, 137, 275, 276; to testify in court, 153, 156; attachment of money due to, 242; money of, paid to Rutger Jacobsen, 286;
    sues Van Bremen, 96; Van Loosdrecht, 153, 165, 169;
    sued for wages, 133, 134; for debt, 135, 136, 137; by Ryverdingh, 259

Adriaensen, Jan, 155

Adriaensen, Pieter, permission to tap, 45; fined for unlawful tapping, 51; sues Cornelis Vos, 121; petition regarding attachment of beer, 202;
    sued for wages, 122, 123; for debt, 294

Adriaensen, Rut, *see* Arentsen, Rutger

Aelbrechts, Femmitge, *see* Alberts, Femmetgen

Aeltgie (Fair Alida), 262, 284. *See also* Jans, Aelgen

Aertsen, Aert, 70

Aertsen, Wouter, *see* Van Putten, Wouter Aertsen

Albert, the carpenter, *see* Gerritsen, Albert

Alberts (Aelbrechts), Femmetgen, examination of, 26; sued for debt, 73, 219; widow of Hendrick Jansen Westerkamp, 182; sues De Wolff and Slichtenhorst, 214, 215, 217; called Geverts, 219; money belonging to, 243; married to Michiel Antonisz, 282; marriage annulled, 283

Albertsen (Aelbertsen), Barent, 185, 272

Albertsen, Willem, complaints against by De Hooges, 36, 43; fighting, 36, 37; settlement with Dyckman, 136; paid for lease of yacht, 140;
    sues Clomp 35; Bronck, 141; Gerbertsen, 168, 171;
    sued for beavers, 31; by Dirck Nes, 32; for stealing a cheese, 36; by Schuyler, for contempt of court, 66, 67; for debt, 74, 108, 130, 140; for return of a jack, 172

Allerton, Isaac, 147

Andriessen (Bradt), Albert, sues Herpertsen, 95, 131; payment to, 131; son-in-law, 136; requests a lot, 185; prosecuted for holding separate divine service and attachment of house rent, 251, 255, 258

Andriessen (Bradt), Arent, oath of burgher, 49; dispute about a gun, 154; loan of money to Director General, 162; testimony, 214, 215, 219

Andriessen (Driess, Van Driest), Hendrick, 20, 140, 298

Andriessen, Luykas, 108

Andryesen, Jan, 190

Antonisen, Michiel, 282, 283

Appel, Adriaen Jansen, *see* Jansen (Appel), Adriaen

Arent the Noorman, *see* Andriesen (Bradt), Arent

Arentsen, Rutger, petition for lot, 16; sues Jacobsen, 54; promise to marry Giertgen Nannix, 57; death, 132; house, 211; settlement of estate, 268
    sued for debt, 53, 71; for slander, 56, 65; for wages, 95, 118; by Bout, 27; by Jansen, 68; by Gerritsen, 85, 93

Ariaen from Alckmaer, *see* Pietersen, Ariaen

Backer, Jacob, 232

Backer, Jochim, *see* Wesselsen, Jochem

Bamboes (Bambus), Herman Jacobsen, prosecuted for violating ordinances, 241, 303; complaints against, for unlawful acts at his tavern, 243, 260, 261, 262, 271; appearance in court, 272;

    sues Margaret Chambers, 275; Jochem Wesselsen, 279;

    sued by De Deckere, 261; for debt, 264, 274, 279

Banker (Bancker), Gerrit, 226, 229, 230, 233, 234

Barentsen (Barens), Foppe, 297, 301, 302, 305, 306

Barentsen, Frans, *see* Pastoor, Frans Barentsen

Barentsen, Jan, 293

Bastiaensen, Harmen, house, 16, 114; misdemeanors, 46, 57; work on Company's house, 47; engaged as surveyor, 79, 187; ordered to pay collector for goods, 84; requests payment of wages, 107; to build bridge, 143; referee, 154, 155; loan of money to Director General, 162; wife Hestor, 210; to be upheld in capacity of surveyor, 217; testimony, 302; prosecuted for violating ordinances, 303;

    sues Sanders, 27; Hendricksen, 53; Jansen, 54; Croon, 72; Adriaensen, 122, 123; Jacobsen, 263;

    sued for receipt for beavers, 31; about a lot, 147, 156

Becker, Jochem, *see* Wesselsen, Jochem

Beeckman, Willem 163

Bembo, Jan, soldier, 84, 142

Bensingh (Bensinck, Bentsingh), Dirck, garden, 21, 64, 157, 158; sale of house and garden, 33; appeal to, 72; purchase of yacht, 93; survey of lot, 117;

Bensingh (Bensinck, Bentsingh), Dirck — *Continued*

    asks for more ground, 131; brother-in-law, 252;

    sues Herpertsen, 58, 65; Ryckertsen, 243;

    sued for abusive language, 130, 276; for canceling purchase of a house, 279

Berck, Willem, 257

Biermans (Bierman), Hendrick, 133, 136, 141

Bogardus, Annetgen, 41, 44, 83, 107, 200

Bont (Bout), Piet, wounded by Jan Gouw, 191; prosecuted by De Deckere, 245; for violence at house of Bamboes, 261, 271; referees to consider case, 277; fined, 280

Boon, Cornelis, 254

Boot, Dirck Claessen, 30

Borremans (Forremans), Frans, 86, 88

Bos, Cornelis Teunissen, *see* Van Westbroeck, Cornelis Teunissen

Boucher, Pierre, 90

Bout, Piet, *see* Bont, Piet

Bout, Willem Fredericksen, bailsman, 40, 46, 71; horse mill, 51, 53, 113; ordered to pay collector for goods, 84; complaints about various actions at his house, 86, 94, 108, 110, 121, 300; request to pay tapsters' excise in lump sum, 97; testimony against Clomp, 107; trade in beer, 138, 142, 143, 148; to build bridge, 143; money due to, 148, 196; sued for sale of horses, 150; loan of money to Director General, 163; appears in court for Stoll, 165; statement on nicknames of houses, 201; wife of, 239; referee, 250;

    prosecuted about lot, 83; for slander and assault, 86; for serving liquor on Sunday, 224;

    sues Arentsen, 27; Jacobsen, 144, 147; Teunissen, 69

COURT MINUTES, 1652-1656 311

Bouts, Geertgen, wife of Willem Fredericksen Bout, 220. *See also* Nanningh (Nannix), Geertgen
Boutsen, Cors, 184, 185, 186, 195, 201
Bradt, Albert Andriessen, *see* Andriessen, Albert
Bradt, Arent Andriessen, *see* Andriessen, Arent
Brant, Adriaen Claessen, **169**
Brant, Jan Claesen, 48, 51
Brantsen, Evert, 46
Bronck, Pieter, lot, 18; fighting at his house, 56, 86, 108, 118; bailsman, 58; asks for extension of time for building on lots, 133; loan of money to Director General, 163; testimony about Jacob Flodder, 191; enjoined from tapping beer, 219; surety for, 236; mentioned, 94;
    sues Michielsen, 29; van Bremen, 43, 276, 278; Herpertsen, 85, 92; Thomassen, 89; Jansen, 154; Pietersen, 171, **178**; Flodder, 178; Gerritsen, 281; Teunissen, 250, 259; Martensen, 285;
    sued by Joost the baker, 20, 24, 28; for debt, 34, 41, 50, 198, 281; by Jacobsen, 35; about his lot, 83; by Albertsen, 141; about payment for grain, 214, 215, 219; by Pastoor, 307
Brouwer, Jacob de, *see* Gerritsen, Jacob, brewer
Brouwer, Pieter, 301
Bruynen, Pieter, 262
Bruynsen (Brynsen), Auckes (Anker), 133, 263
Buildings, occupied by court, 10

Calendar of the minutes, 11
Canaqueese, an Indian, 91
Carstensen (the Noorman), Carsten, lot, 138, 185, 220; suit for recovery of beavers, 236; wife, 242; sued for debt, 275

Carstensen (**Cassersen)**, Hendrick, 45
Chambers (Clabb**orts)**, Margriet, 275
Chambers (Chambre, Clabbort, Chiambers), Thomas, lot, 245; accounts with Slecht, 262; moneys in custody of, 281, 296; mentioned, 106, 226; prosecuted for slanderous remarks about court, 300;
    sues de Forrest, 17; Jacobsen, 224; Jacob Stol, 244; 246; 252;
    sued by Anna de Hulter, 277, 281, 299; for debt, 281
Clabbort, Thomas, *see* Chambers, Thomas
Clabbort, Margriet, *see* Chambers, Margriet
Claes, Marritgen, 133
Claessen, Ariaen, 179, 183, 187, 207
Claessen, Dirrick, *see* Boot, Dirck Claesen
Claessen, Tierck, lot, 264; sues Powell, 253;
    prosecuted for fighting, 245, 247; for being with Lutherans, 247;
    sued by Leendertsen, 254; for debt, 292; for house rent, 306
Clauw, Frans Pietersen, *see* Pietersen, Frans
Cleyn, *see* Kleyn
Clomp (Klomp), Jacob Symonsen, complaint about attachment of money, 94; abusive language, 94, 107, 108, 110; fined, 111; money sent to Director General in sloop of, 162; mentioned, 71, 96, 183, 184;
    prosecuted for fighting, 21; for selling brandy to savages, 69, 70, 71, 74;
    sues Croon, 29; van Bremen, 73, 101;
    sued for debt, 29, 30; for return of boards, 35; for non-delivery of wheat, 66; about lot, 83; for payment of fine,

Clomp (Klomp), Jacob Symonsen —
    Continued
        85; for wages, 172; for failure
        to deliver hogs, 183, 184
Clomp, Jan, 29
Clootendraeyer, Hendrick, 303
Cnyver, Claes Thysen, 130
Cobes (Cobus), Ludovicus, asks
    permission to keep school, 238;
    attorney for Jan Peeck, 291, 297;
    sues the wife of Jeles Fonda, 294;
    sues Frans Barentsen Pastoor, 301.
    See also Jacobussen, Loys
Coenraets, Hans, 242, 250
Coeymans, Barent Pietersen, *see*
    Pietersen, Barent
Coeymans, Luykas Pietersen, *see*
    Pietersen, Luykas
Colebrantsen, Pieter, 262
Coninck (Koninck), Thomas, 149
Cornelis, Broer, *see* Teunissen, Cornelis, from Breuckelen
Cornelis, the Swede, 180, 181
Cornelis, Lysbet, 53, 93, 101, 135, 146
Cornelissen, Arent, *see* Vogel, Arent Cornelisen
Cornelissen (Van den Berch, Van den Hoogen Bergh), Claes, 117, 132, 279
Cornelissen, Cornelis, 277, 278, 282
Cornelissen, Cornelis, the younger, 302
Cornelissen, Gysbert, from Breuckelen, 210
Cornelissen, Gysbert, from Weesp, wife, 53, 102; lot, 61, 89, 111; deceased, 89; guardians of children, 146
Cornelissen, Lambert, 69
Cornelissen, Marten, *see* Van Ysselsteyn, Marten Cornelisen
Cornelissen, Pieter, wife of, 183
Cornelissen, Poulus, 279
Cornelissen (Van Voorhout), Seeger, 169, 172
Cornelissen, Teunis, *see* Van Slingerlant, Teunis Cornelisen; Van Vechten, Teunis Cornelisen

Court, jurisdiction, 7, 8–9; buildings occupied by, 10
Court records, handwriting, 12
Cramer, Barent, 50
Croaet (Crabaat, Crowaet), Abraham Stevensen, 118, 183, 184, 191, 300
Croon (Kroon), Claes Cornelissen, 33, 41, 68
Croon (Kroon), Dirck Jansen, money due to, 141; house nicknamed, 200; magistrate, 236; to request contributions for Willem Jurriaensen, 255;
    sues Bastiaensen, 31, 57; Groot, 284;
    sued about axhandle planks, 29; regarding disputed accounts, 72. *See also* Jansen, Dirrick

Daniel, the baker, *see* Rinckhout, Daniel
Daret, Jan, sued by van Aecken, 28, 29, 33; by Jansen, 34; testimony regarding Catelyn Sanders, 231; witness for Gerrit Slichtenhorst, 307
Davidts (Davits, Davitsen), Christoffel, complaints about selling brandy to savages, 71, 88, 106; letter to from Director General, 190; transfer of claim to Pieter Bronck, 281; sued for debt, 292, 296, 304; mentioned, 93
De Deckere, Johannes appointed commissary, 223; salary, request for, 249; to request contributions for Willem Jurriaensen, 255
De Forest (Forrest), Isaack, 17
De Goyer, Eldert, 141
De Graef, Jan, 293
De Hinsse, Surgeon Jacob, 149, 191, 196, 293
De Hooges, Anthony, offensive conduct of Albertsen toward, 36, 43; petition from, 136; referee, 134, 184; lot, 137; garden, 158; charges against Claes Ripsen, 188; state-

De Hooges, Anthony — *Continued*
ment regarding nicknames given to houses, 198; house, 200; mentioned, 78, 159, 193, 205
De Hulter, Johan, servant, 88, 106, 207; house, 109, 113, 114; brings further suit, 116; sues Albertsen, 172; requests letters of recommendation to the honorable council, 230; widow, 262; mentioned, 131, 190
De Hulter (Thullert), Madam Johanna, agreement with Chambers and Stol about grain, 252; mentioned, 262;
  sues Chambers, 277, 281, 299; Jacobsen, 298; Hendricksen, 299; Gouw, 302
De Karreman, Michiel, 210
De Looper, Jacob, *see* Teunissen, Jacob
De Paus, 168
De Truy, Susanna, 205
De Visscher (Visser), Jan, 52, 58
De Vlamingh, Pieter, 219. *See also* Winnen (Winne), Pieter
De Vos, Andries, lot, 69, 97, 173; request for pasture, 107; garden, 112, 173; attorney for Vosburgh, 155, 173; petition of, 160; summoned to court, 164, 210; requests copy of testimony, 222; judgment against, 224; mentioned, 157, 210; sued by Jacobsen, 225;
  sues Gerritsen and others, 190, 192; Bronck, 281
De Vries, Adriaen Dircksen, 184, 239
De Wever, *see* Martensen, Jan
De Winter, Maximiliaen, 87
De Wit, Tierck Claessen, *see* Claessen, Tierck
De Wolff, Jacob Willemsen, *see* Willemsen, Jacob
Dingeman, Adam, 201
Dirck (Dirrick), Oom, 150, 199
Dircksen, Adriaen, *see* De Vries, Adriaen Dircksen
Dircksen, Jan, *see* Van Bremen, Jan Dircksen

Dircksen (Dirricksen), Theunis, 132, 268
Douw, Volckert Jansen, *see* Jansen, Volckert
Douwesen Gillis, *see* Fonda, Gillis Douwesen
Driesen, Hendrick, *see* Andriessen, Hendrick
Dutch records, act of *1768* providing for translation of, 12
Dyckman, Joannes, on committee to survey lots, 16; on committee to provide for support of church, 28; lot, 61, 196; authorized to inspect houses of tapsters, 81; complaint against, 94; to prepare case, 96; protest against Dominie Schaets' announcement, 99; reads protest regarding Slichtenhorst, 119; cases referred to, 134; to pay Willem Albertsen, 136; to examine accounts of collector, 142; report on lot for Adriaen Jansen, 159; loan of money to Director General, 162; gives presents to Maquas, 171; on committee to confer with Director General, 174; wife, 203, 204, 207, 268, 292; successor as commissary, 223; settlement of Rut Arentsen's estate, 268; mentioned, 60, 62, 102, 106, 127
Dyckmans, Maritge, 250, 275, 278

Eeckelen, Jan, *see* Van Eeckel, Jan Janssen
Eencluys, Hans Jansen, *see* Inckluis, Hans Jansen
Egberts, Egbertjen, 286, 287
Elbertsen, Reyer, 19
Eldertsen (Eldersen), Ysbrant, 211, 292
Evertsen, Jurgen, 86, 88

Fernow, Berthold, 11
Flodder, Jacob Jansen, prosecuted for fighting, 56; fined for not building on lot, 148; complaint against, 191; slanderous words about court, 217, 221; money to be paid to, 221; lot, 264;

Flodder, Jacob Jansen — *Continued*
sues Bensingh, 93; Margaret Slichtenhorst, 260;
sued for slander, 25; about sale of horses, 150, 152; for wages, 172, 175; for debt, 178

Floris, Isaack, 239
Fonda, Gillis Douwesen, 70, 294
Forremans, Frans, *see* Borremans, Frans
Fredericksen, Carsten, 195, 295
Fredericksen, Meyndert, 236, 284
Fredericksen, Willem, *see* Bout, Willem Fredericksen

Gabrielsen, Frans, 37, 39, 40
Gansevoort, Harmen Harmensen, 243
Gardenier, Jacob Jansen, *see* Flodder, Jacob
Gauw, Jan, *see* Gouw, Jan
Geraerdy (Gerary), Philip, 32
Gerbertsen, Elbert, prosecuted for fighting, 56, 57; bail for, 58; fined for failure to inclose lot, 148
sues Clomp, 183, 184; garden, 201;
sued about sale of horses, 150; for costs of summons, 168, 171
Gerbrantsen, Cornelis, 172
Gerret, the cooper, 41. *See also* Jansen, Gerrit, from Swoll
Gerritsen, Albert, garden, 84;
prosecuted for fighting, 69; for violating ordinances, 303;
sues Herpertsen, 85; Arentsen, 93, 95, 118
Gerritsen, Claes, lot and garden, 97, 102; sues van Slichtenhorst, 135, 142, 144; testimony regarding house of Thomas Sanders, 179; accused of giving nicknames to houses, 198, 201; testimony regarding Cornelis Vos, 213; restitution of beavers in his custody, 228;
sued, about taking grain from a barn, 190; about a wagon, 209, 210

Gerritsen, Ellert, 83
Gerritsen, Goosen, crime against daughter, 37; lot, 51; fined for not building on lot, 83; payment of account for beer, 94; testimony in trial of Jacob Stoll, 105; prosecuted by Dyckman, 107; curator of Arentsen's estate, 132, 268; payment to for nails, 137; palisades inclosing lot, 149; requests permission to form corral for cattle, 154; loan of money to Director General, 163; gives presents to Maquas, 171; referee, 173, 184, 212, 244, 250; testimony on use of a barn, 192; house nicknamed, 199; testimony regarding Catelyn Sanders, 231; magistrate, 269; mentioned, 66, 73, 147;
sues Arentsen, 53; Herpertsen, 135; Gansevoort, 243; Vosburgh, 274, 278; Pietersen, 291; Davidts, 292; Teunissen, 292, 303; Van Valckenburgh, 292
Gerritsen, Hendrick, prosecuted for drinking after ringing of the bell, 117; fined for not building on lot, 145; garden, 185; house and lot, 211;
sued by van Hoesen, 284; for slander, 298; by Vandenburgh, 300, 302
Gerritsen, Jacob, carpenter, 57, 108, 130, 281
Gerritsen, Jacob, the brewer, 18
Gerritsen, Wynant, 145, 166
Geverts, Femmetgen Alberts, *see* Alberts, Femmetgen
Glen, Sander Leendertsen, *see* Leendertsen, Sander
Goosens (Goossens), Maria, 223, 247. *See also* Jans, Maria
Gottenborgh, Jan Jansen, *see* Jansen, Jan

Gouw (Gauw, Gou), Jan, sues Jacobsen, 156, 292, 297; testimony regarding fighting at Jochemsen's house, 166; attack on Bout, 191; lot, 220; testimony on fighting at house of Baefge Pieters, 257;
  prosecuted for fighting, 55, 57; for violating ordinances, 303; sued for debt, 153, 247, 274, 302; by Jansen, 235; by Ryverdingh, 239; by Abrahamsen, 305
Greenen Bosch, 7, 220
Groot, Symon, 145, 284
Gysbertsen, Albert, 305

Hansen, Volckert, *see* Jansen, Volckert
Hap, Jacob Jansen, *see* Stol, Jacob Jansen
Hap, Willem, *see* Stol (Hap), Willem
Haps, Geertruy, 280
Harmen, the carpenter, *see* Bastiaensen, Harmen
Harmensen, Dirckie, 289, 290
Harmensen, Harmen, *see* Gansevoort, Harmen Harmensen
Hartgers (Hertgers, Harties), Pieter, referee, 27, 93; magistrate, 42, 126, 139, 236; fined for not inclosing garden, 83; sued for payment for goods, 134, 135; money due to, 141, 196; lot, 145, 212, 276; appointed guardian, 146; loan of money to Director General, 163; gives presents to Maquas, 171; conveyance of houses, 197; house nicknamed, 200; bed sold to, 214, 216; appointed treasurer of court, 214, 215; dispute about pint measure, 220; sentence decreed against advice of, 225; sues Bamboes, 264; grant of land to, 255; gift for repairing Jurriaensen's house, 256; surety for payment for blockhouse church, 263; mentioned, 17, 66, 150, 223

Helmensen, Jan (Jan with the beard), 260
Hendrick, alias the "Styve Snyder," 303
Hendrick, the baker, *see* Hendricksen, Hendrik
Hendrick, the tailor, alias "Cordiael," 303
Hendrick Clootendraeyer (ball turner), 303
Hendricksen, 191, 221
Hendricksen, Claes, loan of money to Director General, 163; surety for Flodder, 172, 175; testimony regarding Maria Jans, 179, 180; lot, 187, 245; house, 197; fined, 242; money in custody of, 242; sues Slichtenhorst, 304, 307;
  sued for house rent, 209; by Swart, 210; for return of beavers, 237
Hendricksen, Cornelis, 53
Hendricksen, Frederick, 291
Hendricksen, Gerrit, 300
Hendricksen, Geurt (Govert), 220, 298, 299, 303
Hendricksen, Hendrik, 278, 285, 303
Hendricksen, Jacob, *see* Maat, Jacob Hendricksen; Sibbinck, Jacob Hendricksen
Hendricksen, Jan, sued by Dyckman, 117; to build bridge, 143; loan of money to Director General, 162; house, 179, 184; sues van Aecken, 179; sues Jan Baptist van Rensselaer, 244
Hendricksen, Marten, bailsman, 40; sued for debt, 55, 58, 64, 66, 154, 155, 194; complaint about Seeger Cornelisen, 168; to contribute for bridge, 169; mentioned, 17
Herbertsen (Herpertsen), Andries, referee, 18, 64, 102, 209; garden, 95; letter to from members of court, 113; memorandum for, 114; magistrate, 126, 236; dispute with Van Valckenborgh, 136; term of

Herbertsen (Herpertsen), Andries
— *Continued*
    office expired, 139; accounts with Keese Waeye, 156; questioned in court on various matters, 158; loan of money to Director General, 162; gives presents to Maquas, 171; house nicknamed, 199; gift for repairing Jurriaensen house, 256; sentence rendered contrary to his judgment, 281; statement on selling liquor to savages, 299; attorney of Goosen Gerritsen, 303; case of slander, 303; mentioned, 49, 131, 133, 138, 165, 168, 290;
  sues Femmetgen Westerkamp, 182; Claes Teunissen, 306
Herpertsen, Marten, lot, 45, 83; sale of house and garden, 94, 109, 113, 114; complaints by creditors, 137;
  sued for debt, 32, 38, 65, 82, 83, 85, 92, 93, 95, 97, 101, 131, 135, 140, 141, 144, 145, 148, 170; by van Hoesen, 58; by the Visscher, 58; by Bensingh, 58
Hertgers, Pieter, *see* Hartgers, Pieter
Higge (Higgins), Thomas, 29, 30
Hoffmeyer, Willem, summoned to court, 118; fined, 277; punished for selling beer to savages, 288;
  sued by Jansen, 235, 247; by Bamboes, 275; for debt, 278, 279; by Wesselsen, 298
Hollenbeck, C. A., 11
Hoogenboom, Cornelis Pietersen, 293
Houses, nicknames given to, 198–200, 210, 213
Houtewael, Cornelis, 172, 175
Houttum, Willem, 156

Inckluis, (Eencluys), Hans Jansen, 194
Indians, sale of liquors to, 69, 70, 71, 74, 88, 106, 164, 167, 286–91

Jacob, the brewer, *see* Gerritsen, Jacob, brewer
Jacob, the carpenter, *see* Gerritsen, Jacob, carpenter
Jacobs (Jacops), Grietgen, 201, 282
Jacobs, Tryntgen, 168
Jacobs, Wybregh (Brecht), 38, 210
Jacobsen, Abraham, 86, 88, 198
Jacobsen (Jacopsen), Aert, 54
Jacobsen, Andries, 231
Jacobsen, Caspar, 18
Jacobsen, Claes, 68, 185, 213, 215, 263
Jacobsen, Cornelis, 32, 35
Jacobsen, Herman, petition to qualify as beer carrier, 218;
  sues Hendricksen, 209; Wesselsen, 282; Roeloffsen and others, 300; Stevensen, 306;
  sued by Gouw, 292, 297; by Johanna de Hulter, 298
Jacobsen (Jacopsen), Roeloff, sues Gouw, 153; Tryntgen Jacobs, 168; Inckluis, 194; Marten the farmer, 244;
  sued for debt, 94, 95, 133; for house rent, 153; by Gouw, 156
Jacobsen, Rutger, referee, 20, 51, 102, 173, 212; boards belonging to, 35; opinion on tapsters' excise, 44; residence, 48; attorney for Jan van Hoesen, 49, 52, 55; money for, from Clomp, 94; letter to from members of court, 113; horse mill, 113; memorandum for, 114; magistrate, 126, 236; payment for boards, 131; curator of Arentsen's estate, 132, 268; term of office expired, 139; garden, 140, 217; hires yacht, 140; requests permission to form corral for cattle, 154; gives presents to Maquas, 171; charges against Claes Ripsen, 188; house nicknamed, 199; testimony, 226, 231; judgment in favor of, 228; rejects Johan de Deckere's request for

Jacobsen, Rutger — *Continued*
    salary, 249; water wheel for a small mill, 255; gift for repairing Jurriaensen's house, 256; money paid to, 285; mentioned, 22, 29, 30, 70, 135, 142, 144, 255, 290;
    sues Clomp, 66; Albertsen, 140; Femmetgen Alberts, 219;
    sued by Fredericksen, 144, 147; for wages, 267
Jacobsen (Jacopsen), Teunis, 18, 188, 224, 225, 303
Jacobusen, Loys, 205. *See also* Cobes, Ludovicus
Jan de Cuyper, *see* Schut, Jan
Jan, the soldier, *see* Bembo, Jan
Jan, the weaver, *see* Martensen, Jan
Jan with the beard, *see* Helmensen, Jan
Jans, Aelgen, 210. *See also* Aeltgie (Fair Alida)
Jans, Jannitge, 239, 278
Jans, Maria, sale of brandy to savages, 179, 187, 191; sues Croaet, 183, 191; dispute about a water pail, 190; must pay for bed, 214, 216; dispute about a pint measure, 220; ordered to suspend tapping, 221. *See also* Goosens, Maria
Jans, Marritgen, 37. *See also* Ryverdingh, Marriecke
Jans, Volckgen, *see* Jurriaens, Volckgen
Jansen (Appel), Adriaen, from Leyden, marriage, 23, 26; lot, 53, 61, 82, 159; referee, 57, 93; testimony of what occurred at the house of Fredricksen, 108, 110; nominated magistrate, 126; loan of money to Director General, 163; charges against Claes Ripsen, 197; statement regarding nicknames given to houses, 198; ordered to build on lot, 263; fined, 284; dispute about an anker of brandy, 305; mentioned, 107, 205;
    sues Westerkamp, 34; Daret, 34;

Jansen (Appel), Adriaen — *Continued*
    Bronck, 34; van Valckenburgh, 34; van Bremen, 43
Jansen, Claes, from Baarn, appointed inspector, 122, 154; report, 155; testimony, 219; fined, 260, 261; referee, 263
Jansen, Claes, from Rotterdam, 122, 150, 199
Jansen, Dirck, 16, 17, 54, 66. *See also* Croon, Dirck Jansen
Jansen, Fop, 267
Jansen, Gerrit, from Swoll, house sold by, 101; testimony, 105, 136; magistrate, 126; loan of money to Director General, 162; house nicknamed, 199; mentioned, 131. *See also* Gerrit, the cooper
Jansen, Harman, *see* Van Valckenburgh, Herman Jansen
Jansen, Hendrick, the cowherd, accused of making lampoons, 248, 251; fighting, 254, 257; prosecuted by de Deckere, 254, 260, 272; mentioned, 271
Jansen, Hendrick, *see also* Reur, Hendrick Jansen; Westerkamp, Hendrick Jansen
Jansen, Herman, 184, 186
Jansen, Huybert, *de guyt*, 154, 233, 284, 300
Jansen, Jacob, *see* Flodder, Jacob Jansen; Schermerhoorn, Jacob Jansen; Stol (Hap), Jacob Jansen
Jansen, Jan, sues Albertsen, 31; money due to, 38; power of attorney to Rem Jansen, 82; holds mortgage on house, 116; power of attorney given to, 156; sued for debt, 221. *See also* Van Eeckel, Jan Janssen
Jansen, Juriaen, 223, 224, 266, 271, 293
Jansen, Karsten, 162
Jansen, Laurens, petition, 41; fighting, 75, 96; testimony on sale of brandy to savages, 88; testimony on shooting by Stol, 107, 111; house, 145, 211; mentioned, 83, 106, 236

Jansen, Marcelis, servant of Mr de Hulter, 88; complaint of assault, 184, 185, 206; testimony, 106, 213, 214, 215, 219, 302; prosecuted for serving drinks during divine service, 235;
   sues De Paus, 168; Pot, 225; Verwegen, 225; Hendricksen, 242; Rinckhout, 253; Loserik, 268; Adriaensen, 294;
   sued by Herpertsen, 281; by van Curler, 305

Jansen, Michiel, 282

Jansen, Paulus, the Noorman, 239

Jansen, Rem, referee, 27, 29, 93, 184, 209; demands payment of bond, 82; fined, 83; loan of money to Director General, 163; lot, 210; house and lot, 211; sues Willem Hap, 222; mentioned, 96, 284

Jansen, Roeloff, 130

Jansen, Steven, wife, 179, 183, 187, 191, 203, 204, 214, 216, 220, 221, 223; assault on, 207; sued by van Loosdrecht, 209, 254, 259, 275; fighting with Jacob Hendricksen Maat, 221; mentioned, 207, 211, 254;
   sues Hendricksen, 55, 64, 154, 155; Arentsen, 68; Jacobsen, 94, 95; Croaet, 184; Hofmeyer, 235; Jan Jansen, 221; Jacob Teunissen, 246

Jansen (Abeel), Stoffel, carpenter, 97, 150, 166, 263

Jansen (Mingael), Thomas, 61, 72, 159, 163. See also Mingael, Tomas Janssen

Jansen (Hansen, Douw), Volckert, to oversee surveying of lots, 16, 48, 51; referee, 18, 22, 52, 93; opinion on tapsters' excise, 44; Becker's attack on, 62; magistrate, 126, 216, 269; sued for debt, 134, 135; money due to, 141; testimony regarding Vosburgh's lot, 159; loan of money to Director General,

Jansen (Hansen, Douw) Volckert— *Continued*
163; gives **presents** to Maquas, 171; house nicknamed, 200; request concerning lot of poorhouse, 216; sentence decreed against advice of, 225, 239; rejects Johan de Deckere's request for salary, 249; grant of land to, 255; gift for repairing Jurriaensen's house, 256; mentioned, 55, 66, 259;
   sues Becker, 23; Bronck, 24, 41, 50; Bamboes, 264

Jeronimus, Geertruy, sued for abusive language and assault, 17, 19, 21, 25; fined, 26; sues Styntgen Laurens and Volckgen Jans, 29, 32; testimony regarding Albertsen, 37; first default entered against her, 149

Jochem, the baker, *see* Wesselsen, Jochem

Jochemsen, Hendrick, garden, 64; sued for debt, 84, 291; summoned to testify, 96; money due to, 141; loan of money to Director General, 162; testimony regarding Stol and Dirck Lammertssen, 166; petition for restitution of money, 218; granted permission for burghers to shoot the target, 220; fined, 241, 247; mentioned, 117, 118, 165, 166, 198; prosecuted for fighting, 75; for smuggling beer, 83

Joost, the baker, *see* Teunissen, Joost

Jurriaen, the glazier, *see* Jansen, Juriaen

Jurriaens (Jans), Volckgen, sues Geertruy Jeronimus, 17, 19, 21, 25; house, 22; sued by Geertruy Jeronimus, 32; payment of money for Jurriaensen, 80; testimony, 142

Jurriaensen (Juryaensen), Willem, sued about lot, 17, 67, 78, 80; house and lot, 19, 47, 49, 52, 55, 62, 191, 199, 210, 238; petition by, 22;

Jurriaensen (Juryaensen), Willem—
Continued
garden, 24; contract with van Hoesen, 63, 67, 78; refuses to accept money, 82; testimony, 118; house, contributions requested for repairing roof, 255; mentioned, 252

Karreman, ship, 180
Ketelhuyn, Jochem, 51, 83, 156, 263
Keyser, Adriaen, 75
Kleyn, Elmerhuysen, 72, 84, 164, 167
Kleyn, Uldrick, 182, 184, 186, 187
Knyver, *see* Cnyver
Koninck, *see* Coninck
Kroon, *see* Croon

Labatie (Labite), Jan, referee, 18, 21; to lay out land, 20; resigns as magistrate to live in the colony, 42; garden, 48; pleads cases, 53; house and lot, 56; lot, 61, 69, 187; magistrate, 126; ordered to return lime, 144; loan of money to Director General, 163; mentioned, 60, 65, 141;
  sues Clomp, 29; Westerkamp, 32; Becker, 58, 119; Hap, 59; Pietersen, 144
La Chair, Salomon, 279
Lademaker, *see* Machiel, the lademaker
Lamberts, Annitge, 260, 261
Lambertsen (Lammertsen), Poulus, 235, 260, 261
Lammertsen, Dirck, 165, 166, 167
Lammertsen, Jan, 187
La Montagne, Jan, 75
Laurens, Styntgen, 29, 32
Lauson (Loison), Jean de, governor of Canada, 90
Leen, Symon, 226
Leendertsen, Gabriel, 82, 141, 145
Leendertsen, Paulus, 60
Leendertsen (Glen), Sander, negress, 16, 24, 27; lot, 56, 112, 113, 212, 276; must pay fees, 59; to collect tax, 77, 111; magistrate, 126, 130, 269; ref-

Leendertsen (Glen), Sander—Continued
eree, 140; money due to, 141; to build bridge, 143; gives presents to Maquas, 171; conveyance of houses, 197; wife, 231; sues Claesen, 254; gift for repairing Jurriaensen's house, 256; surety bond, 264; payment of money to court, 285; mentioned, 247;
  sued for slander, 16; about sale of horses, 150
Liberis, Catharina, 172
Loison, Johan de, *see* Lauson, Jean de
Loockermans, Pieter, 162, 237, 297, 305
Loosdrecht, Jacob, *see* Van Loosdrecht, Jacob Hendricksen Maat
Loserik, Jacob, *see* Van Loosdrecht, Jacob Hendricksen Maat
Lot, Pieter, 145, 158
Lourensen, Lourens, 133, 148
Luyersen (Van Kuyckendall), Jacob, house and garden, 26; complaint about negress, 27; sued for messenger fees, 59; prosecuted for abusive language and assault, 76, 83, 108, 134; must pay treasurers, 130; must file answer to complaint, 131; pardoned, 134; to pay fine, 134; mentioned, 145, 180
  sues Leendertsen, 16; Cathalina Sanders, 24; Flodder, 25

Maat (Maet), Jacob Hendricksen, farmer of the excise, 176; requests that burghers obtain certificate for beer, 176-77; summoned to testify, 179; payment for excise on wine and beer, 195, 222; charges against, 201; attachment of beer, 202; testimony, 204; judgment against, 211; fighting, 211, 221;
  sues Bronck, 198; Jansen, 209. *See also* Van Loosdrecht, Jacob Hendricksen Maat

Macheck Sipoeti (Indian), 290
Machiel, the lademaker, 41, 44, 83
Machielsen, Jan, see Michielsen, Jan
Maerten, the farmer, see Van Ysselsteyn, Marten Cornelisen
Maertens, Poulus, 247
Marcelis, Hendrick, 108
Marten, Swager, see Ottsen (Ottensen), Martin
Marten, the mason, see Herpertsen, Marten
Martensen (Van Alstyne), Jan, 48, 261, 272, 285, 301
Marttensen, Marten, 73
Megapolensis, Johannes, 33, 44, 185
Melius, Wheeler B., 11
Meussen (Messen), Pieter, 297
Meyndert, the smith, see Fredericksen, Meyndert
Meyndertsen, Carsten, 195
Michielsen (Machielsen), Jan, complaint about negress, 27; testimony at trial of Jacob Stol, 105; to build bridge, 143; mentioned, 31;
    sues Leendertsen, 16; Cathalina Sanders, 20, 24; Albertsen, 36;
    sued by Bronck, 29, 72; for messenger fees, 59; for debt, 282
Mingael, Tomas Janssen, 297. See also Jansen, Thomas

Nanningh (Nannix), Geertgen, 57, 213, 214, 237, 239. See also Bouts, Geertgen
Nes, Dirck, see Van Nes, Dirck
Nicknames given to houses, 198–200
Nolden (Nolding), Evert, 43, 44

Otterspoor, Aert, 190
Ottsen (Ottensen), Marten, 74, 180

Pastoor, Frans Barentsen, excused from paying fine, 67; magistrate, 126, 139, 223, 269; loan of money to Director General, 163; gives presents to Maquas, 171; lot, 212; surety for Pieter

Pastoor, Frans Barentsen — Continued
    Bronck, 235; opinion on granting a lot, 245; asks for relief from certain duties, 245; to request contributions for Willem Jurriaensen, 255; referee, 277; mentioned, 276, 278;
    sues Vosburgh, 247, 250, 253, 297, 301; Loserick, 268, 272; van Bremen, 301, 307; Martensen, 301; Vos, 301; Bronck, 307
Paulw, Tomas, see Powell, Thomas
Pearson, Jonathan, 11–12
Peeck, Jan, 145, 275, 291, 297
Pels, Evert, boards delivered by, 149; sued for debt, 155; petition of, 174; money due from van Bremen, 196, 219; wounding of, 210;
    sues Arentsen, 68, 71; van Hoesen, 154; Bronck, 214, 215, 219
Philipsen, Leendert, 140, 147, 156, 292, 306
Pieter, the baker, 293
Pieters, Baeffgen, 190, 257, 261, 284
Pieters, Geertruyt, 173, 176
Pietersen, Abram, see Vosburgh, Abraham Pietersen
Pietersen, Ariaen, 21, 64
Pietersen (Coeymans), Barent, 299
Pietersen, Cornelis, 190, 192. See also Hoogenboom, Cornelis Pietersen
Pietersen (Clauw), Frans, 260
Pietersen, Gillis, garden, 133, 145; sale of house, 144; referee, 184; testimony regarding a fight, 184, 185; sued for debt, 291
Pietersen (Coeymans), Luykas, fined for not building on lot, 145, 168; prosecuted by Dyckman, 157; garden, 158, 174; sued for debt, 171, 178; complaints against of violence, 184, 186; not guilty of charges, 195
Pietersen, Philip, see Schuyler, Philip Pietersen
Pietersen, Ryndert, 219

Poest, Jan Barentsen sues Marten Hendricksen. 64, 66; fencing off lot, 111; farm, 150, 190, 192; mentioned, 192. *See also* Wemp, Jan Barentsen
Pot (Pott), Cornelis, 179, 225
Poulus, the Noorman, *see* Jansen, Paulus
Poulussen, Gommer, 294
Powell (Paulw, Paul), Thomas, testimony, 226, 242; petition of, 229; prosecuted by de Deckere, 250, 277, 280; sued by Claesen, 253; sues Claesen, 292; mentioned, 229, 234, 241
Pries, Evert, 297
Prins, Willem Jansen, 108

Quick, Jacob Teunissen, *see* Teunissen, Jacob

Rensselaerswyck, court of, 9; consolidated with court of Fort Orange, 9
Reur, Hendrick Jansen, 203
Rinckhout (Ringhaut), Daniel, prosecuted for violating ordinances, 251, 277; petition, 229; judgment against, 277; sues Teunissen, 284; summoned to court, 303;
sued about grain measures, 175; for payment of excise, 253; by Bamboes 275, 279
Ripsen (Rips, Ribsen), Claes, 68, 188, 197, 260, 291
Roelofsen, Jan, testimony regarding Jacob Stol, 109; fined for not building on lot, 153; appointed surveyor, 187; to build the block-house church, 263; prosecuted by de Deckere, 273; mentioned, 271;
sued by Bamboes, 272; by Jacobsen, 300
Rosekrans, Lysbet, 56, 65
Rotterdam, Claes, *see* Jansen, Claes, from Rotterdam
Rutgertsen, Ryck, 192

Ryckertsen, Michiel, 145, 243
Ryverdingh, Marriecke, 23, 26. *See also* Jans, Marritgen
Ryverdingh (Reverdingh, Ruyverdingh), Pieter, fees, 17, 30; lot, 61; offers money to Jurriaensen, 80, 82; certificate of delivery of beer and wine, to give, 80, 97; residence, 87; to make up accounts of persons drowned, 94; accounts, 142, 176; money paid to, 237; mentioned, 42, 52, 60, 84, 85;
sues Luyersen and Michielsen, 59; Jansen, 233; Gouw, 239; Jacob Teunissen, 246; Adriaensen, 259; Jan Schut, 275; Bastiaensen, 279

Sanders (Sandertsen), Cathalina, 20, 24, 231
Sanders (Sanderts), Thomas, garden, 65; unable to pay assessment, 119; testimony regarding Stol and Dirck Lammertsen, 166; house, 179, 184; mentioned, 166;
sued by Bastiaensen, 27; for debt, 147
Schaets, Rev. Gideon, lot, 61; garden, 64; announcement from pulpit regarding Van Slichtenhorst, 99, 120, 124; charges against Claes Ripsen, 188, 197; surety for Slichtenhorst, 243; requests money for Schrick, 243; mentioned, 60, 66
Schapenbout, Arent, 58
Schellinger, Jan Tjebkens, 136
Schermerhoorn (Schermerhoren), Jacob Jansen, insult to officials, 20; lot, 53; garden, 64, 67, 107, 112, 157, 158; judgment against, 101; to lay out lots, 108, 131, 133, 150; magistrate, 126, 269; referee, 140; appointed guardian, 146; report on lot for Adriaen Jansen, 159; loan of money to Director General, 162; gives

Schermerhoorn (Schermerhoren), Jacob Jansen — *Continued*
  presents to Maquas, 171; money paid to, 176; testimonial to, 177; gone to Holland, 177, 216; mentioned, 164; sues Herpertsen, 85, 93; Adriaensen, 135; Loserik, 254, 259; Davidts, 304
Schools, 238
Schrick, Paulus, 73, 243
Schut (de Cuyper), Jan, 275
Schut, Willem Jansen, 194, 213, 215, 241
Schuyler (Schuler, Scheuler, Schuldert), Philip Pietersen, cases referred to, 29, 244; lot, 33, 45, 131, 276; sues Albertsen, 66, 67; house nicknamed, 199; interest in a drag net, 220; testimony, 226, 231; surety bond, 264; magistrate, 269
Segertsen, Cornelis, island of, 24; house sold to, 98, 134, 135, 137; claim against Jacob Adriaensen, 137; appointed guardian, 146; request for woodland, 150; sued for debt, 275
Segertsen, Gerrit, 176, 185
Sibbinck, Jacob Hendricksen, 133, 134, 145
Sille, Nicasius de, 123
Slecht, Cornelis Barentsen, 262
Slichtenhorst, Brant, *see* Van Slichtenhorst, Brant Aertsen
Slichtenhorst, Gerrit, sale of brandy to savages, 164, 167; dispute about chest, 214, 215; fighting, 227, 229; prosecuted for fighting, 234, 237, 238; surety for, 243;
  sued for debt, 243; about lease of yard, 304, 307
Slichtenhorst (Slechtenhorst), Margariet, 260
Slingerlant, Teunis, *see* Van Slingerlant, Teunis Cornelisen
Smit, Jan, 55, 57
Staets, Abraham, cases referred to, 21, 52; lot, 48, 61; to collect tax,

Staets, Abraham — *Continued*
  77, 111; magistrate, 126; loan of money to Director General, 162; to present powder to Indians, 175; payment of money to court, 285; mentioned, 22, 55, 60, 61
Stevensen, Abraham, *see* Croaet, Abraham Stevensen
Stevensen, Pieter, 306
Stiggery, Stick, an Indian, 90
Stoffel, the carpenter, *see* Jansen (Abeel), Stoffel
Stoffelsen, Reyer, 291, 292
Stol (Hap), Jacob Jansen, abusive words against magistrates, 26, 27; fighting, 59, 96; testimony on shooting by, 103, 107, 109, 111; ordered to present answer to charges, 119; money due to, 148; horses sold to, 150; house, 197; requests permission to purchase land, 230; prosecuted for fighting, 238; fined, 238; appeal from sentence, 239; sued by Chambers, 244, 246, 252; not punished for beating wife, 248; moneys in the custody of, 296; mentioned, 45, 52, 93, 198
Stol (Hap), Willem Jansen, lot, 48, 157, 187; fighting, 165, 166, 167; testimony, 213, 215, 219; ordered to pay for house, 222; taken to guard house, 252;
  prosecuted, for drinking during service, 235; by de Deckere, 254, 258, 261;
  sued by Bamboes, 279; by Jacobsen, 282
Stuyvesant, Peter, 7, 8, 13, 44, 270
Swager, Marten, *see* Ottsen (Ottensen), Marten
Swart, Gerrit, 120, 210
Symants, Styntge, 19
Symon, the baker, *see* Volckertsen, Symon
Symonsen, Arien, 274

Tappen, Juriaen Teunissen, *see* Teunissen, Juriaen

Teller (Teljer, Tellier), Willem, complaint against, 217; testimony, 226; fighting, 247; to take up monthly collection, 245;
  prosecuted for fighting, 244; for encroachments on public road and slander, 266, 272, 273, 280
Tempelier, Theunis, 218
Ten Haer, Mariken, 73
Tesselaer, Evert, 32, 134, 135
Teunissen, Claes, 250, 259, 292, 303, 306
Teunissen (Theunesen), Cornelis, from Breuckelen, 42, 175
Teunissen, Cornelis, *see also* Van Westbroeck, Cornelis Teunissen
Teunissen (Theunisen), Jacob, 71, 226, 246
Teunissen (Theunissen), Joost, 20, 28, 36, 41, 43, 50
Teunissen (Tappan, Theunissen), Juriaen, denies charges against, 20; sued for debt, 69, 284; fighting at house of, 117, 132; sues Baefge Pieters, 284
Teunissen (Theunissen), Pieter, 172
Theunisen, *see* Teunissen
Thomassen, Cornelis, 95
Thomassen, Frans, 169
Thomassen (Witbeck), Jan, petition, 41; magistrate, 108, 126; loan of money to Director General, 163; gives presents to Maquas, 171; house nicknamed, 199; attorney for Wemp, 210; lot, 212; referee, 253, 254; grant of land to, 255; gift for repairing Jurriaensen's house, 256; ordered to build on lot, 263; examination of an Indian, 290; mentioned, 17, 108, 138;
  sues Albertsen, 130; Schut, 194, 213, 215; Bamboes, 264
Thomassen, Poulus, 89
Thullert, Johanna, *see* De Hulter, Madam Johanna
Thysen, Claes, 163
Thysen, Jacques, 69, 196. *See also* Vander Heyden, Jacob Thysen

Uylenspiegel, Claes, 278, 282

Van Aecken, Jan, sued by Hendricksen, 179; house, 184; house nicknamed, 199; dispute about a chest, 297; mentioned, 147;
  sues Daret, 28, 29, 33; Meyndertsen, 195; Fredericksen, 195
Van Alckmaer, Ariaen, *see* Pietersen, Ariaen
Van Alstyne, Jan Martensen, *see* Martensen, Jan
Van Bremen, Jan Dircksen, indebtedness, 28, 41, 196; testimony regarding Clomp, 70; attachment of money in hands of, 94, 214, 215, 219; summons to court, 219; prosecuted for various offenses, 96; by de Deckere, 245; for wounding Hans Vos, 248; mentioned, 29; sued for debt, 43, 50, 70, 73, 101; for delivery of a hog, 70; for failure to haul logs, 246; by Bronck, 276, 278; by Pastoor, 301, 307
Van Breuckelen, Cornelis Theunesen, *see* Teunissen, Cornelis
Van Couwenhoven, Jacob, 279
Van Curler, Arent, 134, 305
Van den Berch, Claes Cornelissen, *see* Cornelissen, Claes
Van den Bergh (Berch), Arent, 154, 300, 302
Van den Hoogen Bergh, Claes, *see* Cornelissen, Claes
Vander Donck, Adriaen, 193
Vander Heyden, Jacob Thysen, 163. *See also* Thysen, Jacques
Van Driest, Hendrick, *see* Andriessen, Hendrick
Van Duynkercken, Adriaen Jansen, *see* Jansen, Adriaen
Van Eeckel (Ekel, Eeckelen), Jan Janssen, 291, 296, 298, 303
Van Geel, Maximiliaen, 60
Van Groenwout, Juriaen Jansen, *see* Jansen, Juriaen

Van Hamel, Dirk, 239, 299
Van Hoesen (Hoesem, Housen), Jan Franssen, lot and garden, 18, 24, 49, 52, 55, 62, 191, 272; wife, 19, 21, 22, 80, 142; house, 47; contract with Jurriaensen, 63, 67, 78; loan of money to Director General, 162; request concerning Jurriaensen's house, 199, 210; gift for repairing Jurriaensen's house, 256; mentioned, 143, 165;
  sues Jurriaensen, 17, 78, 80; Becker, 55; Herpertsen, 58, 144; Gerritsen, 284;
  sued about house, 47; by Becker, 65; for debt, 154; by de Deckere, 245
Van Ilpendam, Adriaen Jansen, requests promotion to office of secretary, 29; referee, 57; garden, 65; sued for debt, 75; excuses accepted, 83; attack on by Stol, 104, 105; day and night school, 200
Van Kuyckendall, Jacob Luyersen, see Luyersen (Van Kuyckendall), Jacob
Van Linthout, Abraham, 279
Van Loosdrecht (Loserik), Jacob Hendricksen Maat, fighting, 111, 118, 254, 257; attachment of goods, 165, 168; complaint against, 169; summoned to court, 169; lot, 186; mentioned, 203, 271, 281;
  prosecuted by Dyckman, 116; for fighting, 254; by de Deckere, 261, 268, 270;
  sues Maria Jans, 187; Steven Jansen, 254, 259, 275;
  sued by Adriaensen, 153, 169; for payment for house, 254; by Jansen, 259; for debt, 268; by Pastoor, 272. *See also* Maat, Jacob Hendricksen
Van Naerden, Hendrick Jansen, *see* Jansen, Hendrick, the cowherd
Van Nes, Dirck, 29, **32**

Van Noortstrant, Jacob Janssen, 303
Van Putten (Van Petten), Wouter Aertsen, 20, 45
Van Rensselaer, Jan Baptista, court messenger sent to, 60; referee, 134; in possession of farm of Poest, 190; house nicknamed, 200; proposed actions against, 225; sued by Jan Hendricksen, 244; mentioned, 66, 158, 290
Van Schoonderwoert, **Teunis** Jacobsen, *see* Jacobsen, Teunis
Van Schoonderwoert, Rutger Jacobsen, *see* Jacobsen, Rutger
Van Slichtenhorst (Slechtenhorst), Brant Aertsen, assault on, 76, 83; announcement in church concerning, 99, 124; protest regarding, 119, 120; says court has no jurisdiction over him, 125; beavers due to Claes Gerritsen, 135, 142, 144; restitution of beavers, 228; mentioned, 15
Van Slingerlant, Teunis Cornelisen, 185, 268
Van Slyck, Cornelis, *see* Teunissen, Cornelis
Van Thienhooven, Cornelis, 62, 66
Van Twiller (Twillert), Jan (Johannes), 141, 186, 296
Van Valckenburgh, Herman Jansen, 203, 204, 206, 208
Van Valckenburgh, Lambert, summoned to court, 131; dispute with Herpertsen, 136; requests a lot, 185; testimony, 252;
  sued for debt, 34; by Goosen Gerritsen, 292
Van Vechten, Teunis Cornelisen, 233
Van Voorhout (Wip), Claes Cornelissen, 235
Van Voorhout, Seeger Cornelissen, *see* Cornelissen, Seeger
Van Westbroeck (Bos), Cornelis Teunissen, on committee to oversee surveying of lots, 16; appearance in court, 18;

Van Westbroeck (Bos), Cornelis Teunissen — *Continued*
referee, 22, 44, 253; surety, 49, 263; letter to from members of court, 113; memorandum for, 114; magistrate, 126; lease of house, 130; term of office expired, 139; questioned in court on various matters, 158, 168; loan of money to Director General, 162; attorney, 275; requests lot for Mingael, 297;
sues Jacobsen, 153; Croaet, 300
Van Ysselsteyn, Marten Cornelisen, 244
Vastrick, Gerrit, 137
Vastrick, Robbert, 137, 235
Vedder (Vetter), Harmen, 229
Veeder, Symon Volckertsen, *see* Volckertsen, Symon
Verbeeck, Jan, takes burgher oath, 17; complaint about boy running away, 22; referee, 27, 64, 254, 277; to provide for support of church, 28; sued for debt, 29, 30; magistrate, 126, 236; sues Coninck, 149; gives presents to Maquas, 171; on committee to confer with Director General, 174; appointed treasurer of court, 214, 215; ordered to build on lot, 263; mentioned, 164
Vervelen (Verwegen), Daniel, 225, 232
Visbeeck (Viesbeeck), Gerrit, 303
Visscher, Harmen Bastiaensen, *see* Bastiaensen, Harmen
Vogel (Voogel), Arent Cornelisen, 35, 39, 40, 102, 207, 246
Volckertsen, Symon, baker, 67, 201
Vos, Cornelis, garden, 158; lot, 159; loan of money to Director General, 163; accused of giving nicknames to houses, 198; house nicknamed, 201; missing tub of butter, 209; summoned to court for giving nicknames, 210; not guilty, 213; replication to answer filed by, 218;

Vos, Cornelis — *Continued*
sued by Adriaensen, 121; for debt, 284; by Barentsen, 297, 301, 302, 305, 306
Vos, Hans, 248
Vosburgh, Abraham Pietersen, house, 15, 266; surveys by, 16, 17, 117; referee, 27; indebtedness, 102; petition to tap beer, 65; part payment on bridges, 123; to begin bridge, 138; faulty surveying, 146; bridge not built, 149; de Vos answers complaints about, 155; lot, 158, 159, 213, 217, 245; petition of, 160; ordered to appear in court, 160-61, 164, 297; replication again to be sent to, 160, 164; arbitration of dispute, 173, wife, 174, 176; payment for bridges, 178; sues Lammertsen, 235; disputed accounts, 281; mentioned, 112, 157;
sued for debt, 38, 58, 212, 235, 250; by Ryverdingh, 247; by Pastoor, 247, 250, 253, 297, 301; by Maritge Dyckmans, 250; by Gerritsen, 274, 278; by van Ekel, 291, 296, 298; by Cobes, 297
Vrooman, Pieter Meussen, *see* Meussen (Messen), Pieter
Vylens, Claes, 302

Waeye, Keese, an Indian messenger, 156
Wemp, Jan Barentsen, 89, 209, 210. *See also* Poest, Jan Barentsen
Wendel, Evert Jansen, 163, 199, 205, 226, 245
Wesselsen (Becker), Jochem, the baker, wife, 17, 21, 26; pigsty, 22; judgment against, 48, 241; to pay fine, 61-62, 66, 130, 249, 280; testimony in trial of Jacob Stol, 103; attack on by Stol, 105; to sheet bank of

Wesselsen (Becker), Jochem — *Continued*
 kill, 141; loan of money to Director General, 162; testimony regarding sale of brandy to savages, 164, 167; statement regarding nicknames of houses, 199; request concerning Jurriaensen's house, 199, 210, 238, 255; quarrel with Slichtenhorst, 227, 229, 234, 237, 241; petition presented by, 229; sells to savages, 242, 243; denies selling to savages, 250; gift for repairing Jurriaensen's house, 256; beavers in custody of, 274; request for a garden, 299;
 prosecuted for abusive language and assault, 23; for violating ordinance on baking, 55, 61, 251, 280; for fighting, 117, 130, 227, 229, 237, 238, 241; about beer found among savages, 213, 215; by de Deckere, 233, 248, 250, 277;
 sues Van Hoesen, 47, 49, 65; Rinckhout, 175; Hoffmeyer, 298;

Wesselsen (Becker), Jochem — *Continued*
 sued for slander, 18, 19, 25; for debt, 32; about a lot, 52, 119; by Labatie, 58; for assault, 73; for shooting a dog, 140; by Bamboes, 279; by Jacobsen, 282

Westerkamp, Femmetgen, 182. *See also* Alberts, Femmetgen

Westerkamp, Hendrick Jansen, wife, 26, 182; sued for debt, 32, 34; testimony, 62; mentioned, 73

Wever, *see* Martensen, Jan

Willems, Margriet, 22

Willemsen, Jacob, prosecuted for fighting, 117, 130; dispute about chest, 214, 215; petition presented by, 229; testimony, 241, 242; gift for repairing Jurriaensen's house, 256; sues Wesselsen, 274

Winnen (Winne), Pieter, 72. *See also* De Vlamingh, Pieter

Wip, Claes, *see* Van Voorhout, Claes Cornelissen

Witbeck, Jan Thomassen, *see* Thomassen, Jan

Witmont, Jan, 213, 214, 220

Witthardt (Withart), Jan, 134, 135